forever
and ever,
amen

Also by Karol Jackowski

Ten Fun Things to Do Before You Die

Sister Karol's Book of Spells and Blessings

*The Silence We Keep: A Nun's View
of the Catholic Priest Scandal*

*Good Cooking Habits: Food for Your Body,
Your Soul, and Your Funnybone*

RIVERHEAD BOOKS

a member of Penguin Group (USA) Inc.

New York

2007

forever

and ever,

amen

Becoming a Nun in the Sixties

Sister Karol Jackowski

RIVERHEAD BOOKS
Published by the Penguin Group
Penguin Group (USA) Inc., 375 Hudson Street, New York, New York 10014, USA •
Penguin Group (Canada), 90 Eglinton Avenue East, Suite 700, Toronto, Ontario M4P 2Y3,
Canada (a division of Pearson Penguin Canada Inc.) • Penguin Books Ltd, 80 Strand, London
WC2R 0RL, England • Penguin Ireland, 25 St Stephen's Green, Dublin 2, Ireland (a division
of Penguin Books Ltd) • Penguin Group (Australia), 250 Camberwell Road, Camberwell,
Victoria 3124, Australia • (a division of Pearson Australia Group Pty Ltd) • Penguin Books
India Pvt Ltd, 11 Community Centre, Panchsheel Park, New Delhi–110 017, India • Penguin
Group (NZ), 67 Apollo Drive, Mairangi Bay, Auckland 1311, New Zealand (a division of
Pearson New Zealand Ltd) • Penguin Books (South Africa) (Pty) Ltd, 24 Sturdee Avenue,
Rosebank, Johannesburg 2196, South Africa

Penguin Books Ltd, Registered Offices: 80 Strand, London WC2R 0RL, England

Grateful acknowledgment is made to reprint excerpts from the following:
The Constitutions, reprinted with the gracious permission of The Sisters of the Holy Cross.
Letters to a Young Poet by Rainer Maria Rilke, translated by Stephen Mitchell.
Copyright 1984 by Stephen Mitchell. Used by permission of Random House.
Emily Dickinson's poem #483 from *The Poems of Emily Dickinson*, edited by Thomas H.
Johnson (Cambridge, Massachusetts: The Belknap Press of Harvard University Press).
Copyright 1951, 1955, 1979, 1983 by the President and Fellows of Harvard College.
Reprinted by permission of the publishers and the Trustees of Amherst College.

Library of Congress Cataloging-in-Publication Data

Jackowski, Karol.
Forever and ever, amen : becoming a nun in the sixties / Karol Jackowski.
p.   cm.
ISBN 978-1-59448-937-2
1. Jackowski, Karol.   2. Sisters of the Holy Cross—Biography.
3. Nuns—United States—Biography.   I. Title.
BX4705.J2617A3   2007   2006039268
271'.97—dc22
[B]

Printed in the United States of America
1   3   5   7   9   10   8   6   4   2

BOOK DESIGN BY NICOLE LAROCHE

While the author has made every effort to provide accurate telephone numbers and Internet
addresses at the time of publication, neither the publisher nor the author assumes any
responsibility for errors, or for changes that occur after publication. Further, the publisher does
not have any control over and does not assume any responsibility for author or third-party
websites or their content.

Quotations in this book taken from the 1962 Constitutions of the Congregation of the Sisters
of the Holy Cross reflect the pre–Vatican II culture of women's religious communities, and in
no way exemplify the Catholic sisterhood today. In 1982, the Sisters of the Holy Cross revised
the Constitutions to reflect the Catholic Church's understanding and vision of religious women
in the modern world.

This book is dedicated to
my mother superior,
Shirley Jackowski.

contents

forever

and ever,

amen

introduction

There is nothing more interesting to me than what we decide to do with the life we've been given. The choices we make, the paths we take, whom we choose to love, the work we do, how we play, the beliefs we hold to be true—those are the ingredients that make up the mystery of our lives. This isn't a book about nuns as much as it is the story of what I chose to do with my life and the magic that makes up its mystery. This is my story of the first seven years on the least traveled road of becoming a nun; the first steps I took on the spiritual path that led to the fullness of life I know now.

While any one of us will tell you that it takes a lifetime to become a nun, the first seven years are the most dramatic, the most traumatic, and the most formative in a nun's life. Those years transformed us from eighteen-year-old college students into Sisters of the Holy Cross at Saint Mary's in South Bend, Indiana. While college years naturally provide times for one's individuality and personality to be explored and transformed, for the women who became nuns with me they were years of total self-denial: nun of this and nun of that. During these seven years we were melted down and molded into the image and likeness of a nun. Catholic religious communities even referred to those years as a time of formation, which began the day you entered the convent as a postulant and ended formally on the day of final profession; the day of forever and ever, amen.

This is the story of those years and my struggle to become a nun without losing my fun-loving soul. What made these years uniquely dramatic, and for many sisters uniquely traumatic, is that we entered them in the 1960s, at a time of profound cultural and societal change. We were the baby boomers of 1946. President John Kennedy was shot while I was taking a test in religion class. The Peace Corps had begun a few years before, and the Vietnam War was growing more serious. Protest movements for civil rights, feminism, nonviolence, and equality erupted all over the country. Unrest became so palpable in those days that it gave birth to a kind of music never heard before and a way of life we never experienced. The call to hammer out justice, freedom, and love all over the land is the call I heard in wanting to be a nun; and on that tidal wave of protest I entered the convent. The times were "a-changin'," to quote Bob Dylan, and so was I.

Nuns too stood on the verge of revolutionary changes then, though I didn't know it when I joined. Even the Catholic Church and the cloistered lives of nuns couldn't keep out the kind of liberating spirit that charged the country. In 1964 I wore the full postulant habit of the Sisters of the Holy Cross—a floor-length black dress, with black cape and white collar, and a black veil with a narrow white headband—and professed final vows seven years later, unveiled and in a *relatively* stylish navy blue suit. (Regardless of what we wear, it's still not hard to spot a nun in a crowd.) The traditional habit worn for centuries was replaced by street clothes. No longer only face and hands, nuns all of a sudden appeared unveiled; with the change of habit, individuality was born in the sisterhood.

The lifestyle of sisters changed dramatically in those seven years. Like butterflies coming out of cocoons, we no longer lived cloistered or secluded. Groups of sisters moved from castlelike convents in remote privileged areas into low-income neighborhoods and small apartments. As we became part of people's lives in ways that were once forbidden, our homes became social centers, soup kitchens, and shelters. A life once so extraordinary in its secrecy and exclusiveness opened its doors to welcome all. The lives of nuns turned inside out and upside down in those years, causing an unprecedented revolution within the sisterhood, the long-term effects of which continue to unfold.

The changes that took place in women's religious communities between 1964 and 1972 as a result of the Second Vatican Council* were unprecedented. Some historians refer to those years as the "bleeding of the sisterhood." Once a powerful workforce in the Catholic Church, nuns began disappearing from all the old familiar places like schools, parishes, and hospitals. More than two hundred thousand women left the convent in the years following Vatican II, accompanied by a drastic decline in new applicants.

My own experience bore out the trend. In 1964 fifty of us joined the Sisters of the Holy Cross. In 1972 seven professed final vows. Of that seven, three of us remain in the sisterhood. We were the last real bumper crop of postulants. In the years to follow, the number of new sisters dropped drastically from something like fifty to forty, then to twenty, then thirteen, then seven, then years of no new applicants at all. For American religious communities today, a handful of applicants may

*A major meeting of the bishops of the world convened by Pope John XXIII to bring about a renewal of the Church for the second half of the twentieth century. It met from 1962 to 1965.

apply every year or two, at most, but the golden days of fifty to seventy-five new sisters every year is now ancient history.

Why did so many sisters leave the convent during those years? Prior to 1972 it would have been common for a few sisters to depart: some were miserable and chose to leave; others were deemed a "poor fit" by superiors and dismissed. But in the late 1960s sisters began to leave for reasons unheard of before. Our lifestyle as nuns changed so dramatically and so quickly that many sisters faced choices and experiences that challenged their identity as nuns and the reasons they chose religious life. The more ordinary our lives became with the change of habit and lifestyle, the harder it became to define what it meant to be a nun.

As we began living and working with much greater freedom, our lives were no longer controlled by the structure of convent life or suppressed by the will of rigid superiors. Sisters living in oppressive convents (and there were thousands) often sought comfort and community with colleagues in the workplace. As a result, some fell in love with coworkers (often priests) and left the sisterhood to marry. Others accepted their homosexuality and left to pursue relationships. And many became fully committed to social activism, much to the dismay of superiors, bishops, pastors, and even some of the nuns with whom they lived. In 1966, for example, for the first time ever, sisters marched for civil rights in Selma, Alabama. Some did so in defiance of superiors, who forbade their participation in public protest and dismissed them.

These were revolutionary times in the sisterhood. Voices wrapped for years in silence suddenly began to speak. Sisters wanted freedom to make personal choices and decisions about where to live, who to live with, and what work to do. Given the climate of social unrest and conscientious objection, many sought a sisterhood of equals, not one of superiors and subjects.

While I was entering the sisterhood, thousands of the best and brightest sisters were beginning to leave. Many left traditional convents to pursue independent lifestyles, not wanting to abandon religious life but envisioning a more self-governing, self-supporting sisterhood not controlled by superiors, bishops, priests, or the Vatican (all of whom, to this day, legally and effectively govern the lives of nuns). New independent religious communities formed as a result, such as the Sisters for Christian Community founded in 1972, of which I am now a member. Inside and out, the sisterhood became transformed not only by the mandates of Vatican II to modernize but also by the social movements in this country for equality, opportunity, and independence. The way nuns were in 1964 is a way we as American Catholic sisters will never be again.

This is the story of how I became a nun, with a look at the best and worst of both worlds—the isolated world of the cloistered nun and the open ordinary world of the sister today; the secret life we lived behind closed convent doors with all its joys and difficulties, as well as what it was like to change ancient religious traditions so quickly, almost overnight. This is my story of how we lived, how we got along (or didn't), how I changed during the first seven years, why so many sisters left the convent or were sent home, and why I stayed. At a time when nuns appear to be an increasingly endangered species, this book tells the story of how I still find fun, love, and everlasting happiness in a simple life by vowing poverty, a communal life in vowing obedience, and a solitary life in vowing celibacy.

In thinking about how I became a nun, a stream of stories instantly comes to mind, one after another, like a litany: a soulful account of the best and worst of times. The stories give a glimpse into the mystery of the sisterhood, what led me to it in 1964, and what binds me so lovingly to religious life today. Storytelling grew into a sacred tradition that the sisterhood reveres as sacrament—a sacred tie that binds us together. Its importance to us as a source of entertainment rested on the fact that we were the only source of entertainment we had. Before 1968, young sisters at Saint Mary's weren't allowed to watch television (except for Notre Dame football), listen to the radio, go to the movies, or read newspapers and magazines. We read only spiritual books and textbooks. We learned quickly to entertain ourselves.

As young nuns, we listened to stories told by the older sisters that still have the power to make me laugh as I did on hearing them for the first time. In retelling these stories, witnesses always offered new details with unique memories. Some stories took on mythic overtones, revealing experiences we shared in common. Those are the stories that took us into the sacred depths of laughter where tears come from. The stories in this book are like that for me: They reveal the magic ingredients that make up the mystery of my life.

In the sisterhood we naturally become part of each other's lives. So in telling my story, I will introduce you to the women I met along the way who—for better or worse—made all the difference in my world. Here you will meet the sisters who helped me become a nun without losing my fun-loving soul. I see them now as angels who accompany me on my life's journey, and in meeting them you will see what divine intervention looks like in my life.

In telling the story of what I'm doing with my life, it is my hope that you too will see the magic ingredients that create the divine mystery of your own. It is my hope that you too will be moved to the kind of soulful laughter that reveals what a divine comedy life can be. There is nothing more interesting than the story of what we do with the life we've been given. This one is simply mine.

chapter one

hearing the call

Where do we begin?
Begin with the heart.

—JULIAN OF NORWICH

To this day I can't fully explain what compelled me in my senior year of high school to become a nun, except to say that it "began with the heart." The thought had never crossed my mind seriously before then. Even in the seventh grade when most Catholic girls wanted to become nuns, I didn't. While every year on Vocation Sunday we went to church to pray for a call to the sisterhood or priesthood, I prayed not to be picked. I prayed by name for girls I didn't like to get a vocation because I wanted to see them locked up in a convent for life. In my eyes, it was a curse not a blessing.

I prayed for anyone but me to be given a religious vocation, and I had every reason to believe my prayer would be granted. Consistently poor grades in conduct and repeated reprimands by the nuns for "lack of reverence at prayer and in church" were safeguards from my being entrusted with a religious vocation, I was sure. There was a kind of girl cut out to be a nun, and it clearly wasn't me.

Even my family, though Polish and Catholic, was not so religious that they prayed for one of their children to become a nun or priest, as many Catholic parents did. Nor were they fanatic about being Catholic as was the trend in the 1950s. Quite the contrary. Mine was not a family that groomed children for the priesthood and sisterhood, which is why my decision to become a nun shocked them as much as it did me.

In high school, the thought of becoming a nun never got serious until the middle of my senior year, the proverbial eleventh hour. I majored in Fun at Bishop Noll High School in Hammond, Indiana, rarely giving serious thought to anything, much less life after graduation. From all outward appearances, nothing in my early life indicated that I had a religious vocation—especially in high school when my social life took over.

I loved high school and rarely missed a day, because I couldn't bear to be out of the scoop loop. Seeing friends and catching up on what happened the night before was a highly emotional curriculum I didn't dare miss. I thrived on being a hub for the latest information about which couples broke up, who was going steady, fights with parents and siblings, which girls weren't speaking to one another, what happened in class, after-school plans, and daily updates on weekend parties. I never missed a football game, a basketball game, or the parties that followed. I partied so heartily in high school that I earned the nickname "Suds" in my sophomore year because of my capacity to drink.

I loved high school because of the friends and fun I found there; it was my first taste of what I now know as sisterhood. For all intents and purposes, I went to a Catholic girls school. Boys were there, but we only saw them before school, at lunch, at our lockers, and after school. Sisters of the Holy Cross taught the girls in one building, the Christian Brothers taught boys in an adjacent building, and a handful of laypeople taught both. They called that kind of education coinstitutional.

It's true that single-sex education cultivates lifelong bonds of friendship. I still get together now with the same group of girls I hung around with in high school. When I visit Indiana, we still go to the House of

Pizza for beer and the extra-large pizza with sausage and mushrooms. We still go to Miner-Dunn for burgers, onion rings, and chocolate malts. And if it hadn't been demolished years ago, we'd still meet at Fat Boy's for fries and Cokes. What drew us together in 1964 still binds us together today.

My friends felt like sisters in high school. We spent as much time as we could with one another—often a big bone of contention with our parents. Why did we have to call one another the minute we walked in the door after school? What did we have to say that was so important? Why did we need to go out at night when we saw each other all day? And why did there have to be a sleepover every weekend? I still can't answer those questions, but that's what we did. Most parents, including mine, finally gave up.

"Go ahead and go," my mom said in disgusted defeat. "I don't care what you do."

Nearly every weekend there'd be a sleepover, and when there wasn't, we'd make one. I'd call one or two friends, and we'd sneak booze, order pizza, play records (no bedroom TVs then), make prank phone calls, be silly, talk all night, sleep till midafternoon, or until my mother yelled down the stairs: "Get your big asses out of bed!" When I look at the best times of my life, I always see high school.

While nothing about my first eighteen years ever looked as if a religious vocation was brewing, I know now that appearances are not reality. Now I look at those years of fun and foolishness and see a soulful thirst for sisterhood being born. But I didn't see that going on in 1964. No one who knew me did. My becoming a nun was so out of whack with how everyone knew me that it took months before I could tell anyone, and even then I couldn't say it out loud.

I notified my parents that I wanted to become a nun in a handwritten letter sent through the U.S. mail. With the exception of Sister Miriam Edward, my sponsor, I didn't discuss the decision with anyone, not even best friends. I had no heart-to-heart talk in the rectory with a priest and no meetings in the convent with the sisters. There was no dramatic family get-together around the dining room table. There was nothing to indicate that I'd made a well-informed, responsible decision. But why a letter? I don't recall my exact thinking, but a letter felt safe to me. I also remember feeling speechless. I couldn't explain at all why I wanted to be a nun much less why I had to do so suddenly at the age of eighteen. What do you know at eighteen? Nothing, really. I knew even less.

To admit that I was unconscious at the age of eighteen is an understatement, but not at all uncommon. Most lives don't wake up until the mid-twenties, even later, or never. With no inner life to speak of, I had nothing to draw on but instinct, making my decision to become a nun appear even more baffling to everyone, including me. I didn't think the choice through carefully; nor did I consider alternative religious orders. My classmates consulted our guidance counselors, applied to several colleges, visited campuses, and applied for jobs, but I did nothing that responsible. I simply went with the flow of what I knew, and what I knew best were the Sisters of the Holy Cross. I felt no need to look anywhere else. The only advice I followed, I realized years later, was that of Mark Twain: Put all your eggs in one basket, and watch that basket.

My decision to become a nun had everything to do with the Sisters of the Holy Cross, who taught me in my senior year when life all of a sudden demands unprecedented seriousness. Up until that point next steps in life were automatic; no decisions needed to be made. Eight years of Catholic grade school led to four years of Catholic high school. For many of my classmates, four years of college followed, but of that next step I was not so certain. My family couldn't afford college. Being bakers with five children and a business called the Normal Bakery, my family wasn't poor, but we never rolled in that kind of dough. Like most immigrant survivors in our Polish neighborhood with five children in the family, we had what we needed, and struggled to make ends meet at the same time.

Even if my family could have afforded to send me to college, my high school grades were average at best, and my SAT scores no better. I thought that no college would accept me, and I wasn't intellectually ready for the discipline of an academic life. For the high-spirited who paid more attention to her social life than to her intellectual or inner life, senior year became a time of great awakenings and great expectations. The time had come to get serious about taking my first steps toward a future of my own making, a life of my own design. That's when my heart got serious and began speaking up. That's also when I got serious and began to listen. The vagueness and obscurity of "the call" I heard begged for some measure of clarity, some decision, some movement forward, and the Sisters of the Holy Cross helped turn me in that direction.

While my friends began visiting colleges, looking for jobs, or planning their weddings, I found myself strangely, secretly, and uncharacteristically attracted to the life and work of the nuns who taught me. Smart and well educated, independent in their thinking and mysterious in their life, the Sisters of the Holy Cross appeared socially conscious about civil rights—something I never saw in anyone before, much less in a nun.

In 1964 the Age of Aquarius dawned, around the time the Peace Corps was gaining popularity. While thoughts of joining the Peace Corps crossed my mind, the thought of being sent to work alone in the boonies didn't appeal to me at all. I'm still not that kind of brave. I saw in the sisterhood everything I liked about the Peace Corps: the heart and soul of volunteering and the support of community life. Above all, and most important to me, the nuns I knew had fun with one another and fun with us. Knowing nuns with an enduring sense of humor is a rarity I found very attractive. Being a Sister of the Holy Cross didn't kill their ability to be funny, and for me, that's divine intervention at its best. "I wouldn't have to give up fun after all" is the thought that crossed my mind over and over.

Equally appealing was how the Sisters of the Holy Cross looked at teaching. To them it wasn't simply a job; it was a sacred art. The work they did felt holy. For example, Sister Michaela didn't teach me religion, she taught theology. For the first time in twelve years of Catholic education, I learned to love the Bible and understood the gospels as a rule of life. I was in her class taking a test on November 22, 1963, when John Kennedy was shot. I felt just as moved by the sisters who gathered together in the hallway, hugged one another and wept, as I did by the stunning tragedy of the president's death. For the first time I noticed sisters sharing one another's sorrow as profoundly as they did joy. I saw the heart and soul of community life in those sisters and found myself drawn toward that kind of love. Every day we saw how they loved one another, and day by day I saw more clearly a kind of sisterhood I wanted to be part of.

The Sisters of the Holy Cross were a remarkable group of women in every way. Even Sister Mariella, whose personal crusade was outlawing "ratted" hair, became someone we loved to hate. Those were the days of big hair set every night with small frozen orange juice cans, ratted to great heights, and petrified with hair spray. We must have believed the higher the hair, the closer to God. Before every class Sister Mariella took a long, sharply pointed yellow pencil (a Dixon Ticonderoga #2), and walked up and down the aisles, doing the "rat test." Approaching us one by one, she'd slide the pencil in the hairline at the scalp—right between the eyes—then suddenly jerk up. *OW. OW. OW.* Try it and feel the pain. If someone cried, she'd sort of apologize.

"I'm sorry," she'd say, "but it's for your own good. I don't want you looking like sluts."

Even Sister Mariella cared not only about the life of the mind but about how we lived, the choices we made, and how high we ratted our hair. The sisters had standards.

Sister Angeline taught algebra as though it contained the joyful mysteries of life, and she sang as if she had once had her own lounge act. Even Sister Peter Julian, fondly called Petie and much older than the others, introduced us to creative writing as though it contained the secret of everlasting life.

Petie became notorious for two things: first, the Petie Principle. When one of us said something insightful, Petie rolled her head back, her eyes upward (behind bottle-thick glasses), and with hands clasped over her heart in prayer she'd say, "What could my Jesus do more?" That's the Petie Principle.

Petie also assigned weekend book reports (as if we had nothing better to do over the weekend). The Jesus comment remained downright funny every time, but the book reports became so tedious and ridiculous that I (and friends) employed the art of true creative writing by making up the title, the author, the publisher, and the story.

For example, I created a story called *I Turned Black* about a woman who took a drug that changed her skin color so she could experience racial discrimination. Laverne Lavalle became the author and Random House the publisher. I prayed Petie wouldn't check the reference or try to buy the book, and my devious prayer was answered. I received an A for that book report, and to my knowledge Petie never knew and I never confessed. Shortly after I graduated, *Black Like Me* by John Howard Griffin became a best seller. Too bad for Laverne Lavalle. She never sued.

Most influential in my decision to join the Sisters of the Holy Cross were Sisters Miriam Edward and Christopher Marie. With a love of theater, they directed me and Joe Kissela in the lead roles of *Harvey*, Mary Chase's Pulitzer Prize–winning (and our senior class) play about a man believed to be crazy because of a friendship with an invisible seven-foot rabbit. They valued as divine the creative life of writing, art, and theater, and I learned to love these from them. Not only did they rehearse with us every night until after midnight, but they also shared such pure fun with us that everything in me felt compelled to follow. They acted out the funniest scenes, teaching us to do the same, all while laughing uncontrollably the way you do only with best friends. I wanted to know the secret of their happiness, even if it meant becoming a nun in order to find it. That's what "the call" sounded like to me in the beginning: divine laughter.

The only thing I made sure of before applying to the Sisters of the Holy Cross was that they didn't shave their heads and wear wedding gowns when receiving the habit. So much for having "enlightened" criteria in choosing a religious order. Happily I learned that the Sisters of the Holy Cross no longer did either.

Once, before entering the convent, I did visit Saint Mary's in South Bend, Motherhouse of the Sisters of the Holy Cross. Sister Miriam Edward thought it would be good for me to see the place before moving in. The date was July 25, 1964, twelve days after I was accepted, and the day that, unbeknown to us, Sister Madeleva's body returned to Saint Mary's College for her funeral. We arrived just in time for the procession.

Sister Madeleva had been president of Saint Mary's College for twenty-seven years. She was a renowned poet, who knew everyone from philosopher Jacques Maritain to the actor Helen Hayes. In addition to being college president, Sister Madeleva maintained a New York City life. An artist at heart, she wrote several books of poetry; a must-read autobiography, *My First Seventy Years;* and a vocation pamphlet, given to me, titled "One Girl in a Hundred." In that little gem, Sister Madeleva wrote about what it felt like to be called to the sisterhood. "One girl in a hundred," she wrote, was one "who did not even want to think of a religious vocation for fear that God would catch her in the act and impose a vocation upon her." That girl was me.

Sisters Miriam Edward and Christopher Marie drove me and my best friend since kindergarten, Veronica "Vern" Pawlus, to South Bend that day. We joked in the car about having to say the rosary as we rode; it's a universal nun tradition. (The sisters in the front seat lead, and those in the back respond.) We laughed when Vern announced, "First one to see the gold dome gets to lead the rosary on the way home!"

The closer we got to Saint Mary's the more excited I felt, and by the time we spotted Notre Dame's gold dome, I was downright giddy. As we turned onto the campus of Saint Mary's, a tree-lined avenue of one-hundred-year-old sugar maple trees and oak trees welcomed us to a breathtakingly beautiful campus. We fell suddenly silent. Hundreds of Sisters of the Holy Cross lined the avenue on both sides, chanting "Ave Maris Stella" while waiting to welcome Sister Madeleva home. A solitary church bell tolled. Never before or since had I seen or heard anything like it. I felt as if I was coming home.

The campus is far more beautiful than anything I or Hollywood could imagine. When you see it for the first time, it really takes your breath away. Old buildings with bell towers and stained-glass windows stand saluted by every genus and species of tree known in the Midwest, including the rare gingko. Birds, squirrels, and rabbits roam across acres of well-manicured lawns that stretch out in every direction. Scattered throughout the campus and across the lawns appear carefully tended flower gardens in the center of which stand shrines, statues, benches, and kneelers—private little grottoes of solitude and prayer.

I was totally taken by Lake Marian in front of the old library, more of a reflecting pool surrounded by giant whispering weeping willows, planted when Saint Mary's was born. A narrow wooden footbridge with decorative wrought-iron railings led to an island in the center of the lake, on which stood a shrine to Mary, covered with vines and flowers. Candles burned at her feet and two white stone benches offered an invitation we couldn't refuse.

As the four of us sat in silence, I felt so clearly that I belonged there: as though I had some unfinished business to attend to from a past life and needed to come home to take care of it. (Catholic teaching doesn't believe in past lives. But I do.) Looking into the water, I saw oversized goldfish beneath flowering lily pads, swimming to the surface and making that face as if blowing kisses to welcome me home. I sat there feeling certain that's where I was called to be.

In that visit we also saw the new Postulate, the building that I'd be moving into in six weeks. While it was still under construction, we walked around and saw the planned bowling alley in the basement, the courtyard where a swimming pool would be, the private bedrooms, and the tennis courts out back.

"Sort of like a country club for nuns." I said to Vern.

Miriam Edward and Christopher Marie looked at each other as though they knew something they couldn't reveal. I pressed for details, getting in return nothing other than a mysterious laugh, leading me to believe that I'd find out about the "country club" soon enough. At the unknowing age of eighteen, the bliss of ignorance felt fine.

The opportunity of starting college at Saint Mary's while training to become a nun was a dream come true that I never saw as part of my decision. But had I not joined the Sisters of the Holy Cross, I certainly would not have been accepted to Saint Mary's College and may not have gone to college at all. I didn't even know I had a mind. But part of becoming a Sister of the Holy Cross included becoming highly educated before being sent out to teach or nurse. In that regard the Sisters of the Holy Cross were trendsetters.

Sister Madeleva pioneered the movement to ensure that teaching sisters be professionally prepared. In 1949 she wrote "The Education of

Sister Lucy," a groundbreaking essay calling for higher education in sister formation. While many religious superiors at that time objected to educating young nuns for fear they'd lose their vocation or leave the convent after they graduated, Sister Madeleva wrote that "nothing can do more to undermine a vocation than to send sisters out to teach without any preparation." That kind of thinking was revolutionary at the time, in and out of the convent.

Higher education was one of the finest features of the Sisters of the Holy Cross. In the mid-1960s, few women other than nuns, if any, became college presidents and professors, hospital administrators and nurses, high school and grade school principals and teachers. The nuns I knew in high school earned master's degrees. They held as sacred the life of the mind as much as they did the life of the soul, valuing work as a sacrament for women, who at that time mostly worked in the home. What I saw and felt very vaguely then I now know so clearly: the Holy Cross sisters would become the "mother of my soul" and Saint Mary's College the "mother of my mind."

In my adolescent unconsciousness, the only inner life I knew was what I wanted to do. I lived by gut instinct alone. My "prayer life" felt equally instinctual, as did the "call of God" to be a nun. Every day in grade school, nuns told detailed stories about the amazingly miraculous lives of the saints. I grew up surrounded by angels, believing wholeheartedly in miracles and signs of divine intervention. Harboring a strong devotion to Mary, the Mother of God and Mother of Mercy, I believed, as we were taught in the first grade, that regardless of what we did we'd all be able to sneak into heaven under her wide triangular skirt.

I also prayed, as most Catholics did in those days, novenas to saints known to grant requests, and frequently I received what I asked for. So when I began thinking about becoming a nun, I asked for a clear sign that my thinking was a call from God and not anything else. I wanted assurance that I wasn't misdirected, impulsive, or crazy. I planned to pray for something impossible, thinking that a favorable answer would be a sure sign I was picked to be a nun. Asking for the impossible improved significantly the odds of my not being picked, so I thought. As a last resort, I prayed for divine intervention and direction because I really needed it.

Designated for those in distress or emergency situations, I chose the novena to the Infant of Prague in asking for a sign. I prayed the novena nine times in a row at the same time every hour for nine hours, and for nine days as specified, asking for the lead role in *Harvey*. Because my chances of being cast were nonexistent, it felt like a true test, my idea of divine intervention. With the exception of appearing in Christmas pageants in grade school and summer talent shows in the basement of Bernie Smith's house, I had been on stage only once, at the age of nine. It was a voice recital in which I sang two solos: "Once I Had a Secret Love" and "Oh! My Papa." I placed fourth out of five, but only because the fifth girl got sick and didn't perform. That was the end of voice lessons with Mr. McLean. Other than that, I demonstrated no theatrical training or interest.

I stacked high odds against the Infant of Prague on purpose, so that if I did get the role, my nun fate would be sealed. In addition, my classmate Kathy Schreier wanted the role badly and couldn't be more qualified. A talented and experienced actor with a beautifully trained singing voice, she was perfect for the part.

Only because of a dare did I try out for the lead role of Veta Louise Simmons—sister of Elwood P. Dowd, best friend of Harvey—and only by the grace of the Infant of Prague did I get it. Not only did I get the lead, but our performance brought the house down every night. Joe Kissela was cast as my possibly crazy brother, Elwood, and working with him turned into pure magic. Not only did he reincarnate the spirit of Jimmy Stewart (who played the role in the movie *Harvey*), but I swear we both saw Harvey on stage every night, as I believe Patsy Nau, who played my daughter, Myrtle Mae Simmons, did too. That did it. I got far more than I asked for. Having been dealt the nun card, I now had to play it. My fate as a nun was sealed. Hard to believe? You bet.

Given the silliness and mindlessness of my decision-making process, I felt a letter was the only way I could tell my parents I wanted to be a nun. Though absolutely certain that's what I needed to do next, I felt completely unable to explain why. What would I tell my mom and dad, "I lost a bet with the Infant of Prague"? In a letter I could say what I needed without facing the shocked looks on their faces or being inter- rupted with outbursts like "Are you crazy?" "Where did that come from?" "Why?" "Why now?" I didn't want to risk the possibility that they'd think it was all a big joke, as so much of my life had been until then, and as I believed when the thought first crossed my mind. I made it a point not to be at home when the letter arrived. The only thing I remember as clearly as if it happened yesterday are the words of my mother, sitting at the kitchen table smoking Benson & Hedges with fil- ters and drinking coffee, with my letter in hand:

"I don't mind if my boys want to be a priest," she said in a com- manding, definitive voice. "That's a good life. But I don't want my daughters to be a nun."

My parents believed being a nun was a waste of life. Being a priest wasn't quite as bad because they enjoyed a "good life" with what ap- peared to be unlimited independence. For example, the pastor of our parish of Saint Stanislaus lived and traveled with his housekeeper and always drove a new car, which seemed like a very good life to us. Free to come and go as they please, priests frequently went out to dinner, vis- ited families in the parish, vacationed in Europe, had enough money at their disposal, and were generally treated by all like God on Earth. Even celibacy appeared optional. What's not to like?

Being a nun, on the other hand, was equivalent to life in prison. Nuns had nothing, gave up everything, were treated like the priest's servants, and worked hard until they died of very old age. Sisters rarely left the convent for anything other than work and church; they never traveled alone, never ate in public, owned nothing, and had no money or personal possessions. Everything nuns received was turned into the common fund or given to the parish priest. It was a life my parents did not wish for me. Even my Busia, my Polish grandmother, tried to change my mind with a bribe of a trip to New York City for the World's Fair. They all felt that being a nun was a life of deprivation and that I was too young to make such a drastic decision.

"You have no idea what you're getting yourself into," my dad warned me over and over, sincerely wanting to change my mind.

My father, who served in the army during World War II, really knew whereof he spoke. The fact that I couldn't explain why I wanted to be a nun only proved his point. For all I knew, they were right. Nuns didn't speak about what happened in the first nine months: That was a secret they didn't share. I found out later that lips were sealed because the truth was too awful to reveal.

In preparing to enter the convent, all we were told was what to bring: a trunk, two pairs of black shoes, a sewing kit, a girdle with garters (no panty girdles allowed), black cotton stockings, white cotton underwear, a watch, Bible, rosary, one statue, one prayer book of our choice, one box of plain white stationery, twelve white cotton handkerchiefs, leather pen and pencil holder (worn around the waist like a holster), fountain pen, soap dish, toothbrush, hairbrush, and a two-hundred-dollar dowry. Everything else would be provided. Two identical habits were made by one of the sisters at Bishop Noll High School, one for daily wear and one for Sundays and holidays. Sister Scholastica, the chemistry teacher, made mine, and both would be waiting for me when I arrived at Saint Mary's.

My brothers and sisters seemed just as puzzled at my decision as my parents were. My sister Debbie, and brothers Hank and David were in grade school at the time, and I suspect my becoming a nun meant nothing other than more bedroom space. We lived in a modern 1960 tri-level yellow brick house—built by my dad, my Uncle Ziggy, and their friend Alex Ziemny—with four bedrooms, two and a half bathrooms, and a partially finished and stocked bomb shelter in the basement (open metal shelves along cinder-block walls, filled with cereal, coffee, canned goods, toilet paper, paper towel, Kleenex, water, and beer). All of a sudden, my big bedroom on the ground floor (with full bath) was up for grabs. I think the younger ones looked at me leaving and saw mostly the exciting possibility that one of them could actually inherit the earth.

My sister Jackie, older by fifteen months, was speechless too, but only because we weren't speaking at the time. Months before, Jackie and I broke into a hair-pulling, screaming, scratching fight over I-don't-remember-what, after which she moved out of the room we shared on the ground floor and headed upstairs to move in with Debbie. Jackie was an honor student, a cheerleader, and a class officer. I managed to be a C student at best, Booster Club officer, and the class clown. Jackie preferred neatness, whereas I wallowed in chaos. We were another odd couple. We even resorted to a masking-tape dividing line on the bedroom floor, neither of us allowed on the other's side.

My leaving home turned into the best thing that happened to Jackie and me. Distance eventually lent enchantment, and we became sisters forever. But at the time Jackie was glad to see me go. She probably thought I'd finally get what I deserved in the convent. And I did.

For as much as my family disagreed with my decision and didn't understand why I couldn't wait a few years or change my mind completely, never did they withhold loving support or their blessing as they said good-bye.

"I never tried to change your mind," my mom says proudly, to this day.

Everyone thought that I'd be home in six months. No one expected I'd last longer than that. Some believed I joined the convent on a dare, collecting the promised payoff if I lasted half a year. And up to now, I told no one of the bet I lost with the Infant of Prague. I didn't want to highlight the appearance of insanity then; now it doesn't matter. Even I, in my mysterious certainty, harbored hidden doubts. Not that I'd want to leave, but that the nuns would find me unsuitable for convent life and send me home. My chances of being dismissed appeared high, but even that didn't deter me.

While telling my parents was something I could do only in a hand-written mailed letter, telling my high school friends I wanted to be a nun was something I could do only in an altered state of consciousness. I needed to be under the influence of alcohol. It happened on December 31, 1963, at Bone's New Year's Eve sleepover. Bone's real name is Mary Francis, but we nicknamed her Bone because she was so skinny. Bone's parents, Helen and Frank, went to a New Year's Eve dinner and dance that night, trusting us girls to party responsibly. We referred to our parents by their first names, though to their faces they were respectfully Mr. and Mrs. Marcinek. I think Bone's brother, Russ, checked in on us once or twice and just let us carry on, so that's what we did.

New Year's Eve was always a party and a sleepover for us because we'd be too intoxicated to go home. It wasn't a matter of being responsible about drinking and driving (none of us had cars), we simply didn't want to face the music at home if we stumbled in drunk. Even though under age, we somehow always found easy access to alcohol.

Alcohol and cigarettes were the drugs of choice in those days. A little marijuana floated around, which I confess to smoking, inhaling, and liking, but it was not much more powerful than rope and could be found growing along the railroad tracks near our high school. Even so, these were the days of *Reefer Madness*, and smoking dope, we were told, opened the door to heroin, cocaine, and insanity. Alcohol was safe because our parents drank. So did our priests.

I knew that Bone's party would be my last New Year's Eve before joining the convent, and these were my best friends, some of whom I'd known since kindergarten. About ten of us were there, all veterans of the same grade school and high school sleepovers. As best friends, they felt like my sisters, and that was the holy night I decided to tell them about my becoming a nun.

It was well after midnight when I told them. The music still played, but we stopped dancing, eating, and drinking, turned out the lights, and circled around the fireplace with pillows and blankets. In the sleepover ritual, that's when we begin telling scary and funny stories and sharing secrets. Everyone is drunk, which intensifies the emotion, so there was sidesplitting laughter mixed in with heartfelt tears.

I swore everyone to secrecy before I spoke. I feared news of my going to the convent would make headlines in the school newspaper. When I made them swear on the Marcinek family Bible not to tell, some laughingly thought I was pregnant and made jokes about a second Immaculate Conception; though none of us even knew that it meant Mary was conceived without sin and had nothing to do with giving birth.

"I'm going to the convent," I said with dead seriousness and slightly slurred speech.

When everyone but me laughed out loud, Bobs Whelan knew I wasn't kidding.

"Oh my God, you're serious," she said.

None of us knew whether to laugh or cry, so we did both. I recall a flurry of questions about why, where, and when, but none of us were in shape to be that serious. None of us slept, all of us drank too much (Babs and I split a fifth of Sunnybrook), and we were all so hungover the next day that I wondered if anyone remembered what I told them. But they did. Rarely a day went by without my noticing one of my friends sworn to secrecy staring at me and bursting into tears. That was the only reason I didn't tell Vern until after graduation.

"Don't you remember?" she said, when I asked how I told her. "You told me at Peggy O'Malley's brother's wedding and I fell off my chair."

I didn't remember that.

"You didn't tell me sooner," she continued, "because you didn't want me treating you differently."

That I do remember. I didn't want Vern bursting into tears too. Being treated differently after breaking the news made me feel as if I was dying of a terminal disease and our days together were numbered. Even though I couldn't think too seriously about becoming a nun, there was no doubt that life as I knew it was about to end.

While I didn't know what daily life as a nun would be like, I did know that all contact with family and friends would be restricted. I wouldn't see them for years, couldn't write to them, couldn't call, and wouldn't be coming home for five years. There was no way I could continue to be in touch with my friends. I also understood clearly that the kind of fun I knew in high school would soon be over. There would be no chugging Sunnybrook in the convent, no more "Suds," no fries and Cokes at Fat Boy's, no spending hours on the phone, no writing and passing notes incessantly throughout the day, no more drunken sleepovers. When my friends joked about there being "nun of this and nun of that" in the convent, part of me was finding that less and less funny.

While most of my friends headed toward a life of more fun in college and jobs in Chicago, I walked off alone to a life of solitude, silence, study, and prayer in the convent. A big part of me was changing, but it felt like dying. The only life I knew and loved would soon be over, and we all feared that becoming a nun would extinguish all sparks of fun. The Karol everyone knew and loved—Kare—would disappear in the habit of being a nun.

The call I heard to become a nun happened just like that. There is not now, nor has there ever been, anything unusually dramatic or noteworthy about the call I heard. What I do know now about the mysterious beginning of my religious life is that I recognized the call simply as a voice—a still, small, inner voice—a kind of hunch, an intuitive gut-instinct telling me what to do and where to go, like a divining rod showing my thirsty soul where to find water. It was the Sisters of the Holy Cross who helped me discover that I had a mind, a voice of my own, a more thoughtful, reflective, insightful voice. They helped me discover my soul while continuing to follow my fun-loving heart. They taught me to always let conscience be my guide.

I can see now how my dumb feeling speechless about why I wanted to be a nun was due largely to the fact that none of my friends had experiences similar to mine, except for the sisters, who knew exactly what I meant. They understood how everything I experienced in wanting to be a nun at eighteen was entirely inexplicable. I was given Rilke's *Letters to a Young Poet* as a graduation gift from Sister Michaela, in which the following passages were underlined and through which everything I felt in the beginning made sense:

> something new has entered us, something unknown; our feelings grow mute in shy embarrassment, everything in us withdraws, a silence rises, and the new experience, which no one knows, stands in the midst of it all and says nothing . . .

I would like to beg you to have patience toward everything un-
solved in your heart and try to love the questions themselves, as if
they were locked rooms or books written in a very foreign language.
Don't search for the answers, which could not be given to you now,
because you would not be able to live them. The point is to live
everything. Live the questions now, perhaps then, someday far in
the future, you will gradually without even noticing, live your way
into the answer.*

Even with mountains of mysterious certainty, I still delayed as long
as I could the formal steps to enter the convent—filling out the application, taking the psychological tests, getting certificates of Baptism and
Confirmation from the parish—believing maybe that at the last minute
the call would fade in favor of some more normal life choice. But all I
found in the delay was that the time had truly come for me to follow
those sisterly women with whom I felt such an irresistible affinity. The
time had come to take my life to a place where support and understanding might be found for my strange and inexplicable experiences.
I'm still not exactly sure how or why, but the time had clearly come in
the summer of 1964, at the too young age of eighteen, to close my eyes
and jump into what always feels like a massive sea of unknowing.

"Holy ascetic, I have set out to find God. Show me the road."
"There isn't any road," he answered me, beating his staff on the ground.
"What is there then?" I asked, seized with terror.
"There is the abyss. Jump!"
"Abyss!" I screamed. "Is that the way?"
"Yes, the abyss . . . the abyss leads to God. Jump!"†

*Rainer Maria Rilke, *Letters to a Young Poet*, trans. Stephen Mitchell (New York: Vintage
Books, 1986), pp. 83, 34–35.
†Nikos Kazantzakis, *Saint Francis* (Chicago: Loyola Press, 2005), p. 42.

I was accepted by the Sisters of the Holy Cross on July 13, 1964, the Feast of Saint Henry (whose name my father, brother, and nephew share), and two months later left home for the convent. It was the Feast of the Exaltation of the Holy Cross, the day designated for the arrival of new postulants at the Sisters of the Holy Cross Motherhouse in Notre Dame, Indiana. It was the day forever and ever began.

chapter two

initiation into sisterhood

The postulancy is a time of probation, the purpose of which is to initiate the candidate into the religious life and to test her vocation.

—CONSTITUTION 9:41

In the one-way trip from my home in East Chicago, Indiana, to the Sisters of the Holy Cross Motherhouse at Saint Mary's College in Notre Dame, Indiana, I was a silent mystifying mixture of feeling strangely picked by God to be a nun and completely hungover from partying with friends the night before: the "one last fling" before I got flung into the convent.

I said good-bye to everyone in my world—family, friends, and neighbors—as though I'd never see them again, because for all intents and purposes, I wouldn't—at least not for five years. With every farewell I grew quieter, as if each good-bye took another breath away from me. The day I left for the convent I felt nothing inside.

Sisters Miriam Edward and Christopher Marie drove me and my mother to Saint Mary's on September 14. If you've ever driven the Indiana Toll Road, you know how hypnotically flat the land it crosses is—mile after mile of Midwest farmland, with an occasional wave of stomach-turning smells from pig, cow, horse, and sheep manure. Even with the windows closed, the odor can get to you—especially if you're hungover. Part of me felt increasingly nauseated, while the rest of me wondered whether I'd ever experience that world again.

I don't recall noticing the foliage I'd always seen in mid-September. I only recall staring out the window and feeling that the closer we got to South Bend, the more I was filled with a kind of dread I never knew before. Miriam and Christopher made small talk in the front seat, trying to make me laugh, but they couldn't. All I remember clearly were the "No U Turn" signs about every ten miles, like some cosmic joke telling me over and over: "There's no turning back."

For the first time in my life I felt alone. It was the sick soulful feeling I still get when I jump into the unknown with no idea what I'm getting myself into or when I take an unpopular public stand on controversial issues and find myself surrounded by silence. Saying good-bye to the life I left behind scared me, the giving up of everyone and everything I knew and loved, including my self.

About ten miles from the South Bend exit, there's a wide turn on the Indiana Toll Road where all of a sudden the gold dome of the administration building at the University of Notre Dame appears in the distance and across the road to the west, the bell tower of Le Mans Hall, the administration building at Saint Mary's. We were almost there. At that point, all of my dread and nausea turned to terror and tears. In a matter of minutes my mom and sisters would return to East Chicago and I wouldn't be going with them. It felt as though someone removed my hand gently from the knob as the door to that life closed. That's when I spoke for the first time.

"I want you to drop me off and go," I said, still staring out the window. "No hanging around, no socializing, no meeting anyone or introducing me to anyone, no long-drawn-out good-bye. Just drop me off and go."

Of course that didn't happen, and I was too weak to argue. As we exited the Toll Road and turned on to Saint Mary's Avenue, the trees arched over us like angelic ancestors with lacy green wings, motioning us forward. But the sidewalks weren't lined with sisters singing "Ave Maris Stella" as they had on my first visit. In their place appeared a steady stream of Notre Dame boys coming to Saint Mary's and Saint Mary's girls going to Notre Dame. The excitement of one last look at the road not taken flashed before me, as I, their classmate, drove past them to the convent. At the end of the avenue we veered right around the circle in front of Holy Cross Hall, past the Security Guard office, taking another right-hand turn, pulling up and parking in front of the yellow brick building marked "Sisters of the Holy Cross Postulate."

"Well, here we are," Miriam and Christopher announced, as if I hadn't noticed. One of them added a too cheerful, "This is it!"

"You can go now," I said, not even wanting them to get out of the car.

"Don't be silly," Miriam Edward said, getting my suitcase from the trunk. "We're going in with you."

When we pulled open the big turquoise doors, a tall middle-aged nun greeted us. In reality she was no taller than I was, but the habit's headgear added another five inches to her height. She had a round, kind face, a thin-lipped smile, and pale blue eyes I saw once before when visiting the Westville Women's Asylum with my high school health class— piercing blue eyes that when angry changed instantly to gray. Her arms were folded and hidden under the habit's black cape which made her look like a double amputee.

"This is Sister Joseph Marie," Miriam said, introducing us, to my superior.

"And you must be Karol Jackowski," she said, extending a warm hand of welcome from under the cape, breaking into a smile that transformed her stern face into something loving and kind.

"Welcome to Saint Mary's," she added with miraculous smile intact.

After a few uncomfortable minutes of small talk, Miriam, Christopher, and my mother finally granted my wish and decided to go. As they prepared to leave, I started to cry.

"Well, say your good-byes now," Sister Joseph Marie said, extending a comforting arm around my shoulder, "then come and join your sisters. They're waiting to meet you." I was among the last to arrive.

"She seems very nice," my mom said as we walked arm in arm to the car, "and the building is beautiful."

"I know, I know," I said, choking on tears.

"You'll be fine," Miriam Edward added, squeezing my other hand.

"Please," I begged while taking deep breaths and trying to hold myself together, "just go. I can't stand this."

"We'll keep in touch," Christopher Marie said while giving me a hug before taking the driver's seat.

"You better keep in touch," I said, trying to laugh as I let her go. "Don't abandon me here."

"We won't abandon you," Miriam Edward added tearfully, laughing as she hugged me good-bye. "Trust me, you'll be just fine."

"You keep saying that," I said, trying not to burst out sobbing. "I miss you already."

Miriam Edward got in the car, leaving me to say good-bye to my mother.

"Be good," my mom told me with a tearful hug that felt so final.

"Like I have a choice," I said, not wanting to let her go. "I'll write as soon as I can. Tell everyone to write me."

"I will," she said, letting me go. Then with one last kiss before getting in the backseat, she whispered, "Love you."

After our tearful curbside good-byes, I watched as they drove away and turned down the avenue out of sight.

There was no going back now.

I stood outside the postulate for I don't know how long, staring at the road, as if they'd come back to get me and I'd go. I wore a pink suit, white blouse, black flats, and no makeup. Not that I ever wore much makeup in high school, but on the day I left for the convent, I figured, "Why bother?"

The only step left for me to take led through those big heavy turquoise doors. Feeling terrified and weak-kneed, I turned to go in and saw that I wasn't alone. Leaning against the building, away from the doors, stood a sophisticated-looking woman, a little older than I, in a stylish pastel blue suit, navy blue heels, and a face full of makeup. She was smoking. I hadn't noticed her there before. At her feet near a small suitcase were several lipstick-stained butts smoked to the filter.

"Are you going in there?" she asked, exhaling roundish rings of smoke.

"I think so," I said as though I still entertained a thought of escape, adding, "I hate good-byes," while wiping tears with a handkerchief Miriam Edward gave me.

"I know what you mean," she said. "I went through the same thing this morning when I left my family in Boston."

Looking at her watch, she added, "We have a few minutes." It was 3:45 P.M. and we needed to be inside by four o'clock.

"I'm Fran," she said, offering me her cigarette. "Do you smoke?"

"Not really, but I will now," I said. "I'm Karol, but everyone calls me Kare."

Handing me the lit cigarette, she said, "Breathe deep, it's our last taste of the real world."

I did breathe deep and started coughing as the tower bell rang at 3:55 P.M. At that moment one of the big blue heavy metal doors opened slowly. Fran stomped out the cigarette and scattered the other butts into the bushes. Standing behind the door was Sister Joseph Marie.

"Are you ladies staying or leaving?" she asked with a half-smile that gave no clear indication that she was joking.

As she grabbed her suitcase, Fran and I looked at each other as though we were in trouble already, and I mumbled, "Sorry, Sister."

"You must be Mary Francis Monahan," she said. "I'm Sister Joseph Marie, your superior. Welcome to Saint Mary's. I assume you two have met."

"It's a nice place you have here," Fran said mindlessly while looking around the lobby. "I heard you have a bowling alley," she added, which made me laugh.

Sister Joseph Marie ignored both remarks.

The building, as new as we, smelled of fresh paint and construction dust blended with the faint scent of incense. We stood in the lobby on terrazzo floors, looking at beige walls and an abstract bronze sculpture that hung on the south wall, which we later named "Nuns Flying Home." On the north wall hung an oversized seal of the Congregation of the Sisters of the Holy Cross. It looked like a mausoleum and was just as eerily quiet.

A few sisters walked through the lobby, smiling and waving at us with a look of pity, as if to say, "We know how you feel." The south side of the building, called the Sisters of the Holy Cross Postulate, was where the new sisters lived, while temporarily professed sisters in their junior and senior years of college lived on the north side, the Sisters of the Holy Cross Juniorate. The sisters who waved, smiled, and winked walked into the door leading into the juniorate.

"You'll meet them later," Sister Joseph Marie told us with a surprising little burst of excitement, as though a big treat awaited us.

Before us, to the right of the "Nuns Flying Home" sculpture, were two oak doors with bronze handles shaped like upright fish. Opening one of the doors and leading us in, Sister Joseph Marie turned to us and said, "This is the chapel, where we'll meet for vespers."

Built in the center, the chapel linked the two residences, as did small office-like visiting rooms in the lobby, three on each side. Though tasteful and modern in design, the chapel felt as empty as I did, as though

God had just arrived and hadn't yet unpacked. Bronze statues of the Virgin Mary and Saint Joseph hung on the marble walls to the left and right of the altar. Marble floors, a marble altar, and a shiny off-white marble wall behind the altar did nothing to surround us with the warmth and comfort often found in old convents, chapels, and churches. Ours were the first spirits to live there.

"I like the stained-glass windows," Fran said, noticing that the sunshine made rainbows on us. Dozens of pink and red roses flanked the altar, filling the chapel with sweet scents that carried a little buzz. Between the rainbows and the roses I got goose bumps. Maybe God was at home there after all.

"There you are!" two sisters called out, appearing from the door leading to the juniorate. They actually ran to meet us, as you would best friends you hadn't seen in a long time.

"These sisters will show you to your rooms and help you dress," Sister Joseph Marie said, with the mysterious half-smile that I later learned reflected her dismay at the "running" sisters. Running was not part of a nun's religious decorum.

"I'm Sister John Mark," one of them said, welcoming me with a hug and taking my suitcase. Little did I know then that we'd become lifelong friends.

"And I'm Sister Michael," the other said to Fran, offering the same warm welcome. "Follow me," she said, leading us to the postulate.

"They'll take good care of you," Sister Joseph Marie said, walking with us. "We'll meet in the community room at five o'clock and process together to the chapel for vespers."

"They'll be dressed and ready to go," Sister John Mark said, looking at us with a heartwarming smile I found comforting.

We walked through the lobby to the door that opened into the postulate "community room"—a long rectangular room with circular

Formica-topped game tables and wooden chairs with fabric-covered seats, bright orange and royal blue Naugahyde lounge furniture, TV, record player, fireplace, and wooden cabinets along the walls that stored games, recreational equipment, and records. On the east wall, between the floor-to-ceiling windows, hung three Margaret Keane "Big Eye" paintings of orphans, dogs, and cats with big heads and round black alien-looking eyes. The opposite wall was one big window looking into a grassy courtyard with classrooms on the other side. Both bright and private, the community room looked more like a hotel lobby than a convent. The nun's world I entered looked surprisingly modern and ordinary, not like a dark and musty monastery. Changes had already begun in the lives of nuns, though I didn't see it that way at the time.

Over the marble fireplace hung a bronze crucifix with an abstract risen Christ figure with raised outstretched arms—not the bloodied, beaten body I expected to see. Seated in a circle around the fireplace were the other postulants, dressed in habits, sewing laundry numbers on their underwear (I was #1053), and speaking in low voices, but no laughter. All heads looked up when we walked in.

"Well, your sisters have finally arrived," Sister Joseph Marie announced. "This is Mary Francis Monahan and Karol Jackowski. They'll be joining you shortly."

"After we get dressed," Fran added, and several laughed.

An elderly little nun with a sweet Irish face and twinkling blue eyes walked over to greet us.

"This is Sister Electa," Sister Joseph Marie said. "She's my assistant."

"Welcome, welcome," she said, taking our hands in hers. "We've been waiting for you." I liked her instantly. She radiated good humor.

"You're both on the second floor," Sister John Mark told us as she led us to the stairway. "Karol, you're in room 214, and Mary Francis, you're across the hall in room 233."

"Great!" I said, thinking of the fun we'd have up there.

"Well, don't get too excited," Sister John Mark said. "With the exception of today, there's no talking on the bedroom floors."

"And you're never allowed in one another's rooms," Sister Michael added.

"Are you serious?" Fran asked with disbelief.

"Absolutely," both sisters said in unison.

When Fran and I looked at each other and smiled, they added, "We're not kidding."

"This is it," Sister John Mark said at Room 214, opening the door and leading me in. Keys weren't necessary because bedroom doors were to be kept open, except at night. On each door, hand-scripted in perfect calligraphy, was our name. Mine read: "𝕶𝖆𝖗𝖔𝖑 𝕬𝖓𝖓 𝕵𝖆𝖈𝖐𝖔𝖜𝖘𝖐𝖎."*

While generations of postulants before us slept in dormitory cells, I loved being given a room of my own—a six-by-eight-foot beige shoebox with a twin bed, wooden desk chair, built-in desk, bookshelf, closet, sink, and window with a marble windowsill big enough to sit on. Over the desk hung a modern gold crucifix, and on the wall over the bookcase a wood reproduction of an icon of the sixteenth-century Spanish mystic Saint Teresa of Ávila. I remembered one detail about Teresa of Ávila from reading her autobiography in high school: one of her prayers was "God preserve us from sour-faced saints!" Being given her icon seemed like a divine sign. The bedroom window faced south and looked out onto the novitiate thirty feet across the road—the one-hundred-year-old building where generations of novices lived in solitary confinement and slept in big dorms with ten to fifteen others. The thought alone made a room of my own feel like a lifesaver.

---

*We did not receive the title of Sister until we entered the novitiate. As a postulant I was addressed by superiors as Miss Jackowski or Karol.

My postulant's habit lay on the bed like a dead nun. I stared at it, feeling as though I was the soul chosen to give it new life. Sister John Mark set my suitcase near the desk, then opened the closet door where a spare habit hung, taking out a plain brown paper grocery bag.

"Put your clothes and shoes in here, shoes on the bottom," she said, handing me the bag. "I'll come and get them after you're dressed."

Sister John Mark explained how to assemble the postulant's habit, then asked if I had questions or needed help. All of a sudden I felt sick to my stomach.

"No," I said, hardly able to speak. "I think I can figure it out."

"Very well," she said, with a heartwarming smile. "I'll be back in twenty minutes."

Closing the door after she left, I stood at the foot of the bed staring at the habit resting in peace, feeling as though I couldn't move. Within seconds I heard three light knocks on the door behind me.

"Are you okay in there?" Fran whispered loudly.

That broke the spell. I opened the door and there she stood, looking just as dazed and confused as I felt, holding the grocery bag in one hand and her habit in the other.

"I think I'm going to throw up," I whispered.

"No you're not," she said with a mini burst of bravery, coming into my room and closing the door. "Come on, we can do this. We have to do this."

The moment had come for us to cross over. I knew that.

First we took off our "worldly clothes," folding them nicely as if we were laying them to rest, then placing them in the brown bag on top of our traveling shoes.

"There goes our life in a grocery bag," I said, which broke us up into fits of giggles as we folded the bag closed for pickup. Standing in our underwear, we looked at each other as if we were about to die. Fran took the leap and said, "Okay, let's do it."

Layer by layer we donned the postulant's habit. First the black stockings, then the white cotton Fruit of the Loom undershirt, then the black blouse, then the black cotton underskirt with knee-deep pockets, then the black serge overskirt, the black cape, the stiff white collar, the shiny black nun oxfords, and finally the veil, which went over our hair like a scarf and tied in the back. (Postulants wore the veil only in the chapel and in public.) Around our waists we snapped a leather pen and pencil holder.

"We look like pilgrims," Fran said, giggling nervously.

"Amish pilgrims," I said, intensifying the laughter. "But you better wash your face," I added, looking at her in the habit with a face full of makeup. She looked like something you'd see today in the Greenwich Village Halloween Parade.

"Oh my God, I forgot," she said, ripping off the veil, grabbing my washcloth and towel and turning to the sink. She washed her face clean of makeup and re-veiled just in time for the return of the sisters, who tried not to look upset that Fran was in my room.

"Fran just came over to make sure she looked okay," I said.

"You look fine," Sister John Mark said, straightening out my collar while Sister Michael covered more of Fran's hair with the veil.

"You do too, Fran," Sister Michael added, laughing. "You look like you were made for the habit."

Taking the grocery bags with our escape clothes, Sister Michael suddenly turned serious and looked us in the eye. "After today, there is absolutely no talking up here, and never are you to be in each other's rooms. Both are grounds for dismissal."

We stood there, speechless.

"Is that understood?" she asked, not softening the seriousness.

"Yes, sister," we said in unison. We followed them out the door and down the stairs. At the end of the hallway stood a life-size statue of the Virgin Mary, hands outstretched with blue glass eyes that followed us, and a smile that led me to feel that all would be well. The crescent moon under her feet also looked like a big divine grin. As we rounded the corner and headed downstairs, Fran looked up at Mary with anxious eyes, then turned to me, crossed her eyes, and silently mouthed the words, "Help! Save us!"

Within a week we discovered the harsh reality of what we were in for. Day by day Sister Joseph Marie revealed the rules regarding our new lives as postulants. Sister Electa stood at her side smiling, as if to assure us that it wasn't as bad as it sounded, even if it was. First of all, we weren't allowed to walk freely around campus. Rabbits and squirrels enjoyed more freedom than we did. The restricted area for recreation included the front and back of the postulate, the back of which happened to be the nun's burial ground: row after row of white stone crosses, looking like the Arlington Cemetery of God's Sisters.

The thought of socializing anywhere near a cemetery gave us the creeps at first. That's where we were sent on Fridays to meditate on death. But it didn't take long before the Our Lady Queen of Peace Cemetery turned into an outdoor clubhouse of sorts. That's where we met to pass notes, have clandestine conversations, and sometimes smoke. I felt surrounded by the holy spirits who rested there; they were like a comforter of protection wrapped around me. I never got caught doing anything in the cemetery and thanked the deceased sisters for that amazing grace.

Sometimes the college girls in our classes slipped us cigarettes, which we smoked behind the Queen of Peace shrine. In the winter, smoking was easy. Everyone who walked through South Bend winters breathing the frigid air looked as if they could be smoking. Generations of young sisters snuck smokes in the cemetery and never got caught.

Actually, we weren't allowed to talk with the college girls, though we did. In class the postulants sat together in the last row, as if to avoid notice. Some of my high school friends, also students at Saint Mary's, became our Sisters of Mercy, sneaking us contraband like candy, soda, and cigarettes, and sneaking out our uncensored mail. We weren't allowed to talk to professed sisters at the college either, but few of us dared do that anyway. Any one of them could be part of an entrapment scheme and would report us to the superior.

The ban on communication with the outside world also included reading magazines and newspapers and watching TV. Tuning knobs were removed from the communal television and radio to prevent unsupervised viewing or listening, and only the superior knew where they were. In the fall, on Saturdays after lunch, Sister Joseph Marie appeared like Houdini and replaced the knobs so we could watch Notre Dame football, whether we were interested or not. That was one of her superior powers—the keeper of the knobs.

After a few weeks of radio and TV starvation, I made friends with Mr. Horner, one of the maintenance men, who'd lend me his red pocket transistor radio on weekends—from Friday afternoon when he left work until Monday morning when he returned. Once again I was able to listen to American Top 40 hits on WLS. I'd take it by myself to the cemetery, find an isolated spot, and crank up the volume. I like to think the sisters resting there made jokes about being raised from the dead. And for three weekend nights, after lights-out, I fell asleep listening to WLS with my favorite DJ, Casey Kasem.

For months the radio arrangement was perfect, giving me weekends with the real world, that is, until Mr. Horner began lurking in the postulate hallways where he didn't belong and slipping me notes of song titles like "Send Me the Pillow You Dream On" and "Be My Baby." Something about Mr. Horner turned horny and I didn't like it. It nearly killed me to give up the joy of weekends with Casey and WLS, but sexual harassment ended my transistor relationship with Mr. Horner. Without the radio, a big part of me felt unplugged from life and surrounded by silence I never knew before.

The ban on communication with the outside world also meant that visitors weren't allowed. With the exception of Advent and Lent, three members of our family could visit once a month on designated Visitor Sundays; those with large families didn't see brothers and sisters for nine months. Other than family and nuns, no other visitors were allowed without special permission. Only once did Sister Joseph Marie let me visit with my high school friends for an hour.

Rules controlled every aspect of our lives. We were to walk slowly without swinging our arms. We were never allowed to chew gum. We were to laugh and speak softly, waste nothing, and sweep the halls and wax the floors as though the King of Glory was coming for dinner. We put small pieces of paper under the thumb as we held our prayer books, so that the thin pages would be preserved from soiling. If an accident of any kind happened (spilling water, spotting the habit, etc.), an "account" of the incident was to be made to the superior immediately. And if we cleaned our rooms in five minutes, when the rule said fifteen, that meant we probably didn't have a vocation.

We also learned on day one that the proposed bowling alley was the Trunk Room, the area in the basement where we stored trunks and shined shoes on Saturday afternoons. Apparently construction money ran out, and the bowling alley and swimming pool were never built. I wanted to know who made that decision. Given that the bowling alley was a big drawing card for me, my heart sank when I got that news. Several of us felt scammed by false advertising and said so. Sister Joseph Marie and Sister Electa just looked at each other and laughed. We got the message: What you think doesn't matter.

After all was said and we thought we were done, Sister Joseph Marie dropped the bombshell. Opening a small, worn, black book called the Constitutions—the rule book for the Sisters of the Holy Cross—she read Constitution 33 on Silence:

Silence is essential to recollection and prayer; it is therefore the right of every religious. Unless personal duty or courtesy to others prevent, the sisters shall refrain from talking except at times appointed for recreation.

—CONSTITUTION 33:205

A religious living in the presence of God will never disturb anyone unnecessarily. She will show her love of silence by the noiseless way she moves and acts.

—CONSTITUTION 33:209

In other words, most of every day would be spent in silence. Recreation was scheduled for forty-five minutes after lunch and after dinner, but other than that, silence ruled. One of the biggest adjustments for me in the beginning of my religious life was not being able to talk whenever I wanted. How would I get to know the other postulants? What if we needed someone to talk to? We were all homesick, going through the same anxiety and misery. Why couldn't we talk to one another privately without disturbing the others?

None of our questions or concerns mattered, as we kept being told, and those who spoke up in protest were cut short and silenced. Speaking our mind wasn't encouraged, especially if what we had to say questioned the divine wisdom of the holy rule. And if we needed to talk to someone, we were told to talk to the Superior. Yeah, right. Where do we line up?

After the initial shock of not being able to talk wore off a bit, we learned quickly how to communicate without talking and developed a sign language all our own. A tug of the sleeve and a shift of the eye meant "meet me in the cemetery," and a loud fake cough meant the superior was coming. Note-passing, though still a violation of the rule of silence, was a lifesaver. We'd slip notes into one another's prayer books, pass them discreetly in the dining room, or leave them in the cemetery between two designated graves. My cemetery spot for note-passing was about the sixth row from the north fence, between the graves of Sister Lisetta and Sister Edwardine.

I became a prolific note-writer and superb note-passer (I was never caught) and was careful to destroy the notes after reading them so as not to risk discovery by the superior or anyone. The contents of those clandestine notes, often full of complaints, gossip, and subversive activities, surely would have meant big trouble if not dismissal. Complaints mostly focused on superiors and excessively obedient postulants, and we gossiped about sisters who got sent home and what they did that resulted in dismissal.

While talking during the day, or "breaking silence," was judged to be a common sisterly fault in need of correcting, we talked anyhow without guilt. We'd walk outside a few feet apart, heads bowed to give the appearance of being lost in thought, while we carried on soft-spoken conversations with one another. Or we'd sit side by side on park benches in Our Lady Queen of Peace Cemetery, our noses buried in spiritual books while discussing the buzz of the day. It didn't take long to figure out inconspicuously safe ways to say what we had to say while giving the appearance of keeping the rule of silence. We did what we had to do in order to survive, and having someone to talk to always felt like a matter of survival.

After a few months of climbing the walls over not talking whenever I wanted, I began not to mind the general rule of silence. I even appreciated its intent to keep fifty teenagers undisturbed by distractions. For me, the protection of a woman's right to peace and quiet became one of the sisterhood's finest features. I suppose the founding sisters thought that since we did everything together at the same time, day after day, what else was there to say?

Even more important, the general rule of silence created an atmosphere that freed us to focus, concentrate, and do whatever the day set before us, be it study, housework, prayer, or play. The rule of silence taught me to keep still. Freed from distraction, I found silence charged with what I needed to listen. Ordinary everyday silence became my constant irritating companion in the beginning, and in that sacred silence my solitary life as a nun began to unfold.

While we practiced daytime silence mostly in the breach, the Great Silence at night was a far more serious rule according to the Constitutions (33:207), to be "especially observed." The Great Silence began at the close of evening recreation and lasted until after meditation the next morning. Breaking the Great Silence could be cause, we were told, for immediate dismissal. Even so, keeping quiet at night almost killed me at first and nearly led me to explode on occasion. Sometimes I had to talk.

I believed at the time that Great Silence was really a gag order, created to keep us from complaining at the end of the day when we were tired, and some of us sick and tired. My mother tells me that even as an infant I became more animated at night, so much so that it usually took a car ride around the block several times to put me to sleep. The simple fact that I'd been a night person since birth (even though I was born at dawn) provided some explanation for the difficulty I experienced keeping seriously silent at night. This was always compounded by the fact that at the end of the day, I had things to say.

While most of my sisters fell soundly asleep moments after lights-out, no matter how tired I felt, I was wide awake. I'd look out the window, watching the college girls or hoping one of the novices across the street would look out her window and we could send signals. Sometimes professed sisters walked by, and I'd throw notes out the window that said, "Help! Save me!" But little by little, night after night, I began to enter solitude when I began writing, sitting in the dark on the marble windowsill, writing by the soft white glow of the streetlight. Darkness, silence, and solitude replaced the radio, TV, and stereo in rocking me to sleep each night. And they became divine comfort.

I wrote every night from some inner necessity, as though I could not rest until I had done so. I wrote long letters to family and friends (some of which I snuck out and others I never sent), clandestine notes to sisters I passed to them the next day, and funny poems and stories I illustrated and gave away as presents. There's something about darkness that quiets the outside world and brings us closer to ourselves, how we feel, what we think, and in ways that are nowhere as clear during the light of day. After I stopped climbing the walls and learned to keep still, the rule of silence became my best friend.

On Friday, September 18, 1964, five days after I entered the convent, I snuck a letter out to my best friend, Vern, which she saved. One of the college girls in my English class mailed it. Why the need to sneak mail out? Superiors read and censored all outgoing mail, limited to one small sheet of paper. We could write two letters a month, one to family and one to friends; both written on the second Sunday of the month, "letter-writing Sunday." If I wrote something negative, the letter was returned with highlighted sentences that needed to be deleted or made more positive. Once I got a letter back so many times that I finally suggested to Sister Joseph Marie that she write the letter to my family and let them know how happy I was. She accepted my insolence far better than I deserved, and accepted the next draft without question. When push came to shove between us, Sister Joseph Marie always showed me mercy.

Superiors censored incoming mail as well, banning all letters from men. When long letters arrived, we'd be given only the first and last page because if our family and friends had anything important to say, they'd put it in those pages. Some of us protested the reading of our mail and the withholding of long letters as illegal, but silly us, it didn't matter. The sisterhood was a law unto itself when it came to tampering with the U.S. mail, and if we didn't like it, we could leave.

The difference between mail snuck out and censored mail was like the difference between truth and fiction. Below are two letters sent to Vern in my first months as a postulant. The first, dated September 18, four days after I entered, was written on pages ripped from a spiral notebook and snuck out uncensored. The second, sent in December, was written on a religious note card and censored.

Friday Morning
8:00 A.M.
Sept. 18

Hi Vern.

    Gee thanks for all your letters, it sure helps a drooping spirit; I get from 6–9 letters every day from everybody you could imagine. I really love it here so far Vern; I see Peggy O'Malley on sneak visits [Note: Peggy was a high school friend who entered the convent the year before and was in the novitiate]; and there's this girl here, Mary Sue Brennan, who's just like you, giving the finger and all; we even say some choice f-words every now and then. Her and I serve breakfast and yesterday two pot holders started on fire but we didn't get into too much trouble; you wouldn't believe how I am dying for pop; it's really killin' me. All

we have is milk, water, and once on a while orange juice, and what I
wouldn't do for a measly piece of candy. We rise at 5, early huh? We
go to mass, then breakfast, then we do housework, then class. I have 11
hours just like everybody else. I take Theology, American Democracy,
Psychology, and English, and boy do we get homework. There are so
many silence rules like no talking till after lunch or on bedroom floors
or after 7:30 p.m. or inbetween recreations. So in other words 3/4 of the
day is silence; we don't talk at meals either but I haven't kept silence
once and neither has anybody else; it's also an awful lot of prayin'
which I just ain't used to but like everything else we laff it off; every day
we're supposed to say a rosary, 7 dolors, stations of the cross, a 15
minute visit, and all other kindsa goodies which are very irritating; we
have to memorize 15 prayers for next week. Pray that I get it done . . .
I'd write to everybody but we're on a very tight schedule and all the in-
between time I have goes to studying because they really pile the work
on. I always get yelled at cuz I take off my collar when I feel like it, I
have to, it irritates me. All the kids here with me are great, and so are
the nuns so far; the kids are jealous because I get so much mail. Call
Miriam Edward and tell her I said "hello" and I'm very happy and that
I'm sitting in a desert and would love a Coke. I wish she'd bring you
here, I'm dying to see PEOPLE in real clothes; everybody calls us "sis-
ter" and I hate it; the other day we walked to St. Mary's library with
Sr. Joseph Marie for books and all the kids open doors for us and say
"good morning sister." I have so much to tell you but I have class in 5
minutes. keep writing it really helps; I understand your code words very
well and I am really happy. Be good and find a job. I'm really prayin'
for it!!!
  Keep Smilin

Love
Kare

P.S. Don't mention anything about getting this sneaky lil' letter!!! Or I'll get hell baby and I mean H __ __ __

JMJ

December 17, 1964
Notre Dame, Indiana

Dear Vern, Babs, Donna, Bone, and everybody:

Well I guess I should say Merry Merry Christmas and Happy Good New Year . . . We're getting ready for our first Christmas "at home." We'll be ice-skating (you remember how well I skate) and partying with Peggy and the other novices, and eating and caroling and sledding and decorating and finally, sleeping until 6:00 a.m. We'll be kept very busy as you can see, but I'll be thinking of all the Christmases we spent together and all the good times we had. As you probably heard, our New Years Eve is spent in a full day of retreat and so you'll also know that it'll be quite different from last year, huh Babs? [Note: Babs and I downed a fifth of Sunnybrook the year before.] We have the Saint Joseph's River here but it's nothing like the "sunny brooks" we experienced last year! Tell Bone to write because I know I'll be missing her while pondering on old New Years Eve memories. Thank you all for remembering my birthday and for all the letters and cards I received; it really helps. I'll be thinking and praying for all of you especially during my Christmas masses, particularly Midnight Mass. As we were together last year, in a different way we are still together this year. Keep Smilin' God loves You!

Love,
Karol

With every day wrapped in silence, every day also looked exactly the same. With no opportunity to ease into the life of a postulant bit by bit, on day one and every day thereafter this is what our life looked like:

5:00 A.M. Rising bell (6:00 A.M. on weekends and holidays)
5:30 A.M. Lauds (morning prayer)
5:45 A.M. Meditation
6:15 A.M. Mass
7:00 A.M. Breakfast (silence)
8:00 A.M. Housework (silence)
9:00 A.M. Class/Study/Private Prayer
11:45 A.M. Examination of Conscience (midday prayer)
12:00 P.M. Lunch (silence)
12:45 P.M. Recreation
1:30 P.M. Class/Study/Private Prayer
5:00 P.M. Vespers (evening prayer)
6:00 P.M. Dinner (silence)
6:45 P.M. Recreation
7:30 P.M. Compline (night prayer)
8:00 P.M. Great Silence
9:00 P.M. Lights-out

And five minutes before every hour the church bells tolled—one bell, two bells, three bells—according to the time of day.

"When the church bell rings," Joseph instructed us, "we stop what we're doing, pause, and pray 'Jesus, Mary, and Joseph, I love you. Save souls.'"

Over forty years later, the prayer comes to mind when I hear church bells ring.

Given the repetitive similarity of those mostly silent days, the surprising advantage of everyone doing everything together at the same time clearly was found in how well we got to know one another. Actions actually spoke louder than words. For example, when something funny happened at a holy serious time, we saw how even the most devout among us were helpless to stifle a side-splitting laugh.

Everyone in the postulate and juniorate experienced that kind of redemption one morning at five, when someone snuck into the Superior's office and over the P.A. system played as loudly as possible throughout the entire building the "Chicken Fat Song"—Robert Preston's version of an exercise march—with the refrain "GO, YOU CHICKEN FAT, GO AWAY! GO, YOU CHICKEN FAT, GO!" Before being wakened rudely by the traditional handbell (the kind nuns used in grade school to end recess), we bolted out of bed to the "Chicken Fat Song."

More than one hundred of us marched to church that dark winter morning in perfect peppy step to the "Chicken Fat Song" and in waves of laughter that lasted for months. Violations of the Great Silence didn't get any more serious than that, and no one ever knew who did it. Superiors and some of the other postulants suspected me, but I wasn't that brave (at least not yet). And while Mary Sue Brennan never confessed, I suspect it was she. The idea was mine, but I'm convinced Mary Sue did it, and I'm forever grateful to her for such unparalleled courage. That day still ranks as one of the funniest in my life. And if you take the time and trouble to find the "Chicken Fat Song," which I hope you do, you'll understand why.

Even though we lived in rooms of our own and never spoke on the bedroom floors, we still knew how our friends and neighbors were at the end of the day. The walls between the rooms weren't soundproofed; consequently, when someone lay awake with a nagging cough or sobbed over some unspoken anguish, we'd knock on the wall to let them know they weren't alone or slip a note under their door to say something that might help them feel better. Even with the profound seriousness of the Great Silence, especially observed, we found ways to be sisters to one another, and that rule superseded all.

Because of our constant togetherness, the best and worst in us was revealed, accepted, and even embraced. All of the daily togetherness took on such great importance in the beginning, as though surviving its intensity was a holy rite of initiation into sisterhood, a blessed boot camp that bound us together forever. I suppose that was the intent behind Sister Hilda's mandate one day that the postulants form a hot water bucket brigade to melt several feet of snow that fell the night before our new building was to have its postcard picture taken. Sister Hilda was the Superior General's assistant, so her wish was our command. She also oversaw the construction of the new building and took personal pride in every brick.

Sister Hilda envisioned a springtime postcard scene for her building not a mountain of snow, and it took all morning to complete the back-breaking, bone-chilling job. Even the most obedient became disgruntled with the rest of us over losing a morning of free time to melt snow. After inspecting the full length of the front lawn for specks of unmelted snow, Sister Hilda thanked us with an old thawed box of See's candies for all of us to share.

Given how ravenous we were for candy, the gift did little more than pour salt on our sugar-starved wound. Each piece, whitened with age or frost, was bit into with great hope and spit out with a nasty comment about Sister Hilda. Even Joseph Marie and Electa felt sorry for us. Within an hour a big pot of hot chocolate with mini-marshmallows appeared with trays of assorted cookies. That day we wanted to melt Sister Hilda. I was sorry we didn't when we found out later that she was the one who pulled the financial plug on the bowling alley and swimming pool.

While all the mandatory togetherness gave the appearance of one big happy family, it didn't take long to discover that physical proximity alone does not create community. Within weeks we began to get on one another's nerves, and being eighteen-year-olds, some of us had no reservations about telling one another off. Before tensions escalated too far, Sister Joseph Marie gave us a quick talking-to on Constitution 34, which governed Recreation and Conversation, and Constitution 35 on the Spirit of Union and Community.

> *Conversational powers are no common gift, especially among women meeting daily in the same circle. Every sister shall go to recreation with a view to improve the social spirit of the community and to make all around her happy, that they may experience how good and pleasant it is for sisters to dwell together.*
>
> —CONSTITUTION 34:212

> *To preserve and increase the spirit of union, the sisters shall in all circumstances show mutual esteem and loyalty. They shall love one another sincerely, never entertaining feelings of aversion.*
>
> —CONSTITUTION 35: 215

Loving one another sincerely without entertaining feelings of aversion is as improbable in the sisterhood as it is anywhere else. Some sisters were so irritating that I couldn't help but entertain feelings of aversion. Those who demonstrated an insatiable desire for obedience drove me crazy. They loved being told what to do, relishing every opportunity to dismiss practical judgment and comply with the will of the superior. For example, while the rest of us were miserable, Lucy Brown beamed with happiness. While we complained, she complied, never entertaining feelings of aversion about anyone or anything, seeing Jesus everywhere. Being a "living rule," she lived the law of the sisterhood to the letter, with a joyful heart and smiling eyes. While I was told years later by Mother Octavia, the Superior General, that I "smiled with my teeth but not my eyes," the truly obedient always smiled with both.

In our class, several living rules shot the curve for the rest of us. In their honor, my best friend, Mary Ann Pajakowski, whom we called Paj, gave a dramatic reading of a poem in the spring that summed up the feelings of aversion that many of us entertained. It's called "The Sunbeam."

> She was a sunbeam,
> all sparkling and bright,
> shedding her rays
> from left and from right.
>
> She was a sunbeam
> with zeal unabated.
> She was a sunbeam,
> and boy was she hated.

—Anonymous

The monotony of a quiet life did nothing but stimulate Paj's creativity. She also wrote a one-act play for Thanksgiving called "The Ugly Pilgrim Girl" about a young girl so ugly that the pilgrims thought she was a turkey and shot her. I suppose you'd call that a severe case of entertaining feelings of aversion, which is probably why the Constitutions ruled against them. But Paj is still a Sister of the Holy Cross after all these years, which just goes to show you that entertaining feelings of aversion can also be a saving grace. None of the "sunbeams" lasted.

Feelings of aversion also surfaced unexpectedly around the dinner table, where we ate in silence. Because our new building didn't have its own dining room, we marched daily, two by two, across the street to Lourdes Hall where the postulant dining room was located. As postulants, we took all our meals in the same dark refectory where generations of postulants had dined before us. Fake-brown-wood-paneled walls surrounded us, with three floor-to-ceiling windows facing a brick wall yet were covered by heavy beige draperies. I imagine we looked like huge hamsters from the same litter, eating in a big brown box.

The table arrangement appeared military: two rows of long rectangular wooden tables seated nine, four postulants on each side and a professed sister at the head of each table to see that we behaved and to model dining etiquette, though on my first day at breakfast I found that questionable.

Because I was seated at the end of the table, it was my job to serve coffee. Starting with the sister at the head of the table, I poured the hot coffee perfectly (i.e., without dripping), then mouthed the words without speaking: "Would you like cream and sugar?"

She looked up at me with a furrowed brow and said in a loud enough whisper for those sitting to her right and left to hear, "I take my coffee black and bitter, like my life."

I turned away horrified, pouring coffee for everyone else and thinking, "That's a real nice thing to say to someone on the first day. Welcome to hell."

Sister Black and Bitter Like My Life was the buzz of the day. I felt like suggesting that she leave and stop heaping her misery on the rest of us, but I didn't have to. About six months later she did leave. From that day forward, whenever I'm asked if I take cream and sugar, I think of her fondly and joke about taking my coffee "black and bitter, like my life."

As postulants, we were seated alphabetically, with named napkin rings at each place around the table. The head table, at which Sister

Joseph Marie sat flanked by two petrified postulants, faced the rest of us. Seating changed weekly and we all dreaded our week at the head table under the direct supervision of the superior. Over the head table hung a three-foot-tall wooden crucifix, as if to remind us that we were being watched not only by the superior but by the crucified Christ as well. On another wall hung a gilded gaudy gold-framed portrait of Father Basil Anthony Mary Moreau, the founder of the Sisters of the Holy Cross. The look on his face was one of mild disgust, as though what we were eating turned his stomach—though I swear I saw him smile when Baked Alaska was served.

Not only were we expected to be content with the food of the day— even the turkey croquettes and fried Spam with pineapple—but three bites of everything was the food rule, whether we liked it or not. Sometimes I didn't. For example, before I entered the convent, I never saw or ate slimy cooked rhubarb for breakfast or white beady hominy grits for dinner, but that's what I put on my plate. When I looked at Margaret "Mugs" Gallagher, who sat next to me with a scrunched-up face over the bowl of grits, as if to say, "What is this stuff?" I incorrectly heard her whisper that they were "guts." I put three tiny guts on my plate, mashed them around, and pretended to eat them. I learned to scatter food on the plate in such a way that it looked as if I ate everything—a little convent dining survivor skill.

While the meals were usually quite good and of sufficient abundance, the sister at the end of the table often got the smallest cut of meat, the melted scoop of ice cream at the bottom of the bowl, and the slimiest poached egg. Frequently, certain sisters took more than their fair share, much to the silent dismay of the last to be served—which on one fine day was Gloria Glaser, well known to be outspoken about her feelings of aversion, and they were legion.

Gloria liked a lot of cream in her coffee. I did too, but one morning the creamer was empty when it came to me, and I drank my coffee "black and bitter like my life" ever since. Not so with Gloria or anyone seated after Pat Delancy. Pat ranked first among several sisters who quickly earned a reputation for eating more than their share and always taking the best. When passed the meatloaf, Pat forked through all the slices, taking the middle and leaving the ends. She did the same with coffee cake, taking the slice with the most filling. She must have felt she deserved the best, but so did the rest of us.

After mass and morning prayer, Pat would race down the stairs to the breakfast table to make sure she got Cap'n Crunch, and if she didn't, she'd swap her Grape-Nuts or Bran Buds with a sister who did before the rest of us took our places. When my turn came to set up for breakfast and pass out the cereal, my enemies received Grape-Nuts and Bran Buds. (I thought they were full of crap, and the roughage of Grape-Nuts and Bran Buds were my way of helping.) I don't think Pat was malicious or mean-spirited, just unconsciously narcissistic, which is even worse, especially for a nun.

For three days in a row Pat Delancy poured all the cream in her coffee, handing Gloria the empty creamer. Each day I could feel Gloria, sitting next to me, growing madder and madder. She'd bang the empty creamer on the table, ignoring the glare and "tsk-tsk-tsk" from the professed sister. I fully expected Gloria to tell her to "fuck off," but that didn't happen. Gloria's anger focused on creaming the Creamer. Pat Delancy was a marked woman.

On day four I could feel the tension in Gloria mount as the cream sat at the head of the table. I knew a storm had been brewing for days and all hell was about to break loose: a category 5 outburst from Miss Glaser. And true to form, Pat poured every last bit of cream into her cup with a big self-satisfied grin, handing Gloria the empty creamer. That did it. Gloria took the creamer, slammed it on the table, glared at Pat sitting across from her, and breaking the solemn rule of breakfast silence, yelled out loud, "You cow!"

As a result of Gloria's outburst we spent the rest of the day in silence with no recreation, having burst into nonstop laughter we couldn't contain, not even when Sister Joseph Marie clapped her hands and demanded "Silence!" But every laugh was well worth it; even the recreation sacrifice didn't matter. I suspect that every sister who had to sit at the end of the table wanted to do to some nun what Gloria did that morning to Pat Delancy.

Without a doubt, it was the other sisters who got me through the postulate. Our first experience of the power of sisterhood I call the Miracle of Sister Mark. The miracle began at the end of September when we started talking about the nun name we wanted when we received the habit. From day one Mugs Gallagher had her heart set on being called Sister Mark. The rule for nun's names stipulated that you couldn't have the name of a living sister—as though having two sisters with the same name was too difficult for nuns to handle. It didn't matter what we thought, but suffice it to say, that rule did not deter us.

One of our jobs as postulants was to set up meal trays for the sisters in the convent infirmary. With a name tag on each tray, we found out there was a Sister Mark critically ill on the second floor. Some of us began praying for Sister Mark to die a happy death before June 10, the day of our reception, thus freeing the name for Mugs. And Sister Mark died on October 11, soon after we began our prayerful crusade. At first we felt a little spooked over maybe killing a nun, but we were excited at Mugs's having a great chance to get the name she wanted. On June 10, 1965, Mugs became Sister Mary Mark, and that, for us, was a miracle.

We postulants became a major source of entertainment not only for ourselves but for the rest of the community as well. Talent shows highlighted every special occasion, with postulants cast as the stars of the show. The first of many talent shows I participated in took place on Christmas Day 1964—our first Christmas without family and friends. After a Christmas lunch of steak, green beans, baked potato, strawberry Jell-O with bananas, and Baked Alaska (and during which we got to talk), we were told by Sister Joseph Marie to gather in the community room around the Christmas tree. Recognizing our holiday sadness and homesickness, she and Sister Electa worked overtime to make a Merry Christmas.

"It's time for presents!" she announced after lunch, with great joy and certainty that gifts from family and friends would make us happy. "Merry Christmas, sisters!"

We marched in twos from the dining room back to the postulate. As instructed, we pulled up chairs in a semicircle around the Christmas tree and took a seat. During lunch Santa had put presents under the tree, and by the stacks piled high, it looked as though we were very good girls that year. Sister Joseph Marie and Sister Electa handed out gifts sent by family and friends, then we each received a six-week pile of Advent mail tied in a red bow. Those with Advent birthdays received twice as much mail and just as many presents because no mail (or visitors) was allowed during Advent and Lent.

After months of absolutely nothing, being given everything all at once left us numb and slightly nauseated. Spending Christmas afternoon—in my mind's eye a dark, rainy day—opening presents we couldn't keep did little to lift our sad homesick souls. Unless given special permission by the superior, every gift sisters received went into the common fund—which for us was an empty room next to Sister Electa's office. And reading letter after letter about how loved and missed we were by family and friends did nothing more than move us to tears. That's when Sister Electa saw how close to the edge we were, and rang the bell for the start of the talent show.

Our talents were fairly simple. I sang Polish Christmas carols with Paj. Mugs played the guitar with Sister James Maureen (Mugs's real-life sister, who was also a nun, living in the juniorate) and sang "Molly Malone." A group of us lip-synched "Dedicated to the One I Love" and "Ain't No Mountain High Enough." And then Lucy Brown, always the "living rule" paradigm, played her recorder and sang a song she wrote called "The Kingdom of Heaven Is Like a Little Leaven." That was a holiday fun-stopper, as though it was her job to put Christ back into our Christmas. None of this diverted attention from how much we wished we were home for Christmas. That is, until Helene Moynihan sang a song composed especially for the occasion.

In order to understand the heart and soul of Helene's Christmas carol, you need to know that when we entered the convent, razors were not allowed. Those who intended to shave their legs and underarms had razors taken away. I always wondered if they feared we'd slash our wrists on a bad day. Whatever the reason, all razors were confiscated on the first day, as was Tampax because it was "too suggestive." With fake innocence, I asked, "Suggestive of what?" Sister Joseph Marie just turned red and walked away with an armload of Tampax and razors.

Older than the rest of us, Helene had completed college before entering the convent. As a college graduate, she was expected to be more mature and responsible, which was an unfair burden on anyone in our situation. The song she composed for the Christmas talent show caused her credibility to nosedive in the eyes of the superiors, but Helene won our heartfelt admiration.

Set to the tune of "Let It Snow," Helene sang, "Let It Grow." It went like this:

Oh, the hair on our legs is frightful,
and a razor would be delightful,
but since it doesn't show
Let it Grow! Let it Grow! Let it Grow!

Years later I came across a quote by Anna Freud that said, "Creative minds have always been known to survive any kind of bad training." It reminded me of Helene. And ever since that day in 1964, not a Christmas goes by that I don't find myself singing a round of "Let It Grow" for friends and family, and telling the story of my first Christmas talent show in the convent, when Helene Moynihan not only improved the social spirit of the community but gave everyone around her a very Merry Christmas. For one brief moment of pure heartfelt laughter we felt at home.

The only day more singularly difficult than Christmas was New Year's Eve, which for all nuns is traditionally a day of solemn retreat, unlike what it is for the rest of the world. From the time I learned that New Year's Eve would be a solemn day of retreat—meaning silence all day, it felt as if doomsday was approaching. I didn't think I could do it, so much so that I felt that I might have to leave. That is, until Sister Joseph Marie called me into her office a few days before Christmas. In the center of her desk stood a half-full brown grocery bag. I thought my clothes were in that bag and that I was being sent home. Joseph closed the door and asked me to sit down. I broke out in a sweat, wondering what I got caught doing, expecting the worst.

"Some of your high school friends came to visit you today, and I'm sorry you couldn't see them," she said. I think the sick look on my face made Joseph feel genuinely bad for me. Visitors and mail weren't allowed during Advent and Lent. Joseph understood how hard that was for me, accustomed as I was to at least five letters a day.

"They brought you a gift," she said, pointing to the brown bag, adding, "I didn't know you liked oranges so much."

When I heard "oranges," I nearly leaped off the chair. In high school we used to inject oranges with vodka, roll them to blend the booze with the juice, and have screwdrivers with lunch. I also knew that if those vodka-laced oranges ended up on the breakfast table (all gifts were turned in and shared with everyone), I'd be home for Christmas.

Trying to contain the excitement building within, I casually said, "Well, Sister, I do love oranges and my friends know what a great gift that would be. I had one for lunch nearly every day in high school." At least I didn't lie.

I prayed, as never before, that she'd hand the bag over to me, and then added pathetically with downcast eyes, "I'm just sorry I didn't get to see my friends."

Handing me the bag of vodka-filled oranges, Joseph hugged me and said, "Merry Christmas, Karol. Enjoy the oranges."

At that point we were both teary-eyed, for the same and different reasons.

"Thank you, Sister," I said, wishing I could offer her one. Then pressing my luck, added, "May I have permission to write them a thank-you note?"

"Of course you may," she said, smiling as though I were the recipient of a consolation prize.

Words can't describe the enormous relief and joy I felt walking out of her office with the bag of oranges. I felt saved. Someone was looking out for me, making sure I had what I needed to make it. I kept the oranges chilled on the marble windowsill in my room and didn't touch them until New Year's Eve. When the solemn day of retreat arrived, I woke up with a smile. One by one I savored each big Florida orange screwdriver throughout the day, saving four of them for midnight and two for a New Year's party with Sister Concilio, a friend in the convent infirmary. I passed out invitations to three of my friends to meet in bathroom on the second floor at 11:55 P.M., which they did. In perfect silence, we huddled in the tub room, communed with an orange, then, when the bell tower struck midnight, gave each other a big screwdriver smile, flushed all the toilets (the only noisemakers we had), mouthed a silent "Happy New Year" to one another, and went to bed. O Holy Night.

MEALS

Superiors shall combat in their houses whatever may savor of sensu-
ality, in order to forestall even the slightest abuse. Beverages with alco-
holic content shall not be used except on special occasions and with
extreme moderation. No sister may have such beverages at her disposal
without explicit permission of her superiors.

—CONSTITUTION 36:222

Lest you think I was singularly decadent in my consumption of vodka-laced oranges on New Year's Eve, I need to introduce you to Sister Concilio. For postulants, part of the Sunday ritual included visiting the elderly sisters in the convent infirmary. I wasn't thrilled about the prospect of visiting strange old nuns on my day off. The convent infirmary smelled odd to me: a creepy combination of sickness, death, medicine, and disinfectant. The thought of breathing that air on Sunday afternoons turned my eighteen-year-old stomach.

Saint Mary's Convent was where nuns went before they died, or as one sister described it, it was the "waiting room before the Pearly Gates." But visiting the retired sisters on Sunday afternoon wasn't optional—

nothing was. In training to be a nun, whatever we were told to do, we did together. Optional didn't belong in the sisterhood.

I was assigned to visit Sister Concilio in Room 302. Sister Concilio, and her best friend, Sister Evangelista who lived across the hall in Room 303, were known to be live wires. High-spirited and popular, they did exactly as they pleased. Known in the sisterhood as Concil and Vange, they called us "kids."

Concil was a retired high school English teacher, born and raised in Iowa, who spent most of her teaching years in the Midwest. With a mind as sharp as her tongue, Concil had a sense of humor that surpassed both. I don't remember much about my first three visits other than that the door was kept open and I left with deep pockets full of hard candy.

"The young sisters need candy," is what she'd say as she stuffed my pockets with mints, butterscotch, cinnamon, and little boxes of lemon drops. I couldn't agree with her more.

Not only did I leave Concil's room every Sunday with an abundance of candy, but every departure concluded with her holding my hand and promising that she would pray for my perseverance. All the old sisters prayed that the new crop of postulants wouldn't get fed up and leave, as many did. I liked hearing that. They knew postulants needed determination in the beginning more than anything else. The convent infirmary was known in the community as a powerhouse of prayer, and I felt real comfort in being a recipient of that kind of divine power. I needed all the help I could get. But on the fourth visit I left with another reason to persevere.

"Kid," Concil said, as I took my seat in the guest chair across from her rocker, "can you keep a secret?"

"Of course," I said. "We can't talk anyhow."

Even though I had been visiting Concil for just a month, I had the feeling she was about to reveal something important. I knew from the spark in her eye and the devilish tone in her voice that the secret would be a good one.

Concil rose slowly from her rocking chair with my help, and arm in arm we walked over to the door, which she closed and then locked. That's when she looked up with a fiendish grin that sparked her blue eyes, which floated like pieces of sky in her softly wrinkled, intelligent face.

"Take a seat, kid," she said, shuffling behind me to get to the closet door. Opening the left side, she reached behind some shoe boxes and pulled out a worn pink crocheted poodle, the kind designed to cover a whiskey bottle. She held it like a baby.

"What's in there?" I asked, knowing very well it wasn't a stuffed animal.

"Would you like a little C.C.?" she whispered, grinning.

The rest is the stuff of which great friendships are made. Concil poured half-shots of Canadian Club whiskey into little plastic medicine cups, each round making us sillier and sillier. We munched on assorted nuts sent by a former student with whom she kept in touch, and we split desserts she snuck off the lunch trays of the nuns who didn't want theirs. The butterscotch brownies and oatmeal raisin cookies could have won prizes. Over a feast fit for old friends, Concil confided in me about what drove her crazy—like the person who was stealing stuffed animals from the sisters' rooms—and which sisters, nurses, and superiors she despised. Then it was my turn to vent. All the things we would never admit to publicly (except to best friends) we shared on those Sunday afternoons at what we called the Poodle Club, and sealed the divine dirt with shots of Poodle Juice. Not only did we share a little C.C. that day and nearly every visiting day thereafter, but I became one of many young sister accomplices who worked to keep the pink poodle alive.

I visited Concil every week for seven years before she died. On occasion, I'd drive her and other sisters to dentist's appointments at Dr. Toothaker's (which was really his name). On the way home Concil invariably insisted on being dropped off last, so we could stop at Don's Liquor Store on the Dixie Highway near the college. Arm in arm, we shuffled into Don's and a bell over the door announced our arrival at the counter. Concil would dump maybe two dollars in dimes, nickels, and pennies on the spiked rubber mat and, smiling bashfully, peer over her glasses and ask in a sweet old, naive nun way, "Is this enough for a fifth of C.C.?"

I couldn't believe it. Don smiled at her the way I used to do in my family's bakery when an old customer walked in and expected a baker's dozen. Concil clearly was a regular.

"Of course it's enough, Sister," he said, reaching for the Canadian Club among the whiskeys and for a long brown bag.

But that wasn't the end of being Concil's accomplice. My duties also included sneaking out the empties and sneaking in the refills. Those deep nun pockets covered a multitude of sins. Concil believed that's what deep pockets were made for.

If the Sunday weather permitted and usually after a shot or two of C.C., I'd walk Concil out to Our Lady Queen of Peace Cemetery to visit deceased friends. She'd leave pieces of candy or holy cards on their graves after soul chats, which sometimes lasted so long that I was late for vespers—an offense that sometimes got me sent to the chapel after dinner without recreation. While always apologetic for getting me into trouble, Concil was never very sorry.

"But we had a great time, didn't we, kid?" she'd say with the smile that melted any remnant of regret on my part.

After seven years of what the two of us called holy disobedience, Concil's health began to fail and our conversations turned more and more to her days' being numbered.

"Kid," she said, pouring two pill cups of C.C., "when I go, get the poodle. Don't let anyone find the poodle."

"I promise I'll get the poodle," I said with instant ceremony.

Why she cared about the poodle after she died is still beyond me, but she did. I never asked, but she cared. She had me put my hand on the Bible and wrapped her rosary around my fingers before making me swear I would get the poodle when she died.

"Well, let's drink to that!" she said, as if to seal the deal.

"My pleasure," I said, raising my pill cup to hers. "I promise."

The last time I saw Concil was three days before she passed. It was March 9, 1971, a beautiful spring day after an unusually brutal South Bend winter. She never recovered fully from a stroke she suffered, and her heart was failing. I worked as a guidance counselor and teacher at Saint Joseph's High School in South Bend at the time, which was six blocks south of Saint Mary's, and one of Concil's nurses called the school and asked me to come. The end was near.

When I arrived at her room in the convent infirmary, Concil looked as though she was sleeping, each breath more shallow than the last. I pulled up my chair, sat at her side, and reached over to hold her hand, loosely bound by a prayer-worn black rosary with right thumb and forefinger resting on the last bead she had prayed. She opened her eyes when I took her hand, and at first looked as though she didn't recognize me. But then, as if some holy spirit within turned on the soul's eye, her soft translucent face melted into the same smile I saw the day I met the pink poodle.

"O kid . . ." she said, nearly breathless and squeezing my hand softly.

"It's me, Concil," I said, "it's Kare. I'm right here."

Her parting words were delivered with a soft soulful smile, barely above a whisper.

"Get . . . the . . . pooooooooooodle . . ." is what she said. Then she drifted back to sleep.

I got the poodle and left her resting in peace. Sister Concilio died three days later. She was buried with a smile on her face and a little bottle of Canadian Club tucked carefully in the folds of her habit. I saw to that.

As a postulant, I remember being pleasantly surprised that several sisters had alcoholic beverages at their disposal without the permission of the superior, and no one seemed to mind. When I shared a screwdriver orange with Concil at our New Year's Day party, she loved that I had such good friends and such a wise superior. Concil wasn't the only infirm sister with a poodle, and somehow that exception to the holy rule was permitted. One of the finest features of the sisterhood still is its enjoyment of distilled spirits, with moderation of course, but not *extreme* moderation. We are believers of moderation in all things, including moderation.

The fact that the postulancy lasted nine months became a big joke, thanks to a dramatic (I thought deranged) visiting priest whose sermon at an Advent mass about the divine power of the Virgin Mary's pregnancy was punctuated with random painful outbursts of: "N-i-i-i-i-n-e L-o-o-o-o-n-g M-o-o-o-n-t-h-s." Nine Long Months. He acted as if he was in labor and we burst out laughing. Some, including me, needed to leave the church. We lost a day's recreation over the outburst and the ridiculing of Father Nine Long Months, but we didn't care. Like the morning of the "Chicken Fat Song," a big laugh at a seriously silent time proved well worth any consequence. Such times smack of divine intervention.

At the end of our nine long months, though, a new life did come to term. Something happened to us in that period, and the time arrived for taking next steps. Either we moved on to receive the habit and enter the novitiate or we left. That's when I began to see the first steps on my spiritual path that called me further. I understand far more clearly now what I vaguely felt in the beginning of my religious life. Through the magic ingredients of all those funny, bizarre, angry, joyful, and painful experiences, the soul of sisterhood was born in me.

Living under one roof and doing everything together day after day for nine months caused a kind of mysterious soulful gluing to take place, one to another, sister to sister to sister, in ways that would probably not happen otherwise. Even those who drove me crazy felt like sisters, and when the first ones decided to leave, or were sent home, we mourned the loss.

Bonnie Buckemeyer was the first to leave after only one month, and that took all of us by surprise, including Sister Joseph Marie and Sister Electa. We hardly knew her. It happened on the first visiting day with our families, and when the time came for our parents to leave, Bonnie got in the car with hers and took off, leaving behind two bushels of apples as a parting gift. At first I felt so betrayed that I suggested we boycott the apples, but then I relented, took a few McIntoshes, and just felt sad. It was a shock for all of us, as was the departure of anyone. We never knew in advance when someone planned to leave or got sent home. And we never knew why they left unless they told us, which Bonnie didn't. A missing napkin ring at the table was the first indicator, followed by a brief announcement after breakfast: "Erin Dunleavy and Nancy Velasko are no longer with us."

It felt as if those who left or got sent home died a sudden death, never to be spoken of or heard from again. With no due process in the convent, those dismissed were sent home without knowing why, and superiors weren't obligated to give reasons. Whether friend or foe, we suffered the loss of a sister; we were family.

In the beginning I took the spiritual step toward sisterhood and community life, and loved what I found after nine months. I experienced what I always knew with family and friends but feared I might not find in the convent. Being surrounded by sisters who wholeheartedly supported, encouraged, and applauded one another's creative instincts was something I grew accustomed to at home and found among my sisters. They picked up where my family and friends left off, helping me feel at home in what at first felt like such a strange new world. Most important of all, they were fun to be with. Having been given such great times in those "nine long months," I saw clearly how sweet it is to be bound anew by such fun-loving ties. More than anything else, it was sisterhood—the women with whom I shared the first nine months—that helped me see most clearly everything I was meant to be.

Along with the spiritual step toward sisterhood and community life, I also found myself called further into silence and solitude. I learned to keep still in the postulate, and in the silence I began to discover my real voice, the inner voice, the writing voice, the voice of God. With everything suddenly taken away in the beginning, we reached a soulful impasse that threw us back into ourselves, stimulating the impulse for reflection and watering the seeds of consciousness. I found my mind getting sharper in silence, offering me greater clarity about what was happening inside and out. I began to know what I thought and came to know my self in ways I never had before. At the age of eighteen, that felt like a miracle.

What I learned in silence and solitude is similar to the first step in Hindu yogic training: the ability to control your "chit"—thoughts that buzz around in the mind and distract. On the path to enlightenment, distraction is the first stumbling block. In solitude I learned to catch my wandering thoughts and bring my mind under control so that I could become one-pointed, or single-hearted. I discovered the capacity for concentration in solitude—the soul's ability to direct, focus, and apply divine energy—and a wellspring of creative life. As if in divine compensation, I found periods of solitude and introversion were always accompanied by the discovery of a lively imaginative life. I loved the self I found in silence and solitude, feeling wakened to a life I could live forever.

After nine long months, I looked at me and my sisters and saw that none of us had lost our fun-loving souls; if anything, we became funnier while becoming more serious. Given everything that we went through, becoming happier felt like nothing other than divine intervention and reason enough to continue on the path that led me there. Side by side with my friends, I decided to enter the novitiate.

Of the fifty, thirty-eight of us received the habit and entered the novitiate on June 10, 1965. Those who left or got sent home did so for health reasons, personal reasons (they were miserable), or for reasons I'll never know. Sometime in April (I like to think it was April Fools' Day), we met one by one with Mother Katrina, the Superior General of the community, to ask formally for reception into the community. Although we didn't have much individual contact with the Superior General as postulants, Mother Katrina's importance in our lives loomed large. Every month she received written progress reports on each of us from Sister Joseph Marie, and without Mother Katrina's approval, no one entered the novitiate. She had the power to dismiss us at will, and she was known to use it. I rarely saw her smile, never heard her laugh, and the sight of her made me freeze. Her face can best be described as stoic and unflinching, with a puppetlike mouth that reminded me of Mayor Phineas T. Bluster, a blubbering professor puppet on the 1950s *Howdy Doody Show*. Having to meet with Mother Katrina individually in order to enter the novitiate was something we dreaded for nine long months.

With several others we waited our turn in the parlor of the Generalate—the free-standing building next to the Church of Loretto where the Superior General and her council lived. The parlor felt like the Temple of Doom, and since it was near the kitchen, it smelled like whatever they ate for lunch. Displayed carefully on antique tables were well-preserved memorabilia (prayer books, rosaries, medals, etc.) from past Superiors General—things I wanted to touch and hold but didn't dare.

Built-in bookshelves with leaded glass doors lined the walls. They were full of books on community history and the lives of the founders. Of greater interest to me were the old statues, relics, and paintings displayed around the room. A huge gilded portrait of Mother Augusta, the first Superior General, stared at us with haunting lifelike eyes, as though someone were watching from the adjoining room. Everything in that room felt alive, except us. I felt like I was in limbo.

We sat silent and still on antique sofas, which I'm sure every Sister of the Holy Cross had sat on. A foreboding energy hung over the room like a dark cloud, probably emanations from the sisters who had sat where I sat and been sent home. As we waited on the edge of our seats, we really didn't know if we were coming or going.

A junior professed sister summoned and escorted each of us one by one to Mother Katrina's office. As instructed, when entering, we knelt before Mother Katrina and prayed—i.e., begged—to be received into the Congregation of the Sisters of the Holy Cross, and when leaving we knelt and prayed for her blessing. I did all this but not gracefully. Tripping on my habit while standing up to leave, I knocked a pile of folders (our personal files) onto the floor. A look of horror covered her face.

"I'm sorry, Mother," I said, adding quickly, "I'll pick them up."

"Just go!" she told me, clearly upset. I heard her mumble "You fool!" as she moved to pick up the files.

I escorted myself out, not knowing whether I was staying or leaving.

But by the grace of God, the blessings of Sister Joseph Marie and Sister Electa, good karma, and a total miracle, I was accepted. I took the next step into the novitiate.

The Sisters of the Holy Cross
request the honor of your presence at the
Ceremony of Religious Reception
at the
Church of Our Lady of Loretto
Saint Mary's, Notre Dame, Indiana
Thursday morning, June the tenth
Nineteen hundred and sixty-five
at ten o'clock
(central daylight time)

chapter three

solitary confinement

"Remember," one group of sisters was cautioned every morning before breakfast, "what you are in the novitiate, that you shall be for the rest of your lives."*

I look at the two years I spent in the novitiate and see them surrounded by a cloud of unknowing. Even now, forty years later, I still don't understand completely what those solitary years did to me. The descent into the divine madness of the novitiate actually began on June 2, 1965—day one of the eight-day retreat all postulants made before receiving the habit. Those were the days we packed up our life and got ready to leave the private room of our own, walk across the street about thirty feet south, and enter the novitiate. Those were the days we got ourselves ready to begin two years of solitary confinement.

I don't remember praying on that retreat as much as I do packing my suitcase and trunk, feeling *excited* about seeing my family and friends, *sad* over leaving Sisters Joseph Marie and Electa, and *scared* over moving in with our new superiors: Sister Beatrice, the Novice Mistress, and

---

*Sister Charles Borromeo, C.S.C., ed., *The New Nuns* (New York: Signet Books, 1968), p. 22.

her assistant, Sister Martha. Eyewitness reports from veteran novices about their sense of humor were not encouraging. No one even dared give them a nickname. In note-writing we referred to them as B and M, as though it was a secret. The community buzz was that Sister Joseph Marie and Sister Electa were too "permissive" with us—a class-A felony in the convent—and what we needed was "discipline"—something at which Sister Beatrice excelled.

We heard through the grapevine that prior to becoming a nun, Sister Beatrice served the country honorably as secretary to Navy Admiral Nimitz (and got red roses from him on her birthday). She earned advanced degrees in theology and was recognized as one of the community's best theologians. Sister Beatrice excelled in military training, academic training, and nun training—a triple whammy of obedience to God and country.

Sometime during the transformational eight-day retreat, we met for our final hour of spiritual direction with Sister Joseph Marie. She met with each of us monthly to see how we were, and now it was time to wrap up the year and say good-bye. What I recall most clearly from that exit interview is being told not to be afraid of the novitiate. She sensed correctly that I'd probably have a hard time with Sister Beatrice's administrative style and asked that I keep an open mind.

"You'll do fine," she said, hugging me and giving me her blessing. "You're a survivor."

That felt more like a curse. Being a survivor is an abysmal existence, not something you'd ever want, much less look forward to. But our class had earned a reputation as the rebellious ones, and we were worried about being beaten into submission and whipped into spiritual shape. One unspoken message appeared clearly in the stone-cold sternness of Sister Beatrice's face: The party's over. It's time to get serious. You are hereby sentenced to two years of solitary confinement.

Below the existential dread of strict new superiors floated the anxiety over losing a private room in exchange for a curtained cell in a dorm with a dozen others. I prayed all eight retreat days that I'd get a cell with a window and windowsill big enough to sit on, with a streetlight bright enough to write by. On June 10, the day we crossed the street and moved into our new place, I actually got what I prayed for. I was assigned to Saint Joseph dorm (all dorms had saints' names), a big Pepto-Bismol pink room with fifteen-foot-high ceilings, from which hung the oldest and best sprinkler system in the world.

Within each cell stood a white wooden spindle-back chair, a three-drawer dresser, and a white cast-iron twin bed with a worn flat mattress slid on top of a thin piece of plywood (a nun's idea of box springs). Our walls were white cotton curtains. The cells looked like those you see in shared hospital rooms, only half the square footage (and no TV), but I didn't care. Mine came with a big wide-open window and an enormous piece of sky. Blessed be.

Facing west and overlooking a shrine to Saint Thérèse, the Little Flower, in the backyard, this big old window was three times the size of the postulate's, with a long benchlike windowsill for greater writing comfort. And six feet outside the window, taller than the trees, stood a bright, newly installed streetlight, as if made to order. I took one look out the window, saw paradise in a nutshell, and thought of the Petie Principle: "What could my Jesus do more?"

Not only did I receive the cell and window of my dreams, but on the night before we moved, June 9, our last night in the postulate, I also got to cut my own hair. I actually cut my hair (and others') all year, keeping it short enough to accommodate the habit's headgear. I wanted to keep making it perfectly clear that there was no need whatsoever to shave anyone's head. We knew our hair would be cut short the night before the "veiling," and Sister Joseph Marie knew we feared the worst. She and Sister Electa assured us repeatedly that nothing awful would happen that night. Heads would not be shaved. That was a promise.

Even so, when that night came, the unforgettable happened. After supper, as directed by Sister Joseph Marie, we brought a towel and lined up single-file along the wall in the basement, waiting our turn for "the haircut." In the lower recreation room, we stared at empty wooden chairs draped with white sheets, and behind them, in blue gingham checked aprons, stood smiling sisters from the juniorate with scissors and clippers in hand. One by one, we took a seat, bowed our heads, closed our eyes, and prayed for the snipping to stop. The sister barbers knew exactly how much to cut off and did so sparingly and stylishly, thank God. We did not look like marines or mental patients. We just looked as if we had had our hair cut much too short.

But even under the best of circumstances, the hair-cutting experience threw us. Fran Shea melted into tears, mourning the sudden loss when handfuls of curly blond hair dropped into her lap and then fell to the floor. (I saw her slip a small piece into her side pocket.) And when a few living rules asked with bowed head to have their hair shaved off, the constant moaning buzz of the electric clippers made those nearby cry.

I don't know what kept me from screaming "Stop!" or pulling the plug, but I didn't. No one did. All I needed was a little receding of the hairline around the temples. Sister Joseph Marie let me shave it myself. It's strange, but the way my hair looked that night is pretty much the way it still looks now . . . only much shorter and not gray.

I suspect I wasn't the only one who underestimated the emotional impact of having her hair cut too short—how strangely humiliating it felt. (I wondered if they cut it too short on purpose so we couldn't leave.) One by one we walked back to our rooms with white cotton caps covering our heads (these were to be worn always at night), eyes down-cast, and speechless. Some of us wept openly. It felt as though we were cut off from something very big but didn't know what it was.

I felt strangely unplugged that night from whatever had grounded us so comfortably in the postulate. Being a postulant was over. There was no such thing as repeating the year or being granted a deferment. By leaving or staying, we needed to move on. The survivors needed to jump across the street, where once again we stood at the beginning. We entered the novitiate blindly, with no idea what we were in for; and we had to learn to deal with two new superiors, reportedly hell-bent on discipline. For all eight retreat days I looked every statue I passed in the eye, and prayed, "Help Save Us!"

RELIGIOUS HABIT

The religious habit of black material is made as directed. It consists of a fitted waist and a gathered skirt which falls to a length of two inches from the ground; sleeves twelve inches wide extending to the fingertips; a circular cape reaching two inches below the waist and made of the same material as the habit skirt; small close-fitting sleeves; a white collar. The headdress of white material consists of a small inner cap, a band to cover the forehead, and a circular border. A semi-circular veil completes the headdress. The novice wears a white veil.

—CONSTITUTION 5:16–17

The ritual for reception into the sisterhood, which began formally the night before with the cutting of the hair, continued the following morning at sunrise with the "veiling." Sisters Miriam Edward and Christopher Marie appeared at my door with the holy habit in hand; they came in to help me dress. Putting the habit on correctly was a no-brainer, but the headdress took manual dexterity and special maneuvering. There was no worse fashion faux pas for any nun than crooked headgear.

We practiced getting dressed for weeks, working to reduce our time with the headgear to one minute. A few of us even designed a special fold of the headband that gave it a slight upward tilt, like fins on 1960s cars. The Mistress of Novices quickly condemned our signature look as a sin of vanity (individuality) to be rooted out. Individuality kills the purpose of a habit. I'm sure she even quoted the Constitutions on the subject: "Continual attention shall be paid to uniformity, the natural guardian of order and union."

In putting the headdress on for the first time, I felt grateful for the expertise of veteran nuns. Seeing the radiant faces of Miriam Edward and Christopher Marie that morning was exactly what I needed to confirm that all would be well. While the "veiling" turned into a silent, solemn ritual for some novices and their sponsors, mine was blessed with out-loud laughter we tried to subdue but couldn't. Laughter was our way of relieving my stress and anxiety over what would happen that day, and every day thereafter in the novitiate.

In all of the hilarity, they also made me look good and feel better. And even more important, the headgear felt secure enough that it wouldn't fall apart if I tripped or if it got blown off in a storm—my two constant fears. Before we made our first public appearance in the habit, we received the blessing of our black veils. The sisters who gave us wings in the beginning became the first to bless our crossing over into the novitiate. Once again, they walked me, arm in arm, to the edge of the abyss, laughing. I already knew what came next: jump.

Families and friends arrived from all over the world for Reception Day, along with sisters who flew home especially for the occasion. Cars streamed up Saint Mary's Avenue like a parade. While those of us from the Midwest were fortunate to have family visits in the postulate, most sisters from the East and West were seeing relatives for the first time in a year. Finally, we would meet face-to-face the families we knew only through great stories and letters.

Although it may have been overcast, in my mind's eye, the morning of June 10, 1965, was springtime at its very best, with Saint Mary's in full bloom. The reason I know it wasn't raining is because we walked in a procession from the postulate to the Church of Our Lady of Loretto through a nun-lined path of smiling faces, some teary-eyed, full of pride and joy, chanting "Ave Maris Stella" as we passed by.

While we were instructed to proceed with heads bowed, veils pulled to block peripheral vision, hands folded and hidden within the habit's big black sleeves, and eyes downcast, my wandering eyes kept shifting to the right and left, searching for family and friends lined up with the sisters. When I spotted my high school pals, I lost control, smiling and waving like a prom queen. I foolishly felt I could do no wrong. Reception Day was a high holy feast day and we were the stars of the show. We passed phase one of the initiation and the Sisters of the Holy Cross received us into their community. We survived "n-i-i-i-n-e l-o-o-o-n-g m-o-o-o-n-t-h-s." That was reason to celebrate.

The organist, Sister Marie Cecile, pulled out the stops and made all the happy bells ring when we entered the church. Some families and friends applauded, while little brothers and sisters yelled out our names (for the last time). I heard my brothers yell, "Yeah, Kare!" Sisters in the infirmary who normally wouldn't have come down for mass (the audio was piped into their room) did so for our reception. Concil sat among them, front row center, teary-eyed and grinning like a proud grandmother. She gave me two thumbs up and a wink when I passed her, adding a swift little jab at the air as if to say, "You go, girl!" The Church of Our Lady of Loretto was packed with people who loved us. Amid the singing congregation, the organ, pipes, and bells, the clouds of incense and delicate scent of lilies surrounding the altar, I am quite sure I left my body.

Built in 1885,* the Church of Our Lady of Loretto felt full of the peaceful energy that comes from generations of Holy Cross sisters praying there daily. As in a parish church, we received the habit, professed vows, celebrated jubilees, and blessed the dead at the altar of Our Lady of Loretto. That's an enormously powerful concentration of divine energy within those walls. The heart and soul of Holy Cross sisterhood lives and prays in that church; so much so that I'm surprised that it hasn't lifted up and floated away the way the thirteenth-century holy house did—so the story goes.

I was already enchanted by Our Lady of Loreto before I walked into the church for the first time. Because I was born on December 10, the Feast of Our Lady of Loreto, I instantly felt a mysterious bond with her; but when I saw the statue of the Black Madonna in the Chapel of Loretto and heard the story of the flying house, I knew that I was standing on holy ground. Up on a hill overlooking the mighty Saint Joseph River, Mother Angela picked the perfect spot. Built in 1850, the first permanent chapel at Saint Mary's was dedicated to Our Lady of Loreto. Located behind the church, the chapel is a replica† of the Holy House of Loreto, enclosed in the Basilica of Loreto, Italy. According to tradition, that's the same house where the Virgin Mary was born and where the Holy Family lived. Jesus grew up there.

In 1291 when anti-Christian Saracens threatened an invasion of Nazareth, the Holy House was miraculously lifted up by angels and transported to Loreto, Italy (after a stop in Tersato in Dalmatia), where it still stands intact today. Despite questions about the authenticity of

*The present church, whose name is traditionally but incorrectly spelled Loretto (with two t's), was reconstructed in 1955, renovated in 1992, and rededicated in 1993.
†Mother Angela's brother, Father Neil Gillespie, a Holy Cross priest, got the blueprints from Italy.

the means of transportation, the shrine remains a main attraction for pilgrims, which have included Pope John XXIII and Pope Paul VI.

At Saint Mary's, the Chapel of Loretto is attached to the church, hidden behind the main altar, as though the church is born of the chapel, which it actually was. As postulants, before we saw the church for the first time, we were taken to the chapel.

"In order to know who Our Lady of Loreto is," Sister Joseph Marie told us on our second day as postulants, "you need to go to the chapel to meet her."

The Chapel of Loretto is a dark little room, no more than fifteen feet square with four kneelers, which indicated how many were allowed in at one time and how long you could stay if others were waiting. (Nobody likes a prayer hog.) On the altar, within arm's length, stood the one-hundred-year-old statue of Our Lady of Loreto, about four feet high, carved from cedar wood grown in the Vatican Garden (as is the original in Italy) and encased in glass. Well-tended votive candles burned at her feet, illuminating the chapel with a soft golden glow. The figure of Our Lady, with the Holy Child, is dressed in an ornately jeweled triangular robe of embroidered gold and white silk. Only the black faces are visible. Both figures are crowned in gold and strikingly beautiful.

I entered another world when I knelt at her altar; I felt taken in by the darkness of the face and the candlelight, and uplifted by the holiness of the ground on which I knelt. Every time I walked into the Church of Loretto after my first chapel visit, I felt the same pull inward and upward into another world, the world of spirit and soul. I felt as if angels had appeared and moved my soul's house to a place of peace and comfort.

Even those who didn't know about the hidden Chapel of Loretto found the church beautiful and otherworldly. (Only one person I know didn't. My dear friend Michael Dongarra disliked the design because it looked like a "mosaic pineapple.") On entering the church, you first passed individual pews and kneelers for the Superior General and her council, situated strategically to overlook the congregation. (Seating was assigned by rank, so the youngest members sat in front.) It's after passing the superior's pews and walking into the body of the church that your eyes instinctively look up and you get the feeling of being lifted into another world. Circular in design, the church has four vertical mosaic panels, imported from Italy and framed by stylized gold leaves that rise from the floor to the ceiling. The panels celebrate and picture the Tree of Jesse, the Seven Joys of Mary, the Seven Sorrows of Mary, and the Litany of Mary.

As a postulant, I was seated in front on the side with the Seven Sorrows,* and got to know the worst parts of Mary's life very well. But sometimes during meditation on a particular sorrow, I saw other images in the mosaic, like Harvey the invisible rabbit, a UFO with beams, a black dog, and even a monkey. When I mentioned these revelations in spiritual direction with Sister Joseph Marie, she found them funny. I did the same once with the Sister Beatrice, the Novice Mistress, thinking they'd be a funny icebreaker (like finding Waldo), but she reprimanded me for my undisciplined prayer life. She compared my mindless distractions to the biblical "foxes wreaking havoc in my vineyard," which needed to be "rooted out." In other words, kill that silly imagination. She also gave me a book that day, *It's Your Attitude, Sister.* I never said this to her, but I don't have an undisciplined prayer life. I have a playful God.

Seeing the mosaics for the first time can leave you speechless, and like art, it can be just as breathtaking to see something in it you never noticed before. That alone takes you into the other playful world of

*The Seven Sorrows of Mary are: the prophecy of Simeon, which pierced her heart (Luke 2:34–35); the flight into Egypt (Matthew 2:13–21); the loss of Jesus for three days; his being found in the Temple (Luke 2:41–50); the Way of the Cross (John 19:17); Crucifixion and Death (John 19:38); the taking of Jesus down from the Cross (John 19:38); the laying of Jesus in the tomb (John 19:42).

imagination, which William Blake calls the Divine Body in everyone. As you look up at the mosaic panels, your eyes are drawn to the church's circular dome with stained-glass windows depicting the twelve apostles. Suspended in the center is a free-floating polished-steel Holy Spirit in the form of a dove with spread wings that actually move on windy days. Along the walls and in between the mosaic panels stood side altars with white marble statues of Mary, Joseph, Jesus, and with one altar full of sparkling jeweled monstrances containing relics of saints.* Charged with the divine power of so much prayer and ritual, the church was saturated with divine energy from sacred art and blessed artifacts.

Round stained-glass windows overlooked the gallery above the entrance, and the south choir loft with the original organ (renovated in 2000) made up of twenty-eight ranks and more than sixteen hundred pipes. No one made that organ sing like Sister Marie Cecile. Above the bronze crucifix hanging over the altar, like a burst of divine revelation, is a stunning stained-glass window of the Annunciation†—the moment the Angel Gabriel enters Mary's house in Nazareth and tells her she's to be the Mother of God. Beneath the Annunciation window, at the foot of the cross, stood a massive marble altar held up on the muscular backs of two sculpted marble angels, both on bended knee with bowed heads, like Atlases with wings. In the center of the altar stood an elegantly brushed-gold tabernacle with ornately gold candelabra at its side. On high holy days the altar was loaded with burning beeswax candles, extra-large gold vases of fresh flowers, and gold censers for burning incense.

On the day of our reception, surrounding the altar were dozens of white lilies and rising clouds of frankincense, in the center of which appeared, a magisterial figure, the elaborately dressed bishop of South Bend, with gold staff and miter, seated before us on a throne. The choir

---

*The palm trees and side altars were removed in the 1992 renovation.
†A memorial dedicated to Father Neil Gillespie, Mother Angela's brother, who figuratively built the chapel.

was full of singing nuns, and in every pew stood singing sisters and loved ones. There was not a dry eye or empty seat in the holy house. Jampacked with so much love, the church was charged with the presence of God.

There are two things I remember clearly about the reception ceremony. First, the strange experience of seeing one another in our habits for the first time, literally trying to figure out who we were while mass was going on. And second, how terrified I felt kneeling before the bishop, asking to be received into the community, and getting a new name. You could feel the anxiety heighten when it came time to go to the altar, especially when the congregation and the organ became suddenly silent. Carolyn Pratt nearly fainted, but she recovered quickly. I think we all worried about tripping on the habit when we stood up—which I was prone to do—stumbling on the altar steps and dislodging the headgear, or not remembering what to say when we knelt before the bishop as he asked us, one by one, in a booming, overly dramatic voice: *"My daughter, what do you desire?"*

How unforgettably funny it would have been if each one of us had leaned over that microphone and told the bishop what we really desired. For shock value alone and a one-way ticket to East Chicago, I would have whispered "Sex." But our programmed response was memorized. We asked to be received into the Congregation of the Sisters of the Holy Cross; after which the bishop accepted us, then made the announcement everyone was waiting for. There was absolute silence. Anointing my forehead with holy oil, and extending his right hand over me in a blessing, the bishop announced slowly, almost breathlessly: "Karol. Ann. Jackowski . . . from this day forward you will be known as Sister . . . Mary . . . Carol . . . Joseph."

Three months prior to Reception Day we were given the opportunity to suggest three names. I wrote "Karol. Karol. Karol." But superiors made the choice. My spirit soared when I heard "Karol," then dropped flat when I heard "Joseph." And when I saw on the name card a C instead of K in "Carol," I thought someone made a typo. It had to be. I wanted my own name, even though I knew the rule against it. We had to choose the name of a saint and couldn't have the name of a living sister of the Holy Cross. I knew a Sister Mary Carol lived in California, and she was nowhere near death. You'd think my name's being spelled with a K would be an obvious enough difference, not to mention the fact that we lived two thousand miles from each other. Furthermore, Sister Mary Carol was half my size. How difficult could it be to tell us apart? Even George Foreman has no problem naming his five sons George, and they do resemble one another. In being named Carol, I didn't get my name at all. That was another difference nuns couldn't see.

Where "Joseph" came from I don't know; possibly a surprise from Sister Joseph Marie, who knew of my special devotion to the saint. I didn't immediately hate the name, but my heart sank. I felt oddly embarrassed. With no offense to Saint Joseph, I didn't want a man's name. Why would I? Priests and brothers don't take women's names. You never hear of "Father Barbara," "Brother Bernadette," "Bishop Beverly," or "Archbishop Agnes." That's what I must have been thinking when I actually did trip on the habit as I stood up before the bishop, but miracle of miracles, I didn't fall down the steps. I didn't laugh (as my friends and family did), nor did I disrupt the headgear. "What could my Jesus do more?"*

Among my friends, Paj became Sister Mary Jean Dolores and Mary Sue, Sister Brendan Marie. Sue Remick turned into Sister Miriam Rose, and Nancy Gros de Mange got the name she wanted, Sister Mary

---

*Sister Peter Julian, creator of the Petie Principle, was there.

Richard Therese, as did Helene Moynihan, who became Sister Mary Helena, and Ellen Bush, Sister Mary Ellen Bernard. Jane Uebbing received Sister Marian Jean, and Jane Calabria, Sister Mary Jane Ann, her own name. Then we witnessed the Miracle of Sister Mark, and the devastation of poor Sister Adele.

Regardless of how I felt, my name didn't make me cry the way Judy Baldwin did when she heard Sister Mary Adele. I could tell by the look on Judy's face that she hated the name. I thought she'd walk off the altar, keep walking, and we'd never see her again. And I think she really would have left if her hair wasn't so short. It took months to learn the new names, and we only used them in the presence of superiors. Because it wasn't her choice, Judy hated being called Sister Adele no matter who was around, so then we just called her Sister.

Even on our special day, we weren't allowed to eat lunch with our families, but we did have the afternoon to visit, with the rule of silence suspended all day. Our families were scattered in little groups all over the lawn near the church and Holy Cross Hall; it was the perfect setting for everyone to meet and take pictures. On Reception Day, everyone disregarded the rule against photographing novices, especially with men, including relatives.

Families brought food, snacks, and drinks, turning the whole afternoon into one big, happy family feast. We all shared the chocolate sheet cake my dad had made, with butter cream frosting, pink frosting flowers, and the message "Congratulations Sisters." Those whose relatives traveled cross-country received visiting privileges all weekend, while the rest of us, the locals, were limited to Reception Day. Somehow I missed that directive and invited my family back over the weekend. Since we'd have the afternoon off anyhow while the others visited, I didn't see a problem. That, I learned after dinner, was my problem.

At the end of Reception Day, our families and friends left at five P.M. not to be seen again for a full year. We gathered with our new neighbors, the other black- and white-veil novices,* for vespers at 5:15, followed by dinner, at which recreation continued. Nonstop deafening chatter is what I recall. Thirty-eight of us hadn't talked in a week. Add that to all the other novices, and our numbers and volume multiplied overnight. After such a momentous day, we all had a lot to say. That was the first time we really got a good look at one another, trying to match a new name with the habited face. We enjoyed a special surprise dessert of Baked Alaska, prepared to perfection, and received an extra fifteen minutes of recreation after dinner—a full hour—which was an even rarer event. I'm sure the out-of-control noise became unbearable and the superiors wanted us outside.

After dinner, I lined up with a few others to see Sister Beatrice; the designated time and place for questions, permissions, and making accounts of mistakes or accidents (like being late for chapel or knocking over a bucket of water). I was there for two out of three. If there were such a thing as novice report cards, I would have been given an overall grade of D on my first day. Not only did I need permission to see my family again over the weekend, but I had to account for breaking the new dolor beads (the rosary of the Mother of Sorrows that hung from a blue cord cincture around the waist). It happened while I was sitting on a park bench with my mom and dad. I didn't notice that the crucifix slipped between the cracks, so when I stood up to introduce Sister Martha to my parents, the cross got caught in the slats and broke off. Because Martha may have already alerted Beatrice (they told each other everything), I had to make the account. Being last in line, I found myself alone with Sister Beatrice in an empty dining room.

"Hi, Sister," I said, trying to establish a zone of comfort, "I'm Karol Jackowski . . ."

"You are Sister Carol Joseph," she said with a furrowed brow, stop-

---

*First-year novices wore white veils and second-year novices wore black veils.

ping to correct me midsentence. "Have you forgotten already? And I *know* who you are."

"Sorry, Sister," I said, trying not to flinch while feeling like a squashed bug. "I need to ask permission to visit with my family on Sunday . . ."

"Why, Sister Carol Joseph? Do you expect special treatment?" she asked, with arms folded under the cape and a look that could kill. She made my new name sound like a curse. "What if everyone requested weekend visitation?" she continued. "The extra days are for the sisters whose families are not able to visit often."

"I didn't understand," I said, holding my own, "and invited my family back on Sunday. Since we have free time anyhow, I assumed it made no difference." I also wanted to ask, "What's so wrong with everybody having weekend visits?"

"*Assume?*" she asked. I clearly hit a raw nerve. "Sister Carol Joseph, do you know what *assume* does?"

I didn't, so she told me.

"It makes an 'ass' out of 'u' and 'me,' " she declared. She wasn't joking.

To make a long humiliating reprimand short, I was a selfish sister in no position to assume what does and doesn't make a difference in the novitiate. She did, however, begrudgingly say yes to the Sunday visit, but only for two hours. I couldn't wait to get out of there and almost took a chance to skip the broken-rosary account. But I must have felt it couldn't get worse, because I pressed on with it. Again, I assumed it was no big deal.

"I don't know, Sister Carol Joseph," Sister Beatrice said, looking perturbed and shaking her head. Even when I said I could fix it, that didn't matter. I didn't get the point of anything.

"Perhaps this is a sign," she told me, as though I should begin to think about leaving.

I didn't ask what it was a sign of. I didn't want to know what she was thinking.

"I'm sorry, Sister," I said, with downcast eyes, desperate to get out of there. Valuable recreation time ticked away, and my friends waited breathlessly to hear what happened. "I'll be more careful," I added with brave eye contact. I didn't melt.

"Well, I certainly hope so," she said, dismissing me with a scornful look that would become all too familiar. "You may go."

That's how I kicked off two years of solitary confinement. After free floating all day in the pure joy of sisters, family, friends, music, food, and drink, I entered the reality that was newly mine. Sister Beatrice was my superior, and life in the novitiate was off to an unexpectedly bad start.

NOVITIATE

The canonical year, under the direction of the mistress of novices, has for its object the forming of the mind and soul of the novice by study of the Constitutions, by meditation and prayer, by instruction in the observance of the vows and the practice of virtue, and by exercises suitable for correcting faults, regulating the emotions, and developing virtue.

—CONSTITUTION 10:52

A little bit of history is needed in order to understand what happened in the novitiate. Without a sense of the historical forces that turned some Novice Mistresses into monsters, there's a tendency to place personal blame where it doesn't belong. As Paj notes wisely about ours: "From the great view of hindsight, she probably was caught between the warring and strange dynamics of her bosses."

I had absolutely no hindsight as a nineteen-year-old novice, and I placed all blame for my misery on the Novice Mistress, where it didn't belong entirely. Lucky for all of us, those adverse feelings are long gone. Distance didn't exactly lend enchantment, but the further removed I became from the novitiate experience, the more clearly I began to see all the good that was done to me there.

Our novitiate looked like a medieval monastery standing face-to-face with a college campus. Outside it was 1965, and inside we entered the monastic spiritual mindset of the Middle Ages: keep the world out, withdraw from all interest in current events, and be protected from contact with an evil and dangerous world, especially men. Built in 1893, the novitiate was designed to be self-sufficient. In order to keep us in and the world out, we had our own chapel, dining room, and classrooms. We needed to go out for nothing, and we had contact with no one but one another. Living in a cocoon of an existence, we never knew what happened in the outside world.

For example, we learned about the Vietnam War with other announcements after breakfast, with no mention of it publicly again. Privately I learned a little more. After lunch one day, Sister Beatrice announced her "Please See Me" list and I was on it. I ran up there so as not to be last in line—I never made that mistake again. Then I began to feel queasy over what she wanted. I could be guilty of anything.

In the same tone of voice she used to tell me I had done something wrong, Sister Beatrice said that my high school classmate, Tommy Ramirez, had been killed fighting in Vietnam. I received a letter she couldn't give to me (because it was from a boy), which contained news of Tommy's death. After that encounter, I never heard anything that year about the Vietnam War. It didn't exist in the novitiate, except in prayer.

Even though it was 1965 and our lives as nuns would change dramatically in two years, the novitiate we entered demanded a soulful step back in time. With two years of novitiate experience, the first white-veil year is far more cloistered and restrictive. Being sealed in, we didn't go to the college for class, didn't leave the building for meals, and didn't go to the Church of Loretto for prayer. Part of the "hidden year" meant not being seen in public. Even recreation space was restricted further to the backyard around Saint Thérèse's shrine, and, thank God, the cemetery. Only on special feasts and funerals did we join the community for mass in the church—usually as the guest choir—and only then could we visit the sisters in the infirmary. Every Sunday I missed seeing Concil.

We lived together in solitary confinement. Not only did we enter total isolation in the novitiate, but we also found ourselves in an oppressive world with sharp distinctions between superior and subject, distinctions that made no sense outside our front door (and very little inside). Every minute of every waking day—whether praying, working, eating, or studying—the emphasis was on cultivating obedient attitudes like meekness, humility, and docility, attitudes that can smother the soul—at least, that's what they did to mine. Learning to become invisible and submissive was something many of us couldn't do. I found it impossible to believe that the voice of the superior was any more divinely inspired than the voice of the rest of us, and I'd have to lie to agree with every decision she made. But the Constitutions demanded both.

OBEDIENCE

The perfection of religious obedience requires that one renounce her own will and practical judgment in order to conform to the holy will of God, manifested in the Constitutions and in the will of superiors.

To achieve that perfect and joyful obedience which brings peace to the soul, the sisters shall pray for an increase of faith which will enable them to see Christ in their superiors. They shall refrain from all criticism, ill will, and complaint against superiors, as well as from all servile fear and self-seeking. They should also accept without murmur any changes of persons, placements, and employments . . . submission should be full and entire.

—CONSTITUTION 16:129–130

We paid a high price for disagreeing and speaking our minds, being subject to the unexpected wrath of the Novice Mistress, but the price of blind obedience felt infinitely higher. It was the loss of soul. The most blindly obedient were emotionally immature, extremely passive, and couldn't make decisions. Worst of all, they had a paralyzing fear of conflict. In my eyes, that kind of blind obedience brought out our worst features.

First of all, blind obedience became a good excuse for not having to think, which in the novitiate could be very painful. But ready-made answers do little more than suppress self-knowledge (because it doesn't matter), cultivate mediocrity, encourage irresponsibility, and endow moral and spiritual superiority. Who knows what untold damage was done by all who proclaimed proudly, "I did what I was told"? And what's worse in life than having adults, especially nuns, who don't know who they are or what they think?

Second, that kind of blind obedience treated us like children and encouraged a neurotic dependency on the superior, which wasn't good for anyone. Superiors tended to favor docile and cooperative sisters. They perceived them as holier and even rewarded them with better opportunities for things like housework. The most docile got to clean the chapel, deliver meals to the Superior General and her council, and answer the front door. Needless to say, that didn't sit well with me. The consequence of "being myself" exiled me outside to pull weeds out of sidewalk cracks in ninety-degree South Bend heat and scrub bird crap off picnic tables and benches.

With clear-cut convent perks for the blindly obedient, many novices went for it, never anticipating the heartbreaking casualties. Trying to obey blindly nearly killed May Guinane, Sister Francis Eileen, a novice from Ireland brought to this country by Sister Eleanor, the Superior General's treasurer. What May loved most about the United States was

Connie Francis's hit song "Where the Buys Are." She couldn't pronounce "boys" and we joked that it was a divine sign to be a nun. May gave her life to being an obedient sister, and it made her so sick that she couldn't sleep or eat; it got so bad that she ended up hospitalized in the middle of the night, then sent home to Ireland, never to be heard of again. While we didn't know about anorexia and bulimia in 1965, I'm sure that's what nearly killed May (and countless other women) for trying to be so obedient. When it came to obedience in the novitiate, you were damned if you did and damned if you didn't. I preferred to be damned because I didn't.

The way we lived in the novitiate made monsters and survivors of us all. It brought out the best and worst in us, which is what happens in solitary confinement. We got taken down the rabbit hole where insight and depth are found, always a harrowing experience. And the air we breathed was full of historical forces that demanded Novice Mistresses to cultivate submissiveness "full and entire." That was their job, their holy obedience. That's what God wanted them to do.

The nineteen-year-old "good sister," "seeing Christ in her superiors," obeyed promptly and cheerfully, "without murmur." Those were the underpinnings of religious life that made dissent and disagreement such a sacrilege. So if you believe, as many of us did, that obedience means listening to the Holy Spirit in everyone (not only superiors) and finding the common voice, either you spoke up and accepted the punitive consequences, or you kept silent and got depressed. I did both.

According to the Constitutions, a "rebellious spirit" provided grounds for dismissal, especially for those who refused to abandon 1965. Every two months the Novice Mistress submitted reports to the Superior General on the "conduct, disposition, character, and health of each novice"; and every two months Sister Adele and I envisioned a flatbed semi driving our folders to the Generalate. Dissenters walked a fine line in the novitiate. Those who questioned the rules and challenged the superior paid a dear price. We never knew for sure if we were staying or leaving, coming or going. For seventy-two years, the novitiate became increasingly charged with the divine unknowing energy of nineteen-year-old novices learning to survive.

The novitiate building in which we lived was the 1893 original. Unlike the residents of the postulate, ours were not the first spirits to live there. Seventy-two years of novices lived in the novitiate before us, and it felt as if every one of them left a little bit of compassion behind. All old buildings have a life of their own, but when we walked into the novitiate the first time for a "grand tour," I felt surrounded by a lot more than my thirty-seven sisters.

For tour purposes only, we entered through the front door. Only guests, priests, and delivery people used the main entrance; we "hidden" ones exited and entered through the back door, like staff. Entering through the front door was such a heartwarming experience; especially if you approach the building head-on from the path near Holy Cross Hall. Behind you lies a stunning clear view down Saint Mary's Avenue, and before you stands a four-story yellow brick mansion with large white-trimmed windows and a long roofed porch held up by six white gothic pillars. If I didn't know it was the novitiate, I would have felt as if I were visiting royalty, hoping the princess would be granting audiences.

In the front yard of the novitiate stood a thirty-foot-tall shrine to Saint Michael the Archangel (illuminated at night), patron saint of protection against fire. The location is no coincidence. With thousands of layers of Johnson's Paste Wax on every convent floor, that area of the campus needs all the fire insurance it can get. Not only are convent floors aged with wax, but at Saint Mary's all convent buildings are connected, above- and belowground. Through doorways and stairways, the novitiate was connected to the college convent, which led into Rosary Hall, which was right around the corner from the convent infirmary, which led to the Church of Loretto. An underground tunnel system (where, I was told, sisters in the juniorate smoked) connected the convent with the buildings at the college.* At that time, you could go anywhere on campus without stepping outside. And to my knowledge, there's never been a major fire at Saint Mary's College or convent. So far, Saint Michael the Archangel is still making miracles.

Greeting us at the front door a week before our arrival stood our "tour guides," two white-veil novices winding up their first year: Sister Helen Margaret (my high school pal Peggy O'Malley) and Sister Jacqueline Marie, her classmate. Unlike the heavy metal turquoise doors of the Postulate, these doors were old, weather-worn, and oak, with frosted-glass windows in a cross-and-floral design. Above us, to the left, on the second floor, leaded stained-glass windows confirmed where the chapel was; and directly above us, over the front door, were three tall yellow stained-glass windows, also in a cross-and-floral design, indicating more sacred space, most likely a statue or a shrine.

"Welcome to your new home," Sister Jacqueline Marie said, greeting each of us with a hug.

"Home Sweet Home," Peggy added, with a slight tone of sarcasm, a smile, and the sisterly hug.

I felt like Alice in Wonderland. The entranceway looked like a museum and smelled of freshly applied floor wax. People joke about the incredibly shiny floors in convents, as though we had some magic formula or walked on air, but it's no joke. We walked on what looked like

---

*The tunnels were closed for health and safety reasons in 2004.

a glass-covered tile floor; the original three-inch ceramic tiles in a deep beige, with a multicolored zigzag border of maroon, pale blue, and butterscotch gold tile. No wonder they didn't want anyone walking on it; within minutes after someone did, out came the big industrial buffer to restore the flawless shine, as if to restore a work of art.

It's not just the precious floor that's preserved from wear in keeping the front entrance off-limits. To the right and left are crafted wooden staircases leading to second-floor guest parlors. The front doors and stairways were made from the same wood, as if all from one giant oak tree. Hand-carved spindles on a square base, two to a step, reinforce a time-worn smooth oak railing with floral designs at each end. Carved into the sides of the steps are lilylike leafy designs. Face-to-face under each stairwell were two four-seater pews for guests. No one, except priests and nuns, was allowed beyond the inner doors into the cloister.

All of the main doorways and stairways in the novitiate looked like works of art. The spiritual significance was lost on me then, but in the literature of mysticism, doors and stairs are portrayed as ways to God. Teresa of Ávila, the sixteenth-century Spanish mystic, described her soul as a seven-story castle with doorways and stairwells leading to divine revelation. That's why they became works of art in the novitiate. We needed all the help we could get on the way to God. The inner doors to the cloister were similar to the front doors in design, they were on swingers—like kitchen doors in restaurants—and were locked at night. With one tour guide on each side, both inner doors swung open simultaneously.

"These are the Guardian Angel stairs," Peggy said, with a sweeping gesture of the hand, as TV models do when they're showing prize-winners their new car.

The ten-foot width of the main staircase filled the entrance and shined with what always looked like freshly applied varnish. No one knew why they were called Guardian Angel stairs, but I found it comforting nonetheless. In the event of a fire, a huge ball of flame would shoot right up that big wide-open stairwell, consuming all four stories in seconds. So I liked the idea of angels guarding them, and us. Tripping on the habit and falling down the stairs became a daily fear, and to my knowledge that never happened either, at least not with serious consequences. Thank you, guardian angels.

I also liked, and found funny, how every room or area bore the name of an angel or saint. For example, I didn't live in the dorm on 3 North but in the "Saint Joseph" dorm; and it wasn't our backyard but "Saint Thérèse, the Little Flower's" yard. You can imagine the instant intrigue that consumed us when told about our upcoming introduction to the "Seventh Cupboard."

To the left of the front entrance were two big rooms, one across the hall from the other. The sewing room on the right was used only by the seamstress sisters (not me), but the Period Room on the left was used by all. It was a big, all-purpose room, painted mint green with wooden cabinets along the walls, a table, two chairs, and a sink that didn't work. When the hot water was turned on, the sink moaned like a ghost trapped in the novitiate and unable to get out. The cold water sounded like a cruise ship pulling into port. We planned a Hawaiian-theme dinner once, using very effectively the cold-water sound effects at the beginning and end of the meal. (See how easily amused we were?)

The Period Room received its name because that's where we lined up on the first of the month to get weighed and asked if we had our period. While never told that the novitiate could be hazardous to health, some poor sisters nearly bled to death monthly in agony, with a few having periods stop completely the day they entered the novitiate. Either way, within a few months, as psychologists predict, we all had periods at the same time, knocking up the intensity of life a big notch. Imagine the fun.

At the end of the hall we entered the novitiate refectory—the dining room—four times the size of the postulate's in order to accommodate two groups of novices; and until August 15, when the black veils professed temporary vows and moved to the juniorate, three groups lived and ate in a building built for two. Ten tables of nine lined up, five on each side, and centered up-front before a crucifix hung on a varnished plywood panel, stood the head table where the Novice Mistress and six novices sat. The east and west walls were ceiling-to-floor windows with sheer Irish lace curtains that allowed a little of the world in. The brightness of the dining room was a daily treat, as was air-conditioning in the summer. Only one other room in the novitiate bore that luxury: the chapel.

While we were preoccupied with the Seventh Cupboard, our tour guides let the suspense build. We entered recreation rooms on the north side of the first floor—a separate one for each group of novices. (Even though we lived in the same building, we weren't allowed to speak to one another.) Game tables and wooden furniture filled both rooms, with built-in drawer units that served as mailboxes and lockers—places where we left books, gloves, scarves, and other personal items (since you needed special permission to go to your cell during the day). Both recreation rooms had windows for walls; these became spiritual lifesavers. Being able to see 1965 lifted the spirit naturally and kept life in perspective.

With Sister Martha's office strategically located between the two recreation rooms, you can imagine how much fun we didn't have. Across the hall were a restroom, a laundry room, and a supply store. Square white wooden boxes lined the laundry room walls, each numbered and full of fresh folded laundry. Next door was Paj's supply store, a long narrow room with wooden storage cabinets, where we lined up for personal and school supplies—soap, deodorant, toothpaste, toothbrush, notebooks, pens, etc. Paj's "obedience" included stocking the supply store and maintaining inventory. Paj ran it like a mini-Kmart, taking personal pride in service, even handing out made-up coupons for special offers. At the age of nineteen we were still playing store.

But down the hall on the right, near the black veils' community room, stood a series of tall wooden cupboards, all but one, the seventh one, used to store game equipment. Only the Seventh Cupboard was fitted with a padlock.

"No one ever saw it open," Peggy announced, heightening the mystery.

They believed Sister Martha opened it only at night after Great Silence, when no one was around, as though she might otherwise get mugged in the process. Solely in charge of its security and contents, Sister Martha was the keeper of the keys to the Seventh Cupboard. That was one of her super(ior) powers.

Our tour guides revealed that the Seventh Cupboard contained all turned-in gifts. Since we weren't allowed to keep gifts without special permission, everything went into the Seventh Cupboard. So the three-pound box of See's candies you received for Easter sat next to the lavender bubble bath I got for Christmas. By the time any of it saw the light of day, not only had the chocolate turned white with age, but it had acquired a distinct soapy lavender flavor known as the Seventh Cupboard taste. If you sniffed the Seventh Cupboard while passing by, you could easily detect a faint soapy chocolate scent.

Following our leaders, we walked up the first flight of seventeen Guardian Angel steps to the second floor. To the right and left were sterile-looking parlors for visitors, with uncomfortable-looking Victorian furniture, heavy dark draperies, Persian area carpets over sparkling hardwood floors, and religious art in gilded frames. Everyone I saw visiting in those parlors looked uncomfortable, as though it was impossible to feel otherwise. Even when empty, the rooms looked like sealed-off exhibits at a convent museum. I imagined a museum docent announcing, "And this is where the novices received their guests."

The chapel shared the same locked-in darkness as the parlors, except that it felt kinder and gentler. Unlike the parlors, the chapel bore the touching prayerful energy of so many tired novice souls who spent so much of their time there (especially in the summer, in the air-conditioning). Stained-glass windows covered the east and west walls, filtering the rising and setting sunlight. White-veil novices sat on the right, the Saint Joseph side, and black-veil novices sat on the left, the Virgin Mary side.

Two sets of dark shiny pews, seating for four to six novices, lined the center of the chapel, with a single row of side-aisle "bus seats"—two adjoining individual pews and kneelers side by side, which shook like a bus when the air-conditioner kicked on and off (thus the name). We faced a small simple wood altar centered under what looked like a four-posted wooden carport. The same bad brown wood paneling as the postulate dining room covered the chapel walls, but the floors were flawlessly buffed. I can still conjure up the scent of paste wax and incense that filled the second floor. Wonderful Father Grimm from Notre Dame served as our chaplain, greeting us every morning at 5:30 with a sleepy smile and encouraging words. We joked that he got the depressing novitiate job because of his fitting name.

Centered on the second floor near the chapel and in front of the Guardian Angel stairs stood a gold statue of Our Lady of Consolation on a white marble pedestal, placed there, no doubt, because the founders must have known that's what novices needed most: consolation. When passing the statue, novices stopped, genuflected, and said a prayer. Sometimes, if in a hurry, we'd do a kind of fly-by curtsey instead of a full knee-bend genuflection, which was totally unacceptable in the eyes of superiors. How dare we insult Our Lady that way? I found it hard to believe that Our Lady of Consolation cared about the way we genuflected as much as the Novice Mistress did. It felt like a variation on the grade school theme when nuns told us that gum-chewing made the Blessed Mother cry. Nonetheless, with no superior in sight, I always did the fly-by curtsey with a promise of no personal offense to Our Lady of Consolation.

The second floor also housed an office, a classroom, and what we called the "Constitution Room"—the large rectangular room at the end of the hall with lift-top desks where we met daily after lunch for Constitution Class. The novitiate library for white-veil novices lined the south wall and contained only spiritual books. Once again, three walls of ceiling-to-floor windows were the room's saving grace. On the second floor we looked out on trees and pieces of sky. Even so, it wasn't a room of fond memories.

We didn't dare fool around in Constitution Class, although I do admit to frequent note-writing and -passing. Mostly we sat in a state of high alert because we never knew when we'd be called on to recite the constitutions or prayers we were assigned to memorize. The second-floor Constitution Room and classroom turned into spiritual battlegrounds for those who questioned, challenged, or disagreed with the subject matter. Academic freedom didn't exist in the novitiate. Even though our Scripture classes earned college credit, they were taught by Sister Beatrice, the Novice Mistress. When she assigned us to write a paper on the Gospel of John and "the freedom of the children of God," all hell broke loose. What freedom meant to some of us—freedom of thought, expression, and belief—didn't exist for her or in the novitiate. We should have known better than to think we could be honest about freedom without retribution. After all, this may have looked like a college class in the New Testament, but it was actually a convent class on obedience.

On more than one occasion in spiritual direction, Sister Beatrice pulled out my class papers for discussion, all marked up in red. Not only did she reprimand me for unorthodox, rebellious thinking, but I'd get a D or an F on the paper because it didn't reflect the spirit of the Constitutions of the Sisters of the Holy Cross. I also suspected my papers ended up in the bimonthly novice reports submitted to the Superior General. That's the kind of Novice Mistress madness that infuriated me.

A wall-size stained-glass window of the Holy Family with two decorative side windows welcomed us to the dormitory floors. White-veil novices slept on the third floor, black-veil novices on the fourth floor. In the middle of the third floor, above Our Lady of Consolation, was a small study hall and library for black-veil novices who attended classes at the college. Dormitories lined the halls on the north side of the third floor, while the south side housed Sister Beatrice's office and bedroom, and a classroom for black-veil novices. White-veil novices studied the Constitutions, and black veils studied the vows in preparation for the August 15 ceremony of first profession.

At the end of each dormitory floor was the Hanging Room, the designated place for laundry and for ironing habits and veils. Long and narrow, with hooks on the wall, the Hanging Room looked like a grade school cloakroom. From each hook hung mesh laundry bags with big brass safety-pin clips. In perfect calligraphy over each bag, a sign indicated separate bags for Sheets, Pillowcases, Underwear, Little Caps (the white cotton caps we wore at night), Bands (part of the headgear), Bras, Handkerchiefs, Underskirts (the black cotton skirt we wore under the habit), and Veils. When the bags were full, we'd clip them to be sent to the convent laundry, operated by Sister Anna Regina. God forbid that you should make the mistake of putting a bra in the Bands bag. With all of our clothing numbered, it wasn't hard to identify and punish the culprit.

Wrinkled veils and habits were mortal sins in the novitiate. But rather than stand in line waiting for one of two available irons, many of us pressed our veils between the mattress and plywood on our beds; ironing while we slept. And while no one I know committed suicide in the Hanging Room, Sister Francis Virginia hid there during thunderstorms; I suppose she felt safer because there were no windows.

On the day of the novitiate tour we didn't get to see the dormitory floors. Even for us that remained part of the cloister off-limits for a few more days. Our tour concluded with punch and cookies in the recreation room on the first floor and a brief welcome by Sister Beatrice and Sister Martha. Walking through the novitiate for the first time felt like walking through history. Knowing that thousands of novices became "survivors" in that building was an enormous source of comfort. I counted on the holy spirits of those women who passed through there before me to blow some wind beneath my wings and get me through. If they could do it, so could I.

NOVITIATE

During the canonical year the novices must not be employed in any external works . . . They may, however, perform domestic work in the house, but in a subordinate capacity and only so far as such work will not prevent them from attending the exercises of the novitiate.

The order of the day in the novitiate is determined by the mistress of novices. . . . The religious exercises include, daily: morning prayer and meditation of half an hour, Holy Mass, recitation of the office, spiritual reading, study of the Constitutions, particular examen, visit to the Blessed Sacrament, the seven dolor beads, night prayer; weekly: conferences on the spiritual life, confession, hour of adoration, chapter of faults; on Friday, the way of the cross; on Saturday, the singing in common of the litany of Loreto; monthly: direction, as sought or needed, monition, and a retreat of one full day.

—CONSTITUTION 10: 54–55

That's the answer to the question of what we did all day in the novitiate during the first "canonical" year of solitary confinement. We worked (in a "subordinate capacity") and we prayed. Our work assignments were called obediences because we had to do them without question or "murmur." Every month Sister Beatrice posted an obedience list with jobs and names of those assigned to them. We employed no hired help to keep the four-story novitiate clean. We did it all.

We waxed and buffed floors, scrubbed shower stalls and toilets, sanded and varnished (by hand) all four flights of Guardian Angel stairs, cleaned and shined pews in the chapel, even scrubbed pots and pans in the convent kitchen. In teams of five we also loaded and ran the industrial dishwashing machine (like those you see in restaurants), setting up carts of meal trays afterward for the sisters in the infirmary. That's when we found out about the enclosure on the second floor, where sisters with dementia lived locked in to prevent their wandering. We heard through the grapevine that one of those nuns got out, wandered off, and fell over the cliff behind the college Clubhouse, but everyone we asked denied it. Their meal trays were marked NO SILVERWARE.

Working in the convent laundry every day after lunch became a big treat because we got out of the novitiate for an hour. Some worked the mangler, pressing sheets, pillowcases, and veils, while others sat at big square tables folding and sorting underwear and little caps. Several Polish women worked with Sister Anna Regina, the laundry boss, and though banned from talking to us, they did so anyhow when she wasn't around.

Virgie became our favorite. She was a townie, a local woman who lived in South Bend and wore big dangling rhinestone earrings, bright red lipstick, and two arched black pencil lines where eyebrows used to be. Every day Virgie greeted us at the door with a big smile and a heavily perfumed hug, slipping us candy on the way out. I think she felt sorry for us. At the end of the year, the laundry ladies gave us a surprise "congratulations" party for surviving. They saw many novices come and go, feeling just as bad as we did when someone left. Virgie was the mother superior we all wished we had.

When it came to work assignments, the blindly obedient sisters received the best jobs. The chapel ranked number one, followed by cleaning the superior's office and taking care of the refectory (a highly coveted job for the access to food). Every day at 10:15 A.M. and 3:15 P.M. we ate collation in silence, which means "a snack with no talking." Snacks consisted of coffeecake left over from breakfast or extra desserts from lunch. The sisters who took care of the refectory set up and cleaned up after collation, which meant first dibs on snacks. I never got that job. On the obedience list my name always appeared under "Hallway Floors" (washing, waxing, buffing), "Guardian Angel Stairs" (hand-sanding and varnishing), and "Bathrooms and Bags"—the most despised and my most frequent job. Scrubbing shower stalls, tubs, and toilets turned into hellish work in the summer, but "Bags" ranked the worst all year long.

Between the bathroom stalls stood brown paper bags for used sanitary napkins. My job included collecting the bags from stalls on all four floors, taking them down to the furnace in the basement of the convent infirmary, located across from the mortuary. (In those days we embalmed our own.) The advantage of that job was being able to burn clandestine notes and letters along with the bags, and discovering the employee vending machine, across the hall from the infirmary lunchroom. Being a soda junkie who hadn't seen a can of Coke in months, I felt as if I had discovered hidden treasure when I found that vending machine.

I took all my obediences seriously, sometimes too seriously. On one occasion, Sisters Brendan Marie, Mark, Helena, and I were assigned to "Bathrooms and Bags" and decided to give the showers a good spring steam-cleaning. We closed the windows, turned on the hot water in every shower stall, closed the door, and let the water run while we did "Bags." We didn't realize that hot steam would set off the sprinkler system, which worked like a charm. What didn't work was no one knowing how to turn the system off. Sister Beatrice was so angry she canceled recreation for several days, along with the opportunity to attend a Russian history lecture at the college.

Whenever the college needed to fill an auditorium (e.g., the Russian History Lecture Series), Mary Gerber, the program director at the college, called the novitiate. Two minutes before the program began, we entered the college's O'Laughlin Auditorium, filing into the last row. Not many cared about missing a Russian history lecture (except for the chance to get out and maybe see some of our college pals in the crowd), but everyone sorely missed recreation. That hit us where it hurt. The shower incident got me exiled outside to pull weeds from cracks in the sidewalk and clean bird droppings off picnic tables and benches. While Sister Beatrice called me disruptive, I thought I was overzealous.

At least I got to be outside. Being outdoors was a breath of fresh air all-round, but being covered from head to toe in black serge wool felt like hell on Earth in South Bend's hot, humid summers. I also felt haunted by the Talmud's saying, "Every blade of grass has its angel that bends over it and whispers, 'Grow, grow.'" I bent over those same blessed blades of grass, yanking them to instant death.

Even meals became work when seated at the head table with the Novice Mistress. Every month we rotated table assignments, with placements determined by a number chosen in the "table lottery." A small glass bowl on a wooden pedestal contained numbers such as 1-2, 6-4, 3-3, etc., each one indicating a table and place for the month. So if you picked 1-1 that meant you sat at the head table, at the right hand of the Novice Mistress; for some this was the most dreaded choice of all.

High drama always surrounded the lottery bowl. Many closed their eyes before picking, praying for anything but a 1, and you knew by the look on our faces who got a 1 and who didn't. Big smiles and sighs of relief covered the faces of those who didn't, and a dark cloud of gloom enveloped those who did. Friends stood around to protect me, so if I picked a 1, I could throw it back in and take another without anyone's noticing. This was a big novitiate no-no, since we were led to believe that God picked the numbers and put us where we belonged. For Easter that year, I picked a 1-4 and threw it back in, only to get a 1-2, seated at the left hand of Sister Beatrice, one of the two most dreaded spots at the head table—and for a high holy feast day. That meant having to carry on a conversation because on feast days we didn't eat in silence.

On that Easter morning we listened to Handel's *Messiah* before the bell rang for recreation. I listened very carefully to Handel, trying to find something inspirational to say. I liked the chorus of "We like sheep. . . ." I felt moved by a genius like Handel including one whole song about his fondness for sheep.

"Isn't it amazing," I said when the bell rang for recreation, "that a genius like Handel wrote a song about liking sheep."

My comment prompted goofy glares from the sisters at the table and dead silence. Only Sister Adele looked on me with pity because she knew what was coming. I could feel Sister Beatrice stiffen beside me, but she could see it.

"Sister Carol Joseph," she said in an Easter reprimand tone of voice, "you weren't listening. The complete refrain is, 'We like sheep have gone astray, everyone to his own way.'"

Feeling like a smashed marshmallow Peep, I said, "Oh," and nothing more.

With the exception of the Novice Mistress, everyone at the table looked ready to laugh, but no one dared. And after that unnecessary humiliation on Easter morning, I made sure I never picked a 1 again. My sisters understood why, and no one objected when they saw me toss a 1 back in the lottery bowl and keep picking until I got something else.

Another strange mealtime ritual involved washing our own dishes at the table, which at the time made sense but now seems like a disgusting procedure that surely must have violated some health code. At the end of the meal, the sister B servers (A's served the meal, and B's cleared the serving dishes and brought out the dishpans) stood up, walked to the pantry, and returned with "scrape pans"—small round stainless-steel pans with a rubber scraper. One by one we scraped the remnants on our plate into the pan, passing it to the sister next to us. You can imagine what it looked like by the time it got to the last sister at the table. Even worse was the pantry job of dumping all the scrape pans into the "slop can."

After the scraping of plates, B servers set two big stainless-steel tubs of soapy water with a dish mop on the table, where we washed and dried our dishes then set the table for the next meal. While obviously the most efficient way to wash and dry hundreds of dishes in minutes, that nasty procedure also accounted for the numerous times we shared the cough or illness of the sisters at our table. Even washing dishes at the head table turned into a personal disaster for me. I was so nervous when Sister Beatrice handed me her plate that I dropped it into the dishpan, splashing suds in her face. We were dying to laugh, but no one did; the price was too high.

Occasionally, sleeping also became work. During spring and summer mostly, we'd frequently be awakened by the screeching of a bat flying through the dorm. Every dorm had its own bat squad, consisting of two or three sisters with tennis rackets under the bed and newspaper (old *Wall Street Journals* the black-veil novices were allowed to read). In perfect silence, we'd get up, grab our racket, turn on the light, and start swinging. We became quite proficient at stunning the bat with a firm swing, scooping it into a wastebasket with newspaper, then taking it outside and setting it free. In all of our many bat conquests, I am proud to say we never killed a single one.

One night Sister Francis Virginia woke up with a bat lying next to her on the pillow. She very calmly got up, wakened the bat squad, turned on the light, and the bat busters got the job done—all in total silence. Within minutes, when nearly back to sleep, Francis realized what happened and started screaming hysterically. I think we slapped her to calm her down, not wanting to waken Sister Beatrice or Sister Martha. Another sister saw a bat hanging on her cell curtain and the same thing happened. After the bat squad did the job in a jiffy, she went ballistic.

Only once did we experience a bat attack in broad daylight. It happened in the refectory during lunch. The bat seemed to have flown in from the kitchen because Chester, one of the kitchen workers, came running in after it swinging a broom—a double whammy of excitement. Not only was there a bat in the dining room, but even worse, there was a man in the cloister. Under ordinary circumstances, one of the bat squad would have run upstairs for a tennis racket, but no one moved. There was no such thing as an ordinary circumstance in the novitiate.

According to the Constitutions, there was always silence in the refectory during the three communal meals, together with reading. The superior chose the reading which was supposed to be of an edifying, instructive, and interesting nature. The day the bat appeared, the sister doing lunch reading continued bravely but kept looking up at the end of a sentence and ducking when the bat flew her way while the rest of us either laughed or screamed. Sister Beatrice tried to silence us, but we were too far gone. She finally rang the bell for recreation.

Unlike the high ceilings on the dormitory floors, the first-floor ceilings were low. Some sisters hid under the table, while a few others from the bat squad tried to stun the bat with a snap of a napkin (the way we did to one another with a towel in high school gym class). The bat flew back toward the kitchen, followed by the broom-swinging Chester. While being a member of the bat squad never appeared on the obedience list, it was nonetheless a voluntary work of utmost importance.

In the novitiate we learned all work is holy and all nuns are created equal. The sister who cooks and cleans is just as highly valued as the sisters who run hospitals and colleges. All nuns are called to some kind of work, and they don't retire until exceptionally old, seriously sick, or dead. Even the sisters in the infirmary received the obedience to pray for the world. Just as nuns revere as holy a woman's need for sisterhood and solitude, so too do they revere a woman's need to work as a divine right.

"All work is God's work," Sister Beatrice told us when she overheard us complaining about "Bags." Even the most mundane works provided ways to experience divine life, although I wonder if nuns just said that in order to make despicable tasks more bearable.

Nuns aren't the only ones who regard a woman's need to work as a divine right, though they may have been among the first to do so. Social scientists now confirm the one bit of wisdom about women's mental health that nuns have known all along: work improves it. Women who have never worked outside the home tend to have the highest levels of depression and the lowest self-esteem; they feel less attractive, experience the most loneliness, and consider themselves incompetent at everything, even child care.

Consequently, we were taught to lay our hands on the ordinary things and common interests in life as though they were indeed works of God, the most divine work we could possibly do. In the spirit of holy obedience we willingly or unwillingly went where we were sent and did what we were called to do. That's how obedience was lived, even though

I do recall scrubbing a particularly crappy picnic bench and calling to mind Teresa of Ávila's comment to God after being thrown from her horse into a puddle of mud: "If this is how you treat your friends, it's no wonder you have so few."

When we didn't work, we prayed. The list of prayers to say before the end of the day proved to be no small task, especially in the beginning, when our undisciplined spirits dreaded so many hours of solitary prayer. Learning to meditate was a job in itself. I remember sitting in the chapel for morning meditation just trying to stay awake. Nodding off became a common meditative practice at 5:30 A.M., so much so that half of us jumped when Sister Leonard Marie fell asleep and slipped off the kneeler with a thud. Those around her laughed uncontrollably until Sister Beatrice got up from her pew to stop us. The same thing happened when one of the sacristans used too much wax on the pews, causing sisters who nodded off to slide down on their knees. I don't recall the penalty for laughing at the nodders who slipped and slid, but it didn't matter. I loved starting the day off with a good laugh.

Among our daily prayers, I thought some made little sense. For example, every day at 11:45 A.M. we gathered in the chapel for "particular examen," an examination of the day so far and what sins we may have committed, as though there were loads of opportunity for sin in the novitiate. With every minute occupied and supervised, what could we possibly do? All I heard in prayer during those fifteen minutes were stomachs growling before lunch. With the convent kitchen adjacent to the novitiate, the smell of lunch floated up the stairway into the chapel as we meditated on morning sins. Adverse feelings about the Novice Mistress and those who obeyed blindly were my daily sins. And my constant prayerful challenge was how to live with those I didn't like without hating their guts. After all, they were my sisters, just as I was theirs.

Night adoration was one prayerful practice not listed in the Constitutions. Located on the second floor of the convent infirmary, the Adoration Chapel received its name because the Blessed Sacrament was exposed for adoration on its altar twenty-four hours a day; with sisters assigned round the clock in two-hour adoration shifts. As white-veil novices, our shift was 1:00 to 3:00 A.M., the middle of the night. With thirty-eight of us sharing the shift, each of us sat once every three weeks, but even then we dreaded the job because we still needed to rise with the others at 5:00 A.M.

Assigned in pairs, we spent that night sleeping in a special two-room dorm with private bath called the Adoration Dorm, so as not to wake the sleeping sisters. While we were told to get completely dressed, most of us slipped the habits over our nightgowns and wore slippers instead of nylons and shoes. Chances of someone's checking seemed slim at 1:00 A.M. Two black-veil novices relieved us at 3:00 A.M., but they too appeared half dressed. Sometimes Sister Ephraim, one of the elderly sisters in the infirmary, came in and relieved us early, but she sat up in the balcony and probably couldn't see and probably didn't care.

Thank God we did night adoration in pairs. We kept each other awake, sitting there and chatting quietly before the Blessed Sacrament, taking turns with naps. When a sister died, they moved her casket into the Adoration Chapel at night where we'd keep her company. Sister Brendan Marie and I once thought we saw the dead nun move, so I got up and closed the lid. Praying that her eyes were still closed, I opened it again before we left, but neither one of us felt comfortable sitting next to a dead nun.

Depending on my night adoration partner, on the way back to the novitiate at 3:00 A.M. we'd stop at the vending machine in the basement for a nightcap. Thanks to my father, who smuggled in rolls of dimes, nickels, and quarters on visiting day, I treated all my friends to clandestine sodas. Even so, according to Constitution 115, "the 'peculium' or pin money under any form is strictly forbidden."

RECREATION

Recreation is spent in common . . . it is a means of keeping in a healthy condition both mind and body, neither of which can be constantly and heavily taxed without injury.

Every sister shall go to recreation with a view to improve the social spirit of the community and to make all around her happy, that they may experience how good and pleasant it is for sisters to dwell together.

—CONSTITUTION 24: 211–212

Because we spent most of our days in work and prayer, we treasured time for recreation. The Constitution on recreation is the shortest of them all. I suppose the founders figured we needed no direction in that area. On Saturday and Sunday afternoons, as well as on feast days and holidays, we received extra time for group recreation. In addition to the forty-five minutes after lunch and dinner, sometimes we'd get together with the black-veil novices for a movie (such as the Holy Cross vocation movie, *No Higher Way*), with the new postulants for talent shows, or with the sisters in the juniorate for a picnic supper. But as white-veil novices, those times were few.

During summer months, all groups received swim time down at Lake Joy. When the plug got pulled on the postulate swimming pool, the sisters invested in digging a big hole out on the nature trail, filling it with water, and calling it Lake Joy because they figured that's what we'd find there. And we often did—when it didn't turn into Lake Algae, Home of Swamp Thing. All the chemicals in the world didn't kill the algae and weeds that grew in Lake Joy, but we didn't care.

We played down there without superiors and that alone felt like an all-expenses-paid vacation in the Bahamas (not literally, but you get the idea). Lying on a sandlike beach in approved bathing suits (i.e., no bikinis), we tried to get a good tan. I don't know why. In the habit, all you can see are faces and hands, but even so, tanning became a big deal and made us feel almost normal. Unbeknown to us at the time, but as I later learned, some sisters in the juniorate actually sunbathed nude on the roof of the building, that is, until helicopters hovered overhead, forcing them to duck and cover.

We spent a considerable part of our recreation afternoons down in the basement of the novitiate, which always felt haunted by playful novice spirits. Some Saturday afternoons were designated for Arts and Crafts—or as we named it more correctly, Arts and Craps, because of the junk we made. Long before the rest of the world, we painted rocks with "Love," "Peace," and "Joy." We also made twig crosses, pressed leaves and flowers, and made little books of poems and quotes with donated wallpaper scraps. With no money for birthday and feast day gifts, we gave one another worthless treasures made in Arts and Craps.

Located across the hall from the art room was a big recreation room with old soft sofas and chairs, a piano, and a Ping-Pong table. Sister Rita Michael, a musical genius on guitar and piano, played "Golliwog's Cakewalk" more times than I care to remember. All guitar players in the group practiced down there, while the rest of us lounged around or played Ping-Pong. Toward the back of the lower recreation room was the Flower Room—a little closet where Sister Miriam Rose put together floral arrangements in vases for the chapel and in small glass bowls for the refectory tables on feast days or funeral days. Every time a sister died we saw flowers.

Something else happened in the Flower Room that we didn't see. Sis-

ters Georgina and Lydia—a white-veil novice and a black-veil novice—
got caught in a little lesbian hanky-panky, resulting in immediate dismissal at midnight, never to be spoken of again. It was a blatant violation
of the Constitution's rule against "particular friendships."

CHASTITY

*Purely human friendships shall be avoided because these inordinate at-
tachments endanger chastity and may even destroy union with God.*

—CONSTITUTION 15:120

In order to prevent particular friendships, we were told to recreate
in threes never twos, but we did twos anyhow, without endangering
chastity or destroying union with God. Most of us had best friends, and
if sexual activity did occur, it was so secret no one knew—at least I
didn't. Stunned to hear that Georgina and Lydia were dismissed so suddenly, we didn't discover the reason until months after they left. Even
so, the novitiate never became a hotbed of lesbian activity. Sisters who
felt they needed to have sexual relationships decided to leave rather
than be sent home. And I cannot envision a place more inhospitable to
sex than the convent, especially the novitiate. Maybe that's why
Georgina and Lydia ended up in the Flower Room.

The purpose of such an austere novitiate, we were told, was to form
our minds and souls through prayer. At least four times a day we gathered for communal prayer, with free time set aside for private prayer—
the kind of time and prayer I loved most because of its sweet call to step
aside and enter into solitude. The time for solitude in the novitiate
wasn't as plentiful as you'd expect. Time together far outweighed time
alone. With ordinary days so closely and constantly scheduled with communal activities, solitude became a treasured thing.

Even though time alone felt at a premium, I found that the world of sisterhood consistently offered, even made mandatory, time for solitude. Religious life never looks on solitude as a waste of time, a twisted form of passivity, or pathological narcissism. Nuns in particular behold solitude not as the lot of the lonely but as their divine companion. I experienced solitude as a boon of inner activity: inner seeing, inner hearing, inner feeling, and inner knowing.

After a few months in the novitiate, and much to my surprise, I ended up treasuring solitary prayer far more than communal prayer. Such prayerful solitude let me loose to tend to the creative and playful spirits stirring within me, as well as the disturbing and restless spirits that usually accompanied them. As soon as I was alone, as soon as I learned to stop fooling around and keep still, I found myself passing over quite easily into that other inner world, into my most soulful self where all learning from experience occurs.

I fed solitude the best and worst parts of my days and how I felt about them. In doing so, I began to hear the still, small, inner voice of what I call God. I listened for what the Spirit had to say about my burning questions, my whining complaints, my strange experiences, heartfelt hopes, and unspoken prayers. I waited to hear what my soul had to say about the strange life of the novitiate, listening for divine advice. Meditation and prayer became a kind of inner consultation for me. It became a way of begging for some explanation, for some understanding of what was happening to me and why.

At first, my capacity for keeping still lasted no more than ten or fifteen minutes. I chose to spend all of my solitary prayer time outside the convent walking, rather than inside the chapel meditating. Whenever I couldn't keep still, I took myself outside and walked the cemetery, pacing back and forth, up and down those rows of white stone crosses, reading all the nuns' names aloud to myself, like a litany of the saints. Then I did the same with their family names engraved on the back. The earliest sisters received the most unusual names, like Sister Mary Five Wounds, whose last name was Mahoney. She died in 1886 on February 26, my dad's birthday. I imagined her sisters calling her Five Wounds Mahoney and thinking of her as the niece of mobster Baby Face Nelson.

I also remember finding Sister Mary Circumcision, wondering if she died of embarrassment when she got that name and what her sister friends called her. One old nun who knew of her told me they called her Cirky for short. Whatever made my spirit restless in the beginning found comfort in constant walking the rows of stone crosses. I was calmed by those restful and peaceful spirits.

In learning the meditative disciplines of the soul, I slowly learned how to shift from the outer to the inner world and sit still with God. Having all my props pulled out in solitary confinement, I began to see my self in an entirely different way. Not only did prayer offer divine comfort in all kinds of soulful suffering, it also kept away bitterness and the tendency to whine and blame when I was tired. Whenever I follow my restless and puzzled spirits to their God and mine, I almost always find myself lifted up and carried through by them. Only in solitude can I be most attentive to the mystery behind what happens and the divine wisdom that life's mysteries offer. Little by little I was given a divine sense of what was rock under my feet and what was sand. In the first year of cloistered confinement I learned to love the solitary life as much as I did the communal life. I learned to love the heart and soul of sisterhood.

I ended up liking what happened to me in my first year of solitary confinement. Under all of its misery I began to find places within me that couldn't be disturbed or destroyed. By the end of that year I was no longer thrown off-center by Sister Beatrice's reprimands. Parts of me felt untouched by adversity and indestructible as I lived through it. I don't know if it was the descent into the depths of solitude, the months of meditation and prayer, the lifesaving support of my sisters, or the divine madness of our daily life in the novitiate, but I suspect all of the above helped me love the kind of person I was becoming. I felt better at the end of that year, not worse—more serious and funnier, much more solitary and much more of a sister, especially to those who drove me crazy. By the end of my first year in solitary confinement, I was beginning to feel like my very best self.

Even so, the best part of the white-veil novice year was that it didn't last forever, and we were no longer the new kids on the block. New postulants were being groomed behind us, and before we knew it, we were giving them the grand tour of the novitiate and holding them in suspense over the mysterious contents of the Seventh Cupboard. The black-veil novices would be making first profession and moving to the juniorate, and we would be receiving the black veil and moving to the fourth floor. Most important of all, we survived the most difficult year of sister formation. And most surprising of all, Sister Beatrice didn't send me home. That's what I call amazing grace.

chapter four

first profession of vows

NOVITIATE

The formation of the second-year novices continues under the direction of the mistress of novices. The novices devote themselves to the study of vows in preparation for first profession. In addition, they take courses ordered toward the apostolic works of the Congregation. The religious formation of the novices must be the chief concern of this year.

—CONSTITUTION 10:66

While technically still "under the direction" of Sister Beatrice, our second year in the novitiate was relieved of a great deal of intensity by the arrival of new white-veil novices. In a private ceremony we put on the black veil and with it a measure of freedom. Sister Beatrice's main focus of attention was the white-veil novices, while a kinder, gentler Sister Martha oversaw the everyday concerns of the black veils.

Half the size of Sister Beatrice, Sister Martha looked unnaturally thin, with dark, deep-set eyes and pale, drawn facial features, as though she were malnourished. She ate the tiniest portions of everything served and sometimes didn't even finish that. Looking back now, I'm sure she suffered from an eating disorder, but in those days it was looked upon as asceticism. We marveled at her ability to drink boiling hot coffee, bubbling in the cup, and even joked that she had asbestos pipes. No less a disciplinarian than Sister Beatrice, Sister Martha bore none of the burdensome responsibility of preparing us for first profession; a blessing in itself. That was the exclusive job of the Novice Mistress.

As black-veil novices, we returned to classes at the college "ordered toward the apostolic works of the Congregation." In other words, we continued with courses in our major, as well as theology and philosophy. While we concentrated our studies in subjects of our choice—English, history, chemistry, or sociology (my choice)—we also earned nearly enough credits for majors in theology and philosophy. Religious formation remained the chief concern. Most important of all, we left the novitiate daily and returned to life as college students. At least for a few hours a day, we left the Middle Age mindset of the novitiate and re-entered the world of 1966. Our classmates welcomed us back as if we were veterans returning victorious from war.

The new group of white veils got along with Sister Beatrice much better than we had. Far more lighthearted and nowhere near as challenging of authority, the new novices were fun to be with, and that alone lifted the spirit of the novitiate. Looked upon as the entertainers, they sang, danced, played musical instruments, and had what it took to make Sister Beatrice laugh. We deserved a break like that as much as Sister Beatrice did.

Two of the group's funniest were Sister Gretchen (Linda Heidinger) and her guitar-playing sidekick, Sister Suzanne Marie (Suzanne Brennan). To this day, I've yet to see anything funnier than Gretchen's manic running through the lower recreation room of the postulate, with Barbra Streisand's "Gotta Move" blaring on the hi-fi in the background. That performance was outdone only by a hilarious lip-synched version of Streisand's "Ave Maria," which the superiors didn't find funny, but we did. Both Streisand albums mysteriously disappeared after that.

While we remained the pesky gadflies, the white veils became playful court jesters. Even when they caused an untimely and unseemly uproar, their punishment appeared minimal.

A case in point: Sister Laverne's laughably unintentional error in breakfast reading.

MEALS

As often as is practicable there shall be silence in the refectory during the three community meals, together with reading. The matter chosen for reading . . . shall be of an edifying, instructive, and interesting nature.

—CONSTITUTION 223

The rule of silence at meals was always practicable, which meant every day except holy days and holidays. I also suspect that not talking at meals was accompanied by reading in order to avoid the monotony of silence and muffle the irritating sound of clanking silverware. While eating, we listened to stories of the lives and gory deaths of the saints, excerpts from spiritual classics like *The Imitation of Christ*, volumes of community history, and the names of the sisters whose anniversary of death was that day so we could remember them in prayer.

Read to at every meal, we tried to listen carefully since random quizzes were given in Constitution class, and God forbid that you failed. In the old days, you would have been told to kiss the floor for something like failing a quiz. In our day, we were sent to the chapel to kneel for an hour, as though that would refresh our memories and give us the correct answers. Either way, we paid a dear price for wandering minds.

Sisters chosen to read at meals were those with a pleasant voice and an expressive manner, and usually they were well regarded by the superior. I was not one of them. I couldn't do anything serious in silence without laughing, and the thought of reading to my peers was far beyond my minimal level of self-control. While everyone took turns reading, with most given the job for a month, I got the boot after one meal. Not only did my dramatic reading of the brutal death of martyrs incite laughter, but reading the names of the deceased sisters of the day cut my tenure as a reader mercifully short. I could not, without my laughter being magnified by the microphone, announce the names of some deceased sisters. We read their nun name, followed by the family name and the year they died. Names like these did me in:

Sister Mary of the Circumcision (Chanson) 1898
Sister Mary Prezentatione (Tong) 1883 and her sister . . .
Sister Mary Purificazione (Tong) 1900
Sister Mary Resurrection (Tucker) 1947
Sister Mary Exaltation (Daly) 1926
Sister Mary Cunegunda (Hilkens) 1919
Sister Mary Monegunda (Hanlon) 1931
Sister Mary Transfiguration (Stumphauser) 1925

I was dismissed as a reader for disrespecting the dead, but nothing could be further from the truth. It wasn't their fault that they were given those names. I would visit those sisters in the cemetery, always feeling their delight over giving us a good laugh at the beginning of the day, even at their expense. And obviously, they couldn't care less.

The Novice Mistress selected readings, and we were at her mercy. Being a theologian, Sister Beatrice took great care in selecting readings "of an edifying, instructive, and interesting nature." Most memorable was the article by a Catholic priest, Father Anthony Padovano, on the vow of poverty and the paradox of being so rich while owning nothing. Father Padovano became a prominent theologian, with his writings read widely and regarded highly by everyone in the sisterhood, not just Holy Cross, and they still are. (He has since married and left the priesthood.)

Several sisters excelled in reading at meals, but only Sister Laverne stands out to me as unforgettable. With a firm, commanding voice and a theatrical flair, she read profound thoughts slowly, sometimes breathlessly, often pausing between sentences, allowing us to reflect on the meaning. Some feared Laverne because of her domineering presence, but I found her both funny and smart with an edge of cynicism and sarcasm—a spark of life in a sea of white-veiled docility.

While we always looked forward to readings by Laverne, we also avoided eye contact and strained to stifle outbursts of laughter during the unusually dramatic pauses she had during Father Padovano's article. But in the end we lost control completely. She genuinely didn't seem to notice, but in reading the last sentence of the article, one that brilliantly clarified the "enigma" of being so rich while living so poor, Laverne's voice inched toward a crescendo of dramatic flair as she leaned over the microphone and whispered slowly, "And this . . . is the perfect . . . enema."

At every table, quick glances shot back and forth, as if to say, "Did you hear what I heard?" then laughter from those who knew what she said and couldn't contain their hilarity. Laverne had no idea what was so funny, which may have saved her in the eyes of Sister Beatrice, who tried first to ignore the laughter, then to stare and scare us back into silence. But even the white-veil novices laughed beyond control. Rather than blame and ban Laverne from the reading table, Sister Beatrice rang the bell and opened recreation. *That* was the perfect enema.

On another occasion, we were given an afternoon of recreation at the Clubhouse, a one-story white wood cabin on campus near Holy Cross Hall, which was used by Saint Mary's College students for meetings, mini-retreats, and parties. It was equipped with a kitchen, a small dining room, and a big lounge area, and the walls were lined with windows and surrounded by sky-high pine trees. Comfortable stuffed wicker sofas and chairs encircled a huge wood-burning fireplace. The strong smell of cigarettes and beer lingered in it always, probably from the most recent college "kegger." I loved the Clubhouse.

When tensions ran high in the novitiate, even among the white veils, Sister Beatrice sent us to the Clubhouse to blow off steam. One of those times, the white-veil novices decided to put on a play of "Snow White." There we were, twenty-year-olds playing fairy tales. From our group, Mary Sue (of "Chicken Fat Song" fame) played Snow White, and of the white veils, Sister Winifred Marie from England took the part of the wicked witch with the poison apple. At the insistence of the white-veil novices, Sisters Beatrice and Martha attended the performance. In our experience that was never a good idea, but we decided it wasn't worth an argument.

"Would you like an apple from Saint Mary's?" Winnie asked Mary Sue in a crackling voice with a British accent. The chuckling began.

Mary Sue took the apple, bit into it, then broke into an unforgettable death scene. With one hand she clutched her throat while throwing the apple to the floor with the other. She feigned choking and gasping for air. In a stunt worthy of an Oscar, she flung herself on the floor and started flopping around, then went stiff, and died. While we sat on the floor rolling in laughter, Sisters Beatrice and Martha looked horrified, and ended recreation immediately.

We marched back to the novitiate in silence. Mary Sue was nearly sent home for "desecrating the holy habit," while Winnie escaped without notice. Even though the docility of the white-veil novices could be irritating, it wasn't. We appreciated the fact that they diverted a significant amount of Sister Beatrice's time and attention away from us. They were her favorites, and that was our blessing.

forever and ever, amen

On August 15, 1966, the newly professed black-veil novices moved across the street to the juniorate and we moved up to the fourth floor. Once again, blessed be, I received a cell with a window, this time in Saint Teresa's dorm—a smaller dorm with sky-blue walls and eight cells. My cell was in the front of the building. The window faced east and looked out on Saint Michael's shrine, Holy Cross Hall, and Saint Mary's Avenue (the escape route). I could sit on the windowsill or lie in bed and watch college life.

Every fall, before the first home football game, the Notre Dame freshmen got drunk and paraded over to Saint Mary's for the traditional panty raid. The girls hung out of windows waving bras and panties specially purchased for the occasion while the boys yelled for an underwear souvenir. I was tempted to open the window and wave my white Fruit of the Looms in an attempt to draw a crowd to the novitiate, but I was not that brave or that stupid. I would have been home by sunrise if I had.

Eight of us lived in Saint Teresa's dorm that year, with Sister Ann Loretto in charge of the light switch, a responsibility she felt gave her extra power. Ann Loretto was a short, stocky bundle of nervous energy who struggled to become a "living rule" with little success. Each morning at the rising bell, it was her job to flip on the light and get us up with the traditional greeting, "Let us bless the Lord!" We mumbled a groggy "Let us bless the Lord" in response. And every night at 9:00 P.M., she'd flip the light off and announce, "Into your hands we commend our spirit," whether we were ready for bed or not. Whoever was given the cell with the light switch decided on a few extra minutes of sleep in the morning or a little extra time at night to get ready for bed. Every dorm but ours enjoyed that simple, harmless luxury.

The reason some sisters needed more time at night was that showers were limited to five minutes, with a schedule posted on the shower door. If you were last on the list, and the sisters before you took longer than their allotted five minutes, your time was shortened in order for everyone to be in bed by lights-out. While other dorms allowed flexibility for the last to shower, Sister Ann Loretto watched the clock. The second the little hand struck nine, she'd flip off the light and announce, like a centurion, "Into your hands we commend our spirit."

We threw shoes and slippers at her cell in protest, yelling in a loud whisper for her to turn the light back on. But Ann Loretto wouldn't budge. When that didn't work, we'd pretend to go the bathroom, slip our hand into her cell and flip the light back on. In retaliation, she'd kick the curtain, trying to keep us away. Given seven of us and one of her, the odds favored us heavily. This little ritual went on nightly for months, until she finally gave up in tears and left the novitiate shortly after. Sister Ann Loretto tried desperately to be a "living rule," but it only drove her, and us, crazy.

During the day, cell curtains were to be drawn and beds made (unwrinkled and with hospital corners) for random inspections. An unwritten rule in the novitiate stipulated the number of items allowed on top of the dresser. Intended to discourage clutter, the rule permitted no more than three items to be on display—a clock, a statue, and another object of choice. On top of my dresser stood a small black alarm clock, a statue of Mother Mary, and four hand-painted rocks received as gifts from my friends, which were hardly visible from the hallway.

My top drawer, however, was loaded with clandestine goods from college pals: candy, movie star magazines, nonspiritual books, a shoebox of notes and uncensored letters, and a Holy Cross nun marionette we made in Arts and Craps, with blue glitter eyes, hooked nose with a wart, and big ruby red lips. We named her Mother Mary Dymphna after Saint Dymphna, patron of the insane and our idol.

One Saturday afternoon, while we were down in the basement shining shoes, chatting, and probably listening to Sister Rita Michael play "Golliwog's Cakewalk," Sister Lucy, a favorite of Sister Beatrice, came down and announced that Sister Beatrice wanted to see me in my cell. The rest of us looked at one another and our hearts sank, thinking my hour had come: I was being sent home. In those days getting the boot was like Russian roulette. We never knew when someone would be dismissed or why. According to the Constitutions, the list of offenses that warranted dismissal included practically everything.

NOVITIATE

The chief causes for which a novice may be dismissed are the following: contagious or hereditary disease, want of mental or physical health or of mental qualifications, difficult temper; disregard for truth, obedience, the Constitutions and community procedures; carrying on clandestine correspondence, proud and complaining spirit, faulty judgment and indiscretion, habitual violation of silence, worldly dispositions, want of devotedness, absence of goodwill; and in general faults that are regarded disqualifying in the judgment of superiors.

—CONSTITUTION 10:64

That just about covered my whole life as a novice. Full of disqualifying faults, the list was no idle threat. Sisters deemed a "poor fit" could be sent home in the middle of the night, just like that, with no opportunity for recourse or due process. Or if the departure took place during the day, the others would be sent down to Lake Joy or out for a walk on the nature trail in ninety-degree heat, with peanut butter sandwiches and nothing to drink while the sister left. I suppose they expected we'd make a scene if we knew one of our own was being sent home, which some of us surely would have. So when Sister Lucy came down with the grim news of my being summoned by Sister Beatrice to my cell, our hearts had every reason to sink.

I walked slowly up four flights of Guardian Angel stairs, step by step on a death march to the guillotine, calling all angels to come with me. Sister Beatrice stood in my cell near the dresser with arms folded beneath her cape. With furrowed brow and pursed lips, she stared at me with a look that said, "You're dead."

Pointing to three extra items on my dresser, as though they were the worst things she'd ever seen, she asked, "Sister Carol Joseph, what's this?"

"Rocks," I said, feeling faint and foolish for stating the obvious.

Then taking the rocks with one hand, she opened the top dresser drawer with the other to toss them in. I gulped and felt certain my novice days were over. When she saw the top drawer's clandestine contents, I'd be going home with no questions asked. Sure enough, she stared in the top drawer, dropping the rocks with a look of horror.

"Sister Carol Joseph!" she said, picking up the "Story Book of Life Savers" (twelve rolls of candy in a booklike package). "What's this?"

Hardly able to speak, I whispered, "Candy."

Then she spotted the movie star magazine with a bare-chested Fabian and Frankie Avalon on the cover, holding it with a pinched thumb and forefinger, as if it were diseased.

"Sister Carol Joseph, what's this?" she asked again in a higher tone of voice, as if too shocked to say anything else.

Before I could answer, I saw her stunned expression change instantly into utter disgust when she laid eyes on "Mother Dymphna," the Holy Cross nun marionette. As she picked it up by the strings, the puppet's head tilted back as if in a dead faint. It looked the way I felt. I prayed that Saint Dymphna would save me.

"Sister Carol Joseph, what's this?" she asked yet again, almost in a scream, as if she'd never seen anything more ghastly or disturbing.

Before I could squeak, "A puppet," she dumped the marionette, Life Savers, and magazine on top of the dresser, freeing both hands, now trembling, to pick up the book wrapped in brown paper with HOLY

BIBLE hand-printed on the front. The brown paper covered the novel *Manchild in the Promised Land*—nowhere near X-rated, but anything other than spiritual books were banned in the novitiate. That was the Holy Bible I took to the chapel for *lectio divina* (spiritual reading).

That did it. Struck speechless, Sister Beatrice couldn't even repeat the haunting refrain, "Sister Carol Joseph, what's this?"

I'd never seen her angrier. She stacked the book on top of the magazine, along with the Life Savers, Mother Dymphna puppet, and rocks. The shoebox of clandestine notes and uncensored letters was next. My already sunken heart stopped. *If she gets her hands on those,* I thought, *several of us will be home for dinner.*

My sisters in the basement must have been praying for a miracle because Sister Beatrice slammed the top drawer shut as though the shoebox had become invisible. She loaded the clandestine evidence into her arms and walked out. I expected to hear, "Follow me" but didn't. She left me standing there, not knowing if I was staying or leaving. I didn't move for I don't know how long, thinking she'd come back with my brown bag of clothes. When that didn't happen, I went back down to the basement where my silent sisters sat dying to know what had happened, some in tears thinking I was already gone. Looking visibly shaken, my partner in crime, Sister Adele, said I looked like a ghost. All weekend we thought I was in the process of being sent home. We believed angels kept Sister Beatrice from opening the shoebox. Those notes and letters got burned when I did "Bags" the following morning, never to be kept again.

This is all to say that even though the white-veil novices provided a little distraction for Sister Beatrice, her sights still focused on weeding out the malcontents in our group. She and I continued to butt heads in vow class, particularly when discussing obedience. Sometimes the dialogue became so heated—especially when Sisters Adele, Brendan Marie, Miriam Rose, and I voiced our opinions—that Sister Beatrice walked out of the classroom and into her office across the hall, closing the door.

After one particularly explosive discussion, she didn't even come down for vespers and dinner. That was deadly serious. I remember Sister Mark, ever the peacemaker, trying to reason with Sister Beatrice, asking if she would just not leave in the middle of a disagreeable discussion; but she always did, as though she couldn't help herself. Some of us were more than she could bear.

Few of us agreed with the concept of blind obedience, and I think Sister Beatrice, being a theologian, understood our point, but she couldn't admit it. All she could do was walk out. We drove her to tears, she drove us to tears, and in an odd way that became our special bond. I remember sitting in the classroom after she'd walk out, none of us knowing what to do. Do we tell Sister Martha? Do we send Sister Lucy in to see how she is? Do we sit there in silence until classtime is over? Or do we too get up and leave? The four of us always got up and left, since we were the ones who pushed Sister Beatrice over the edge. Believing we'd eventually be sent home, we had nothing to lose.

Being twenty years old and strongly, even rigidly judgmental of those who didn't think the way I did, I was nowhere near understanding that there are as many ways to the truth as there are people who cross my path. I couldn't believe any truth could be found in blind obedience or in those aspiring to be "living rules," since I had not yet discovered divine love, which allows another to be different. We were right, the Constitutions wrong, and the time had come for change. That was our relentless battle cry. Why I wasn't dismissed immediately for insubordination is a mystery I still don't understand.

As novices, we had no idea how close we were to everything changing. With no outside contacts, we didn't know what other sisters thought, nor did we realize that Vatican II issued documents calling for the transformation of the Catholic Church, inside and out, including the sisterhood. While Sisters of the Holy Cross published articles and books on the ways in which our life as nuns needed to change, we had no access to their thinking, as you might expect, given that we were sisters.

Most prominent among the prophetic voices speaking out at that time was Sister Charles Borromeo (Mary Ellen Muckenhirn), a good friend of Sister Beatrice who occasionally came to take her out to dinner, something that mystified us completely. How could they be friends? In 1965, Sister Charles Borromeo edited a book of essays, *The Changing Sister,** in which sister theologians, artists, historians, and sociologists from different religious communities addressed subjects such as "Sociology and Community Change," "The Meaning of Virginity in Religious Life," "The Sister in the New City," "The Sister in Secular Life," and "The American Sister Today." And in 1968, she published *The New Nuns,†* reflecting issues that emerged two years later: "Can Sisters Be Relevant?" "Nuns in Ordinary Clothes," "Protest Movements in Convent Life," "Nuns in the Inner City," "Renewing Religious Power Structures," and "Bureaucratic Dysfunction in American Convents." Chapter titles alone reflected what happened in religious communities after Vatican II but not in the novitiate. We discussed nothing until the time had come to change.

If I recall correctly, we learned about the habit changing and taking back our birth names in a house meeting with Sister Beatrice shortly before Christmas 1966. All the novices gathered in the chapel, fearing something awful was about to happen. Sister Beatrice stood at the lectern used by the priest for homilies, and after an opening prayer to the Holy Spirit, she read a letter from the Superior General addressed to all Sisters of the Holy Cross. She looked and sounded as if she was fighting back tears.

---

*Sister M. Charles Borromeo Muckenhirn, C.S.C., ed., *The Changing Sister* (Notre Dame, IN: Fides Publishers, 1965).
†Sister M. Charles Borromeo, C.S.C., ed., *The New Nuns* (New York: Signet Books, 1968).

I sat there motionless, hardly believing what I was hearing when she read that we would be changing the habit and taking back our baptismal names, if we so desired. No one moved, but you could feel the excitement mounting. We didn't dare to even look at one another for fear that we'd lose control and begin dancing in the aisles. After the letter was read, no questions were allowed. We were only asked to pray for the guidance of the Holy Spirit as we began to respond to the directives of Vatican II.

Most of us were elated at the unexpected good news. Only a few novices felt as Sister Beatrice did and began to weep. For the first time in history, the Catholic Church publicly admitted its irrelevance in the modern world, calling on sisters and priests of every order to change. As nuns we lived an eighteenth-century lifestyle in the twentieth century, differing in the same way anyone would from two centuries ago. With our religious life about to change quickly and dramatically, most of us jumped with joy over the possibilities. Merry Christmas to us.

Not everyone welcomed change in the Church or in the sisterhood. Some Catholics today still condemn Vatican II for changing the mass from Latin to English, as if Latin were the sacrament instead of the Eucharist. Many Catholics resented our giving up the habit, just as many nuns did, believing holiness resided in the habit, not in the sister. The habit covered a multitude of sins: regardless of how miserable and mean a nun in habit was, she was revered nonetheless. No one would challenge a nun, no matter how abusive she could be. If you've seen the movie *The Magdalen Sisters*, the consequences of such blind acceptance and reverence are tragically clear. The habit covered a multitude of sisterly sins, but in their dressing all alike, the truth about nuns would be revealed: it's what's inside that counts.

In Vatican II's Decree on the Up-to-Date Renewal of Religious Life, the bishops recommended that religious habits be "simple and modest, at once poor and becoming. They should meet the requirements of health and be suited to the circumstances of time and place as well as to the services required by those who wear them."* Our Holy Cross community resolved the immediate practical problem of suddenly out-fitting thousands of sisters with new suits by giving us a choice: either make a new habit out of the old habit, or wait for the manufacturer to deliver the overwhelming order. Only a few waited.

Making our own habits was fine for those who sewed. For example, Sister Gretchen created a stylish outfit of a fitted jacket accented with one-of-a-kind buttons (sent by a friend in California), and an A-line skirt with waistband and zipper. She also accessorized with multicolored neck scarves. When the guidelines specified suits in blue, black, or brown, Gretchen appeared in outfits combining all three. While the rest of us looked like pilgrims, Gretchen had style. Inside and out, she was the consummate artist.

With minimal sewing skills, I made a plain collarless jacket with hooks and eyes (no buttons), and an A-line skirt with Velcro—Amish style. However, buttonholes and zippers weren't "proud" in my eyes, just far beyond my pathetic sewing skills. Eventually hundreds of plain blue and black suits arrived, with Sister Fara in charge of the newly desig-nated Suit Room. Since Fara was older and was among the first to wear a new suit, she became an excellent example for her fearful and re-sentful peers.

As black-veil novices, we began visiting the sisters in the infirmary again, with every Sunday afternoon consumed by talk about the changes happening in our lifestyle. Many old sisters, who had lived secluded lives for decades, naturally resisted any change, as did others, including some novices, like Sister Penelope and Sister Virginia Mary, who had en-tered the convent to escape the world. Even though the change was "op-

---

*Vatican Council II: The Conciliar and Post Conciliar Documents, ed. Austin Flannery, O.P. (Collegeville, MN: Liturgical Press, 1975), p. 621.

tional," it offered little comfort to hundreds of sisters who feared a loss of respect, loss of vocations, trouble with hair, worry about what to wear, about expenses, and about their figures. For overweight sisters, the old habit hid their weight problems, and for those whose hair was shaved or badly cut, the headgear did the same. Many sisters wept at the thought of changing anything.

In and out of the sisterhood, we experienced bitter resistance to any kind of renewal, optional or not. All who fought change asked the same question: "If you want to live like everyone else, why did you join the convent?" All who supported change responded, "We don't want to *live* like everyone else; we want to *look* like everyone else." We still wanted to live simply and celibately in community. Even my buddy, Sister Concilio, asked that question. Concil would hardly speak to me when I told her I was making a suit and taking my name back.

Easter Sunday became the designated day to shed the habit and appear in suits, but Concil didn't want to hear any of it, and neither did most sisters in the infirmary. I knew the disagreement turned serious when the poodle never came out of the closet, and our visit was cut short because Concil had nothing more to say. Sometimes she couldn't even look me in the eye. I kept going back week after week, even though the old sisters made a point of letting us know we were no longer welcome. They blamed the young sisters for the upheaval in their lives, not the pope. In their judgment, we were the ones most eager to change the only religious life they lived and loved.

It's true that we had worn the habit for just three years and experienced it more as a barrier between us and the college students at Saint Mary's than a source of reverence and respect. I also found it uncomfortable. Those believing heat never bothered nuns in the summer because we "got used to it" were mistaken. I never got used to layers of black wool in hot, humid South Bend summers, and the headgear hurt the ears and put dents in our foreheads. I couldn't wait to wake up on Easter morning and put on a suit, and getting my name back felt like getting my life back. For me, religious life had nothing to do with what we wore and everything to do with who we were and what we believed. Pope John XXIII, the divine architect of Vatican II, called the Christian the eighth sacrament and the only one unbelievers will receive. For me, the sisterhood is solely a matter of becoming the eighth sacrament.

Not only did convent life begin to undergo massive transformation inside and out, so too did life in the Catholic Church—a double whammy of heartache for those who resented any change at all. The most immediate changes in the Church took place in the liturgy. Priests who once celebrated mass in Latin with their backs to the people all of a sudden spoke English and turned the altar around so that they faced the community. The altar was brought down closer to the people, and the communion rail—a barrier between the priest and the people beyond which no one but altar boys were allowed—was removed. In Vatican II the Church rediscovered itself as the People of God, and everything once so private and mysterious about the mass suddenly opened up to recognize the divine presence of the people who are the Church. We witnessed a second Pentecost.

In the spirit of renewal, liturgists and musicians began translating Latin hymns into English, while others created new music for a new Church. While guitars, flutes, tambourines, and even trumpets replaced the organ at mass, most disturbing for those resentful of change was reception of Holy Communion in the hand, rather than on the tongue. Once led to believe that we'd be struck dead if we touched the sacred host, and that if we chewed, instead of letting the host dissolve, we'd break Jesus' bones, now all of a sudden we took the host in our hand, chewed before swallowing, and were no longer bound to fast the night before receiving Holy Communion.

The meat-eating ban on Fridays was also lifted. While for centuries we suffered fear of mortal sin if we ate meat on Fridays, all of a sudden we did so with no sinful consequences whatever. Almost overnight, the Catholic Church and the sisterhood jumped from the Middle Ages into the twentieth century. No wonder Catholic heads were spinning and so many of the blindly obedient felt duped.

While change blew all around us like a spring breeze, daily life in the novitiate remained the same. Habits and names may have been in the process of change, but the heart and soul of the novitiate were frozen in time. The dissonance between life in and out of the novitiate became increasingly palpable. For example, in philosophy class we read Sartre and Nietzsche, wondering if God was dead, while Sister Beatrice made us sit in the Constitution room for an hour after lunch because on the way to the cemetery to bury Sister Marie Rosaire, the community's beloved artist, Sister Louise, jumped to avoid stepping on a worm and those around her laughed.

A tight lid sealed the novitiate in order to keep out revolutionary thinking. We were still bound by blind obedience, even though the Vatican Council in its document on Renewal of Religious Life posed the question: "Is it not possible to have conflicts between the superior's authority and the conscience of the religious, the 'sanctuary of a person where she is alone with God, whose voice echoes in the depths of her soul?' "* The voice of the superior remained the exclusive voice of God. That belief did not change overnight. In some religious communities and seminaries, that belief has yet to change and probably never will.

While Vatican II called for collegiality and dialogue in decision mak-

*Vatican Council II: The Conciliar and Post Conciliar Documents, p. 693.

ing and policy formation, such open-mindedness did not come to us with new suits and baptismal names. Charitable speech still refused to allow honest differences to emerge and rejected any thinking too controversial or critical. We weren't the only ones in the sisterhood still chafing under the command-obedience community structure, but the intensity of the experience magnified because of our isolation.

As far as we knew, the only things changing were our clothes and our names. The rest of our religious lives remained the same. While many didn't believe that, surviving the novitiate and being recommended by Sister Beatrice for profession of temporary vows demanded that we act as though we did. We needed to hang in there until August 15, when we moved to the juniorate.

Between the time of breaking the news about the change of habit and Easter Sunday, the day we appeared in suits, the only topic of discussion was how sisters felt about the changes. Those who advocated the total transformation of our lives as nuns tried to relieve the fears and bitterness of those who resisted. Even Sister Concilio came around after I threatened to stop visiting.

"I'm not going to keep coming to see you," I told her, standing in the doorway, "if you won't even look me in the eye."

"Well, kid," she said, giving me the eye with a squinting stare, "then pull up a chair and sit down."

That began a new stage in our friendship. Not even heartfelt differences could keep us apart. Concil didn't bring out the poodle that day, but she did every visit thereafter. In all of our discussions I began to see more clearly why it was so difficult for her and the other sisters to change so radically and so fast, and she began to understand that I was the same loving sister regardless of what I wore. That happened to a lot of us with our friends in the infirmary. Sisterhood eased much of the fear, bitterness, and resentment. The love shared with one another healed the divisiveness that threatened to tear us apart. And when Concil's nastiness appeared from time to time, I'd threaten to kill the poodle and that made her laugh. As long as we could laugh, I knew all manner of things would be well.

The night before Easter Sunday 1967—Holy Saturday—looked a little like prom night on the fourth floor of the novitiate. Some set their hair with cardboard tubes from toilet paper rolls, while others ironed skirts, blouses, and jackets, and finished stitching the hem on the new veil, which looked like the postulant veil in that it covered the hair partially and was tied in the back (we used Velcro). We wore new shoes—black flats or pumps—with sheer, flesh-tone nylons, not black cotton. We placed the spare old habit, headgear, black stockings, and oxfords in another brown bag, just as we had our worldly clothes the day we entered the postulate. Once again we put an old life into a grocery bag in exchange for a new one. But this time we slipped out of the eighteenth century and leaped forward two hundred years.

Because of an ice storm on that Holy Saturday night (typical of South Bend winters, which seemed endless), walking to the Church of Loretto on Easter morning was precarious enough for those in new shoes, but for those like Mugs who insisted on a higher heel, it proved downright dangerous. Two of us took her arms, holding her upright as she slipped and slid, and two walked behind to break a possible fall. None of us wore winter coats, and we were far too vain to wrap our new homemade suits in the habit's black wool shawl. But the winter cold was a small price to pay for the liberation we felt. We didn't care if three feet of snow fell. We felt as if it were spring. We too rose and shined with new life.

Most of us woke at sunrise on Easter, before Beth Mulvaney walked the halls clanging the handbell. We couldn't wait to get dressed, and those with set hair needed extra time. I rose early because I wanted to stop by and see Concil before going to church. I wanted her to see me before she heard about me from anyone else. Several of us visited friends in the infirmary before Easter mass. Usually the doors to the sisters' rooms were open, but that morning many of them were closed because the old sisters didn't want to see the young sisters in suits. With Concil's door also closed, I knocked before entering.

"Concil, it's Kare," I said. "Can I come in?"

I heard nothing, so I opened the door quietly, thinking maybe she was asleep.

"Concil?" I said again in a loud whisper. "I'm coming in because I want you to see me before I go to church. Is that okay?"

Walking in slowly, I could see that she was awake, staring straight ahead, saying nothing.

"If you won't look at me, I'll leave," I said, standing beside her bed. "But I think you should. Unless you never want to see me again, you have to look at me sometime. I'm not naked."

That made her laugh softly. She turned her head toward me and, with a fading smile, did a slow body scan, as if it took all her strength to look at my veil, my hair, my suit, my legs, and my shoes. Then it took just as long to reverse the look from toe to head. Never in my life have I been sized up and down as I was that morning by Concil. In the end, she still said nothing. She just looked away, staring out the window.

"Well?" I said, determined not to leave until she responded. "What do you think?"

She turned her head toward me, looked me in the eye, glanced down at my feet, and finally spoke.

"Well, kid," she said with a painful smile, "you got nice legs."

That was the breakthrough I had prayed for. I leaned over and kissed her forehead.

"Thanks, Concil," I said. "I'll be back this afternoon. Happy Easter."

In response, she took my hand in hers and, kissing it tearfully, whispered, "Pray for me." Now it was my turn to pray for her perseverance.

I left Concil's room feeling as though that was the hardest thing she had ever had to do. I was so happy she rose to meet me—and on Easter Sunday. As I left the infirmary, several sisters standing in the hallway saw me coming, went into their rooms and closed the door. I felt sad that our great joy became their great sorrow.

Our reception in the Church of Loretto was not much warmer. I heard many "tsk-tsk-tsks" as I walked past the side pews where the retired sisters sat in full habit, as if to demonstrate massive protest. And when we returned to our pews after Holy Communion, many hissed in disapproval, while others looked away, pretending we weren't there. We were either despised or invisible that Easter morning, and all we could do was pray for one another—pray that the changes we embraced would not tear us apart but would eventually bring us closer together.

Even though all changes appeared optional, no one pressured the sisters in the infirmary to change, though many of them, even Concil, eventually removed the headgear in favor of a more comfortable veil, and traded in the layers of their habits for jackets, blouses, and skirts shortened, like ours, to midcalf. As a matter of fact, Concil became among the first to do so.

"Perhaps you could fix my hair and help me pick out a suit," Concil said out of the blue on a hot summer Sunday walk.

"Seriously?" I asked, stopping and looking at her with a big smile.

"I'm thinking it would be cooler," she replied, with a smile that anticipated grateful coolness in the heat.

"Of course I will," I told her, giving her a hug. "By the time I get done with you, you'll be the best-dressed nun in the convent."

She loved the thought of that and the changes began that day. First I fixed her pure white wavy hair for the modified veil, then helped her pick out a suit at Sister Fara's Suit Room, with several white blouses (she wanted the kind we wore, with a Peter Pan collar). The divine ability to change is what kept Concil young at heart, and the hardest change of her life didn't stop her. She even took to task some of her colleagues in the infirmary who made a point of criticizing and gossiping about those who wore suits. Some of her friends refused to talk to her or look at her.

"Oh, stop it," she'd tell them, shaking her finger in reprimand, "we're sisters. Treat me that way."

RELIGIOUS PROFESSION AND VOWS

About three months and a half before the second year of the novitiate, every novice may make a formal request in writing to the superior general for admission to profession.

The mistress of novices shall submit to the superior general a complete report of the character, conduct, health, exterior deportment, intellectual and moral qualities of each novice, as well as her own opinion on the admission of the novice to vows.

If the novice is judged suitable, she shall be admitted to first profession; otherwise, she shall be sent away.

—CONSTITUTION 11:71–73, 75

I had no reason to believe that I would be "judged suitable" for first profession, expecting to be "sent away," as many had been that year. Most left on their own because of personal misery; a few, like Sister Francis Eileen, were sent home for health reasons; and those suspected or found guilty of sexual activity disappeared in the middle of the night. That's what happened to Sisters Lillian James and Deborah. Unbeknown to us, they snuck over to the juniorate and spent the night with Sisters Julian and Steven Joseph. Because they reappeared in the dorm before the rising bell, we didn't know they had gone, but all four were dismissed at the same time.

I believed I'd be dismissed before profession because I couldn't see Sister Beatrice giving me a good recommendation. From day one we had been adversaries, with the negative feelings so strong between us that I sometimes thought it had to be karma from a past life as though I once did to her what she did to me, and the novitiate was payback. Whatever the reason for our difficulty in getting along, I attribute to Sister Beatrice the reason I'm still in the sisterhood. Had she not recommended me for profession, I don't know where or what I'd be today. And the fact that she did remains one of the joyful mysteries of my life.

If you're wondering why I didn't leave, I asked myself that question daily in the novitiate. With life so miserable, why stay? Why endure the agonizing suspense of waiting to be sent home? There were so many times when I announced to my friends "I'm leaving tomorrow" that it became a big joke because I always stayed. My answer then and now is that I somehow felt that I was exactly where I belonged, no matter how awful the circumstance. I followed my heart, and that's where it led me. I also knew that Sister Beatrice wouldn't be my superior forever, and I believed if I could survive the novitiate, all would be well. For me, it wasn't a matter of leaving; it was always a matter of endurance and perseverance.

I also realized that independent of the poor relationship with Sister Beatrice, I loved what happened to me in solitary confinement. Everything I am today I learned in the novitiate. Those haunting words "What you are in the novitiate, that you shall be for the rest of your lives" proved to be true for me. That's not to say I haven't changed a bit in forty years (quite the contrary, thank God). But in my years of solitary confinement, I met parts of myself I never knew before.

What I found first and foremost in the novitiate is a deep love of the contemplative life. Just as the call to sisterhood reveres as holy the need for community, so too did the call to prayer help me discover how sacred the need is to be alone. Nothing is more essential to the experience of divine life than preserving, protecting, and exalting the right to daily periods of solitude, especially when living in the same house with sixty others. Without scheduling time to be alone, which two years of solitary confinement did to a fault, community life can eat you alive. In the postulate I discovered how comforting it was to live in community, and in the novitiate I found how sacred the need is to be alone.

My love of the contemplative life became far clearer when I entered the novitiate. Though I heard the call to solitude in the postulate, I never gave it a fair chance to be heard. Background noise and mindless activity had always been my comforts. Even in the postulate, my greatest accomplishment was learning to be still. Solitude and I were near complete strangers in the beginning, but when we met face-to-face in the novitiate, it felt like love at first sight.

Part of the reason it still feels so normal, even necessary, to enter into solitude, particularly at the beginning and end of the day, is because everything about our lives in the novitiate prepared us, focused us, and disposed us to do just that. Every confined day filled us with matters religious, thereby cultivating and nourishing a magnificent obsession with all things mysterious and divine.

Even now, when I'm free to read whatever and whenever I want, my preference is still for those subjects that connect me to the world of religious life and the workings of the spiritual life. Since we were taught to live otherworldly lives in the novitiate, it's no wonder I still find myself drawn to the world of spirit. In learning that "appearances are not reality," I grew more attracted to the reality I couldn't see.

Writing is the first divine call I heard in solitude while sitting on the windowsill in the dark, writing by the glow of the streetlight, often to the sound of crickets, hooting owls, and screeching bats. I still do the same every night, only now I'm accompanied by the sounds of city streets: honking horns, screeching brakes, fire trucks, ambulance sirens, car alarms, barking dogs, motorcycles, loud street talk, and even louder music, especially on hot summer nights when neighbors sit on the stoop until sunrise. I have the novitiate to thank for teaching me how to turn off the distractions of the outside world and listen to the world within.

Keeping a journal became a very good spiritual exercise for me. Because of its solitary nature, writing draws us naturally into contemplative activity—inner seeing, inner hearing, inner feeling, inner knowing—the sacred world of insight and divine revelation. It leads to our "sanctuary . . . where we are alone with God, whose voice echoes in the depths of our soul." The call I heard in the novitiate to write came from the inner world of contemplative activity and always sounded like a dear old friend, the Holy Spirit who's been calling me for years. Writing became a sacrament of my solitude, an ordinary spiritual exercise that grants extraordinary peace and insight, a way to recognize and honor the joyful and sorrowful mysteries of my life.

I know now, far more clearly than I ever knew then, that the call to pray and the call to create are both sweet sisterly soulmates of contemplation. I learned to love the contemplative life in the novitiate, and out of that love grew the religious life I know now, the solitary life of a writer.

The other life I experienced in solitary confinement was the sisters' commitment to poverty, celibacy, and obedience. It was the purpose of the novitiate to prepare us for a simple life, a solitary life, and a communal life. What I began to discover is how all three became me and how I became all three. While I argued for two years (and many years thereafter) that poverty was far more than having nothing, celibacy was much deeper than not having sex, and holy obedience could never be blind, I still found that all three were a very big part of me.

It was my disagreement with Sister Beatrice about the kind of vowed life we were called to live that I was sure doomed my being accepted for profession. But the vow of poverty didn't divide us. In the beginning of my religious life, poverty was a shock to my system, a kind of "nothing" I never experienced before. No TV, no stereo, no radio, no newspapers, no magazines, no phone, no fridge, no books (other than religious ones), no leisurely bubble baths, no happy hours, and during Advent and Lent no mail and no visitors.

At first, I felt totally deprived, but after the initial shock wore off, I rather liked the "nothing" feeling that comes with deprivation and the free time that accompanies it. The communal experience of poverty also offered a new kind of comfort. We all had equal amounts of nothing. Unplugged from our former lives at the same time, we found ingenious ways to survive the boredom and pain of withdrawal: skits and talent shows, Arts and Craps, Hawaiian cruise dinners, indoor picnics, Halloween costume parties, and lip-synching rock concerts. My imagination thrived in the novitiate.

Another fine feature of a simple life was how poverty freed us from preoccupation with money. Everything sisters earn goes into a common fund from which each is given what she needs. Even in religious communities where sisters are self-supporting and tax-paying, the best and most socially responsible consequence of vowing some degree of poverty lies in having just enough left over to offer the kind of hospitality and assistance to others called for by our Christian commitment: sharing what we have with the least among us.

Far more than simply a matter of having nothing, the vow of poverty is also a vow of hospitality to all in need. At least we envisioned it that way in the novitiate. Even though convents at that time were off-limits to outsiders and not very hospitable, we knew that would change. The renewal called for by Vatican II asked nuns to accept the challenge of Christianity in building communities without walls.

But even in the novitiate, we didn't disagree about building our lives around some degree of simplicity, some measure of sharing with those in need. That kind of poverty is the divine key to creating equality both in and out of the sisterhood. Imagine the peace we'd know if we all vowed that kind of poverty. Quite clearly, it wasn't the vow of poverty that caused irreconcilable differences between me and Sister Beatrice.

Even when I was at the age of twenty, the vow of celibacy was no problem for me either. Way before I knew anything about celibacy, I was always mystified by how nuns weren't at all interested in being married, particularly in a world that valued a woman according to the man to whom she belongs. Not only did an unmarried lifestyle seem most fitting for community living, it also seemed necessary for preserving a kind of freedom and availability expected of us as nuns. Because we are single, unmarried, and childless, we're free to belong to everyone. In vowing celibacy, I choose to make myself available to everyone I meet, not as a wife, lover, or mother, but as a sister.

While most women I know hear some call to sisterhood with other women, some call to solitude, and even a call to the contemplative life, all draw the line when it comes to celibacy. Most people look at celibacy and see nothing other than an abnormal and unhealthy lifestyle because all they see is no sex. Just as marriage is far more a matter of love than it is of losing the freedom of being single, so too is celibacy far more a matter of the sisterly way we love than of not having sex. Even Gertrude Stein recognized that "sex is a part of something of which the other parts are not sex at all."

It's the "other parts" of sex that celibacy reveres and preserves as holy, the soul-to-soul connections I know with so many friends who've become my sisters. I never experienced celibacy as a torturous, miserable life with no sex. Never have I felt tormented from lack of sexual activity. Nor is my life deprived of soulful, intimate relationships that are also pure fun. My solitary life is everything but lonely.

For me, celibacy is freedom to come and go wherever and whenever I'm called, and not the lonely consequence of no marriage, no children, and no lover. While I find that vowing poverty teaches me to treat others with equality, vowing celibacy teaches me to love others the same, as a sister. I treasure the independence celibacy gives me, like the gospel's "pearl of great price," a gift of the otherworld that gives my life its mysterious edge. Just as nuns revere as holy the call to sisterhood, solitude, and work, so too do we revere the oddness and "madness" of celibacy as a divine call.

I had no problem in the novitiate with celibacy's ban on sexual activity because the friendships I found with my sisters gave me all the satisfaction that I needed and far more happiness than I ever expected. We were so strong and happy when we stood together, and in that way our spirits could not be broken. In that way we were able to survive two years of solitary confinement. The soul-to-soul closeness I felt with my sisters never needed or wanted sexual activity.

The only reason I felt Sister Beatrice would not recommend me for profession was the vow of obedience. I could not and would not promise, even for one year, to be blindly obedient, and that was no secret. According to the Constitutions, in taking a vow of obedience we promised to obey the commands of superiors in everything, renouncing our own will and practical judgment (without murmur) because the voice of the superior was the voice of God. It's not that I didn't believe Sister Beatrice's voice was the voice of God—I did. But I also believed that we too speak with a voice of God, and listening to what we had to say was an important part of being obedient. God speaks to all of us through our conscience, and we're all bound by the divinely natural law to follow conscience faithfully, never being forced to act contrary to what we believe is true.

I had no problem vowing obedience as long as it meant that we listened to one another and found the truth we held in common. Because we lived in community, I believed in our sacred responsibility to listen to what everyone has to say. The ordinary sister not only sees problems from a different angle than her superiors, but she is often much more in touch with the details and difficulties of everyday life. And if we're making decisions that affect the lives of others, it's essential that everyone in the community be part of the decision-making process. Nothing is more deadly to the holy spirit of community than silencing the divine voice of its members, because it's then that we silence the voice of God. So when Sister Beatrice asked if I could in good conscience vow obedience according to the Constitutions, I tried lying and saying yes, but my eyes said no, and that much she could see clearly. I felt there was no way she could recommend me for profession of vows.

RELIGIOUS PROFESSION AND VOWS

The novices before pronouncing their first vows shall make a spiritual retreat of at least eight full days. The first profession must be made in the house of the novitiate.

—CONSTITUTION 11:75

During the eight-day retreat before final profession, the final weeding out of the malcontents took place, and I fully expected to be among them. The final test was brutal. Each of us needed to meet individually with Mother Octavia, the Superior General of the Sisters of the Holy Cross, to ask for admission to first profession.

Having endured Japanese concentration camps in World War II as a Catholic sister and a nurse, Mother Octavia was revered in the community not only as a survivor but as a spiritual powerhouse. Her voice was truly the voice of God. Because she paid divine dues none of us knew, anything we experienced as "suffering" paled in comparison, and we never forgot that fact. Our life was in her hands as much as in Sister Beatrice's.

Once again, as we had done two years before with Mother Katrina, we waited one by one in the parlor of the Generalate, waiting our turn to kneel before Mother Octavia and pray to be accepted for profession. By that time some sisters like Lucy and Rosita chose to leave during the retreat, as others would, but not by choice, after the meeting with Mother Octavia. It wasn't hard to feel that you could be one of them.

We didn't have much personal contact with the Superior General as novices, but Sister Beatrice did. She met bimonthly with Mother Octavia to submit written reports on our "conduct, disposition, and character," and provided in writing her recommendation regarding our admission to first profession.

On the occasions when we did see Mother Octavia, with one look she conveyed that she knew everything we did and said, because she watched us very carefully, like God. Needless to say, we appeared before her in fear and trembling. I remember sitting in the parlor that day, partly terrified and feeling oddly free, as though I had already been sent home. I think at that point I just cast my fate to the wind and commended my spirit into the hands of God. If my time had come to leave, let it be.

Ellen Gibson came out before me, looking like the living dead.

"What happened?" I asked, standing up to take my turn, feeling suddenly faint.

She couldn't speak. Her eyes filled with tears, and she shook her head as if to say, "I can't talk about it." I thought she was being sent home. Later I found out she was simply undone by the experience.

I started walking toward Mother Octavia's office, when her secretary, Mary Ealy, asked me to be seated for a few minutes while Mother Octavia took a break. I envisioned her bracing for another dismissal: mine. I sat there praying the "Memorare," my favorite prayer, over and over:

Remember O most gracious Virgin Mary,
that never was it known,
that anyone who fled to thy protection,
implored thy help,
or sought thy intercession,
was left unaided.
Inspired with this confidence
I fly unto you,
O Virgin of Virgins, my Mother.
To you do I come,
before you I stand.
O Mother of the Word Incarnate,
despise not my petition,
but in your mercy hear and answer me.
Amen.

After the longest ten-minute wait of my life, Mrs. Mary Ealy escorted me to Mother Octavia's office with a comforting smile I saw as pity. Whatever was about to happen to us, Mary Ealy felt sorry. She could see terror in our eyes, and as a mother, not a nun, her heart went out to us.

When I walked into Mother Octavia's office, I heard Mary close the door behind me.

"What do you ask?" Mother Octavia said with great solemnity as I knelt before her.

"To be admitted to first profession in the Congregation of the Sisters of the Holy Cross," I replied, my head bowed. I didn't make that up. We memorized the traditional response.

"You may be seated," she said.

Sitting in a wooden chair in front of the big old desk that had been used by every Superior General before her, I faced what looked like a mound of folders full of Sister Beatrice's bimonthly reports. I was shocked and my heart sank when that pile turned out to be my file: three times the size of my postulant file. I couldn't even imagine the contents. Mother Octavia opened the fat file and turned page after page in stone-cold silence. Each page took another breath away. I was in there nearly an hour, longer than anyone before or after me. I don't recall everything she said, but I do remember clearly the parting blow that did me in. It happened after a long discussion on obedience that I felt beat around the bush.

"Sister Karol, are you prepared to live a life of obedience?"

"Yes, Mother, I am."

"And do you agree with everything that the vow of obedience asks of you?"

"Yes, Mother, I do."

"And do you believe the voice of the superior is the voice of God?"

"Mother," I finally said, feeling exhausted, exasperated, and wanting to get out of there, "I feel like you're asking something about the vow of obedience, but I don't know what it is."

"Very well, Sister Karol," she said, leaning back in her chair with a sense of omnipotence. "Let me put it to you this way."

With arms folded under the cape and looking pleased, as though she was about to set the fatal trap, Mother Octavia leaned back and said, "Tell me, Sister Karol. What would you do if the community needed a chemistry teacher in Flint, Michigan, and you were told to go?"

That was it. She put her cards on the table, asking the ultimate question of blind obedience. Eye to eye, we stared at each other. If I lied, she'd know because my file provided evidence to the contrary. If I told the truth, I could be home by sunset.

Out of the depths of my holy disobedient soul, I spoke.

"Well, Mother," I said calmly, maintaining eye contact without breaking into a cold sweat, "given that I've never taken chemistry, I'd ask for a year off to study what I was expected to teach."

If looks could kill, I'd be dead. I even surprised myself with that response, and I must have looked pleased, because Mother Octavia sat there speechless, seething.

"You may go," she said abruptly, closing my file with downcast eyes.

"Go where?" is what I wanted to ask, but I didn't dare. Back to the novitiate? Home? She said nothing further, so I stood up, thanked her, and left. She saw no more sisters that day.

I returned to the novitiate and was met by Paj, Mugs, Helene, Nancy, and Mary Sue, waiting in fear that I'd been given my walking papers. Even though we were still on retreat and weren't permitted to talk, we met in the cemetery anyhow, where I filled them in on what happened. I still wasn't sure if I'd gotten the boot, nor were they. But if I had, we all agreed that I came up with a divinely inspired response to the most damning question of all. I didn't lie. I told the only truth I knew. So if I was sent home, I'd depart in a mini-blaze of glory.

The only way we knew we'd been accepted for profession was that we weren't sent home within twenty-four hours. On August 15, 1967, there was a miracle at Saint Mary's. In a private ceremony, I made my first profession of vows in the novitiate chapel and in the presence of my sisters. One by one, we knelt before Mother Octavia and read aloud the following formula, handwritten on white parchment:

In the name of the Father and of the Son and of the Holy Spirit.
In the name of Our Lord Jesus Christ
and under the protection of Mary, His Immaculate Mother,
ever Virgin, Mother of Sorrows,
I, Sister Karol Ann Jackowski, make for one year,
the simple vows of poverty, chastity, and obedience,
in the Congregation of the Sisters of the Holy Cross,

promising to persevere in it for one year
in the exercise of the employments which,
according to the Constitutions,
my superiors may assign me.
Such are the obligations I take before God
and in the presence of Mother Octavia
who accepts them in the name of God
and of the Congregation of the Sisters of the Holy Cross.
Amen.

I was so nervous kneeling before Mother Octavia that I choked on every word. When I finally arrived at Amen, you could hear an audible sigh of relief from my friends. I had done it. With the profession of vows, we received a sterling silver heart-shaped medallion surmounted by a cross. The medallion bears the image of the Mother of Sorrows (Mary with seven swords piercing her heart) and the words *"Congrega-tio Sanctae Crucis"* on one side, and on its reverse the words *"Mater Dolorosissima, ora pro nobis."* It was worn suspended on a black cord. On the day of our first profession, we received the heart of the Sisters of the Holy Cross. On that miraculous day, they accepted us as one of their own by giving us their heart.

To this day I have no rational explanation of how I became accept-able for profession. What I do know is that it had everything to do with the mysterious recommendation of Sister Beatrice, without which none of us could have made it that far. By the grace of God and the gra-ciousness of Sister Beatrice, I survived solitary confinement. As I recall, of the thirty-eight who entered the novitiate, approximately twenty-five of us professed first vows, with my circle of friends intact.

I can't say that my feelings for Sister Beatrice changed dramatically that day, nor, I suspect, did hers for me. That wasn't part of the miracle. At most we looked at each other knowing each had done the best she could, given the circumstances, and parted ways giving each other that blessing. In leaving the novitiate, I left behind the awful feelings, taking only the best with me. I was mystified by whatever it was that moved Sister Beatrice to let me stay, and I did not want to tread on that grace with bad feelings. She was my Holy Cross and my sister. After I left the novitiate, we rarely saw or spoke to each other. But over the years I've come to see and understand more clearly that anyone who enters our life that profoundly, for better or worse, is always an angel of God. I know I didn't see Sister Beatrice that way then, but I do now.

All I remember about that miraculous day was the excitement over leaving the novitiate and the pure joy of moving back across the street to the juniorate that night, and in a few days heading home to East Chicago for my first home visit. Having survived the worst of times, we left our years of solitary confinement behind and entered what felt like the Promised Land. Several of us knelt and kissed the ground outside the juniorate before reentering those big turquoise blue doors. We made it. We survived. Mercy.

chapter five

everything changes

JUNIORATE
*The period which immediately follows the first profession
has for its purpose to continue the religious and spiritual
formation begun in the postulancy and novitiate and at
the same time to develop and prepare the young religious
for their apostolic work in the Congregation. The juniorate
shall last for two years.*

—CONSTITUTION 12:92–93

In moving to the juniorate on August 15, 1967, the Feast of the Assumption of Mary, we returned to our beginning. The new building we moved into as postulants, we moved back into as professed sisters; only this time after entering those big blue doors we took a right instead of a left. The presence of talking and laughing sisters in the lobby was the first noticeable difference. Three years ago silence ruled that morguelike lobby, and no one dared speak or laugh out loud anywhere. Some sisters returned from playing tennis and greeted us with hugs and squeals of welcome. They entered their second year in the juniorate as we began our first. Having lived together in the novitiate, we knew one another well, and being with them again felt like a class reunion.

With the change of habit and names, something else transformed the juniorate. There was no rule of silence, at least not in the seriously prohibitive way we knew it before. Sisters Leo Anthony and Valery became our superiors. They were newly appointed and had neither good nor bad reputations to precede them. Both appeared warm, welcoming, and sympathetic to the difficulties we experienced in the novitiate. I envisioned the healing of our wounds with the balm of kindness and understanding. Neither one looked as if she ever furrowed her brow or pursed her lips in disapproval.

The next divine revelation appeared as we walked through the recreation room. Some sisters watched news on TV, while others read the *Wall Street Journal* and the *South Bend Tribune*. TV knobs were replaced permanently, never to be removed and hidden again, and world news was no longer forbidden. Overnight, we moved from the dark night of the soul into the sweetness and light of the Promised Land. Being welcomed with heartwarming smiles was in itself heavenly, but being shown to our new rooms with the encouragement to relax felt as if we had died and gone to heaven. *Relax.* I hadn't heard that word in two years, much less received encouragement to indulge in its luxury. For the first time in three years, it felt as though we walked into normal. It seemed as if it was 1967 inside and out. Blessed be.

In leaving the novitiate and moving into the juniorate, we also left behind dorm life with a curtained cell and returned to private rooms. I say rooms because we received two single rooms, side by side; one for sleeping and one for studying. Because our numbers had diminished by half, there were far more bedrooms than sisters to occupy them, so we each got two. Not only was more living space such a great gift for us, it also solved the practical problem of how to keep the empty rooms clean. Unlike the four-story postulate, the juniorate was built with five floors of bedrooms to house the two groups of student sisters in 1964.

While full then, two years later it stood half empty; the historic decline in membership had already begun. After twenty-four months of dorm life in a curtained cell, I ached for a room of my own.

I didn't hate dorm life. We certainly enjoyed some of our best laughs up there, and we came to know one another in ways private rooms don't offer. Everyone in the dorm shared sleeplessness when someone suffered a cold or talked in her sleep or woke us with a nightmare. On hot humid nights with no fans, those with windows pulled the curtains back (a big no-no) in order to create a cross breeze for the unfortunate sisters stuck in the middle or in the corners. And if someone sobbed in misery, we broke the biggest rule of all by gathering together in her cell to offer comfort. Not even Sister Lucy reported us for doing that. There were times when concern for one another trumped all rules. Even the terror of being discovered in one another's cells during Grand Silence by Sister Beatrice didn't stop us from coming to the aid of our heart-broken sisters. The best and worst part of dorm living was the closeness that bound us together.

For me, the lack of privacy turned into the worst part of dorm life. So many nights I wished for four walls and a door to close behind me, a light switch of my own, access to a sink and shower without waiting in line, and a mattress with box springs instead of a cotton mat with plywood board. So the night we entered the juniorate and got not one but two rooms (and two sinks) of our own, I felt a big part of my life given back to me twice; my first one-bedroom apartment with added access to wash-ers and dryers on every floor. For the first time in three years we washed our own clothes because for the first time in three years we actually had real clothes—not habits cleaned three times a year in the convent laun-dry but blouses, slips, underwear, skirts, jackets, and nylons. Never in my life, before or since, did I find such pure joy in doing my own laundry.

We also returned to enough showers without a schedule and the comforts of modern plumbing; unlike the situation in the novitiate bathrooms of being scalded with hot water if a sister flushed while you showered without yelling "Toilet!" first. Once again we flushed freely without fear of inflicting pain on showering sisters. Gone also were the days of discreetly schlepping "bags" of sanitary napkins to the furnace. Thanks to modern technology, bathrooms in the postulate and juniorate were equipped with individual "burners," little furnaces between stalls for disposal. I never carried "bags" again and no longer needed to worry about burning clandestine correspondence either. The censoring of incoming and outgoing mail ended as well, and with it came the freedom to write whenever and to whomever we wanted, even to boys. One by one the ancient walls between the convent and the real world crumbled and all kinds of holy spirits blew in. O happy day.

Returning to a room of my own felt like divine intervention. Located on the third floor and facing north, my rooms overlooked the tennis courts. In the distance stretched acres of cultivated convent farmland with fields of soybeans, corn, and cattle (eventually transformed into feast day steaks). At the time, the sisters employed and housed a family from Holland to care for the farm—Hank and Gretchen Weinholtz and their two children. From my windows I watched Hank plow the fields, with the kids trailing after him. Beyond the tennis courts and farm, I envisioned but couldn't see the same toll road I had traveled three years before with Miriam Edward, Christopher Marie, and my mother.

A few of us stayed up late that night, sitting around talking, laughing, and celebrating our unexpected newfound freedom. I sat on the windowsill way past midnight, welcomed by a loud cricket serenade, as though they too celebrated our arrival in the Promised Land. And looking up at wide expanses of jet-black sky full of stars, I envisioned angels throwing sparkling white confetti in honor of our surviving the novitiate.

Although I was exhausted from the emotionally intense events of the day—profession of vows and leaving the novitiate—part of me felt wide awake, with nothing but enormous relief over the fact that I had made it.

The campus was full of festivities that day. Not only did we profess temporary vows in a private ceremony early that morning, but at 10:00 A.M. in the Church of Loretto, we joined the community and the guest choir in celebrating the final profession of vows and the jubilees of sisters commemorating anniversaries of profession. August 15 was a high holy day for the Sisters of the Holy Cross, and the families and friends of the celebrants filled the campus to celebrate with us.

Even though our families and friends were not among the crowd (first profession was a private matter), I was deliriously happy that day. Not only did I get through professing my vows in front of Mother Octavia without fainting or laughing, but I woke up that morning knowing it was my last sleep in the novitiate. I was giddy with excitement because the whole day was one big party. After lunch we visited with the families and friends of the sisters we knew, but mostly I counted the minutes until 4:00 P.M. That's when we grabbed our bags, kissed the novitiate good-bye, and moved to the juniorate. By 5:00 P.M. we were all moved in. At 5:15 we joined the other professed sisters in the juniorate chapel for vespers, followed by a picnic supper in Saint Thérèse's yard.

I floated on a cloud of happiness all day. That morning I woke up terrified, feeling I'd never be able to kneel before Mother Octavia and profess my vows; and that night I ended up in a room of my own with no rules about lights-out and silence. In maintaining the holy spirit of Grand Silence, all we needed was respect for peace and quiet. It was that simple, and it was just the beginning of the liberating changes we found waiting for us in the juniorate. Inside and out, life suddenly felt wide open and full of fresh air, as though we too had been assumed into heaven with Mary on the feast of her Assumption—an unexpected miracle of the day.

What we woke up to the following morning, however, reminded us that some things didn't change. Just when we felt safe from Sister Beatrice and the tyranny of the novitiate, our first day in the juniorate turned into a rude awakening. Judy Baldwin and Sue Remick received notice that they weren't staying at Saint Mary's. They weren't being sent home, at least not yet. In what looked like a new plan to further test the vocation of malcontents, some newly professed sisters received the "obedience" to live in reputably miserable convents, work in jobs for which they were not prepared, and attend classes to finish their degree, inevitably pushing them to the breaking point of leaving (which both Judy and Sue did, in 1970 and 1971, respectively).

I asked Judy to refresh my memory about what happened that day. She wrote:

> The day after first vows, Sue Remick and I were told we would not be staying at Saint Mary's . . . Susan was going to San Mateo to teach and attend classes, and I was sent to L.A. to find a college to attend.
>
> Because Sister Edmund Campion couldn't possibly go to San Mateo to teach elementary school [as though it were beneath her], I ended up going there, and Susan and I co-taught (or was it more co-managed?) the 2nd grade while we took classes at three different colleges. Aside from being one of the most terrifying teaching assignments I've had, San Mateo kept Susan and me either crying or laughing hysterically—no in-between.
>
> You, Paj, Mugs, Nancy, and the rest of the gang sent frequent care packages, while I wished desperately that I was somewhere else.

The novitiate experience was excruciating for Judy and Sue in ways most novices never knew. So smart and insightful, so free-spirited and articulate, they consistently and conscientiously objected to everything irrationally authoritarian, never fearing the consequences. They too marveled at the fact that Sister Beatrice and Mother Octavia allowed them to make first profession. In addition to surviving solitary confinement in the novitiate, we shared that miracle. We also felt heartsick the next day that Sue and Judy had to leave. Blaming Sister Beatrice and Mother Octavia for the "superior" devious move, we felt that we'd never forgive them.

The day before she left, Judy and I sat in silence for hours near Lake Marian in front of the college library, watching bugs race across the surface of the water. We hated her leaving, my staying, and knowing all we could do was let it be and hope for the best. The day Judy and Sue left became a day of mourning. They were leaving us with sadness far too precious to be taken away; I remember sitting in the dark that night in tears, praying that our separate paths would never stop crossing. Thanks be to God, they haven't.

VACATION

Through the wise solicitude of their superiors, the sisters shall take an annual vacation for change and rest from their ordinary duties.

Mindful that this period is part of the short and precious time granted them by God for their sanctification, the sisters shall make holy use of their vacation.

—CONSTITUTION 41:243–244

Along with names and habits, so too did our personal lifestyle change in the juniorate. We went home for the first time in three years that summer, without needing to be accompanied by an older professed sister, as the previous rule had stated. Ten unsupervised days at home was like a dream come true. The expectation to wear the habit and attend mass daily while on vacation remained, but I did neither. Walking the streets of my neighborhood and hanging out with friends in my poorly made suit and veil was no vacation; nor did I intend to disrupt family plans with early rising for daily mass.

My family found it strange enough for their daughter to come home in a habit, much less to turn the house into a convent. For example, the first morning I woke up in my old bed around 10:00 A.M., when I heard my eight-year-old brother, David, outside the window with his buddies, peeking through the curtains on the ground floor, telling them, "That's what she looks like when she sleeps." That did it. I gave up the habit, put on my old jeans, shirts, sneakers, and returned to normal.

I did wear the habit a couple of times that week, mostly by request for neighborhood visits. Across the street from our house was Kinelka's, a big, dimly lit gymnasium-size store with timeworn creaky wooden floors that smelled of the Polish sausage and sauerkraut simmering on the stove in the adjacent kitchen. The owners lived in back of the store. Kinelka's provided everything our Polish neighborhood needed: dresses, suits, play clothes, shoes, coats, work overalls, boots, knitting and sewing supplies, and my favorite section in the center of the store, called Oceans of Notions. Small boxes lined up in rows on a long wooden table contained buttons in every size, shape, and color—I love buttons—shoestrings, ribbon, safety pins, hooks and eyes, pins and needles, etc.

We got Buster Brown shoes there and, in the words of my mother, "the best boys' underwear" for my brothers. My Busia bought housedresses, nightgowns, and underwear from Kinelka's too. Given that they were friends, she'd always stay, have coffee, and smoke Old Golds (without filter) with Mrs. Kinel on the back porch, swapping Polish gossip from the old country.

Much friendlier and kinder than "the Mrs.," who earned a well-deserved cranky reputation, Ann Reno managed the store. According to my mom, "You got much better deals when Ann was there." Whenever a shipment of clothing arrived, Ann called the house to tell us "some nice new numbers came in." Everyone in the neighborhood shopped at Kinelka's because of its family-friendly business. Long before credit cards, they kept tabs running in a little brown spiral notebook for Polish customers who paid weekly whatever they could afford. Sometimes we traded clothes and shoes for bread and baked goods from my family's bakery. It was that kind of neighborhood and that kind of business.

Stopping in to see neighbors topped the list of "Things to Do on My Summer Vacation." My mom mentioned that Mrs. Kinel expected a visit because she had "a little something" for me. I got the feeling it was a habit-worthy occasion so I got dressed, braced myself, and begged my mother to come with me. After a teary-eyed Mrs. Kinel oohed and aahed over "Sister," she pulled out a thin square black box from under the counter. Lifting the lid and separating the thin gold tissue, she displayed three pairs of thick black silk stockings as though they were ancient artifacts from Poland, which, now that I think of it, they probably were.

"I've been saving these nice little numbers for you," she said, dabbing tears with a heavily scented handkerchief she pulled from her bosom, adding, "God bless you."

"Oh how nice," my mom said, filling in for my speechlessness.

"Thank you so much, Mrs. Kinel," I added with a little lie, because my days of black stockings were over, "I could really use these."

Embracing me with a big bone-crushing hug, Mrs. Kinel whispered, "Pray for me."

"I will," I said, breaking the hold while asking, "Is Ann here?"

Looking toward the back room, Mrs. Kinel called, "Ann, come see Karol . . . I mean Sister Karol."

"That's okay," I said, feeling the "Sister" title unnecessary, "you can always call me Karol."

Ann came out smiling, and she too turned teary-eyed when she saw me. She motioned for me and my mom to come to the back room where she secretly slipped a little box into the bag with the stockings.

"Just a little something for you, Sister," she said, squeezing my hand. "Don't tell the Mrs.," she added, as though she'd be in big trouble if I did.

Neatly folded in the box were three white linen handkerchiefs embroidered with pink and blue flowers, which I sincerely appreciated because Ann did the embroidery. She too gave me a tearful but not crushing hug and whispered, "Pray for me, Sister."

After a few minutes of chitchat, we left with bag of goodies in hand. Being dressed for the occasion, I decided to visit Pexie's, too—the liquor store across the street. Of the four corners where we lived at Northcote Avenue and 149th Street in East Chicago, there was Kinelka's, Pexie's Liquor Store, and Smitty's, a bar and grill where on Fridays we picked up fried fish and frog leg dinners (with fries and coleslaw) wrapped in newspaper. Mr. Pexie (last name Piotrowski, but called Pexie) came out and waved as we passed on our way to Kinelka's, asking me to stop by. He and his wife stood outside waiting, as though I might sneak back home without visiting. At that point I felt a little like a neighborhood prize for "Show and Tell," but these were people I grew up with; they were part of my extended family. Mr. and Mrs. Pexie, Alex and Jean, also teary-eyed, gave me something they thought "the sisters might like," a big bottle of sloe gin.

"The sisters will really like this," I said grinning, handing my mother the Kinelka's bag so I could accept the great gift with both hands. "Thank you so much."

Mr. and Mrs. Pexie also asked for prayers, as did everyone I met in the neighborhood. While I felt far more like Karol than Sister, clearly I had become more "Sister." No one asked me for prayers before I entered the convent. Given my reputation then, I'm sure they prayed for me. Relatives visited too, wanting to see me in the habit, so I dressed and then undressed for the occasion. And in leaving, they too became teary-eyed, asking for prayers. In and out of the habit, I was now the nun who prayed more than the former Karol they prayed for. Mercy.

Nearly everyone responded that way except my high school pals, who screamed, hugged, and asked what I wanted to drink—as if they needed to ask. With the exception of vodka-laced oranges in the postulate, some cheap altar wine (that's all we had) at Passover seders in the novitiate, and shots of C.C. with Concil, I hadn't had a drink in three years; so that too became a daily event on my ten-day vacation. I plunged headfirst into normal when I went home. and I didn't come up for air until the time arrived to put on the habit and return to Saint Mary's.

All three gifts came back with me to the juniorate, along with some goodies from the Normal Bakery. Concil loved the silk stockings, I loved the handkerchiefs, and on Friday nights we began loving "happy hours" in my spare room with TGIF sloe gin fizzes. I took the train back to South Bend—the South Shore Line, fondly called the vomit comet because of the nonstop jerking, stomach-turning rides. On my first home visit, I realized that I could never go home again as simply Karol; I would also be "Sister."

When we returned to Saint Mary's after our home visit, some of us arrived with food and drink we kept in our spare room for late-night snacks and parties. Spare study rooms turned into mini-lounges at night. Jane Calabria's mom, Pam, made divine chocolate cake with chocolate frosting and kept us supplied with big buckets of party mix that we devoured with a sloe gin fizz. After three years of snack deprivation, we made up quickly for lost time.

I came back also with rolls of dimes, nickels, and quarters so we could get soda from the vending machines at the college. Having money was still a big no-no in the sisterhood, but we knew many professed sisters with access to money. I didn't take seriously the ban on personal spending money because so many sisters didn't and suffered no unpleasant consequences as a result. For that reason alone, I took my chances.

Sister Mercita, who looked like jolly Mrs. Claus, was one of those with money who also lived with us as a residential "role model." Older and wiser, Merce worked at the college library by day and came home to the juniorate at night. We loved her, and she loved the young sisters. Also funny and high-spirited, Merce roomed with Johnnie Walker Red, which she shared freely, and often took us out to dinner, which was an enormous treat. She also introduced me to smoked oysters. In her eyes, they were the perfect complement to scotch on the rocks with a twist.

Merce inherited a family trust fund, whereby she received a generous monthly stipend. I never figured out how she pulled that off, but as far as I know, she did to the day she died. And in the true spirit of poverty, Merce became increasingly generous in return, even to the point of covering for us in times of trouble, which is how she and I bonded.

Shortly after returning from vacation, a note went up on Sister Leo Anthony's bulletin board asking for the sister who broke the third-floor washing machine with change in her pocket to report immediately. Everyone knew that I had money, because it became a "private" common fund. I even financed novices like Sister Gretchen, who needed quarters for clandestine phone calls to her California pals. I suspect everyone but Sister Leo Anthony knew my money broke the washer, and the heat was on for someone to step forward. I even think Sister Valery knew but didn't tell.

I thought quickly, and Merce came to mind first. Just as quickly I ran to the library and begged her to save my soul and fess up to the crime, which she did immediately. She picked up the phone, called Leo Anthony and apologized for being so careless with her laundry. I remained devoted to Merce for that sisterly save, and from that day forward, we became the best of friends.

Sister Mercita was our guardian angel in the juniorate. At night she'd walk the halls checking to see how we were, always interested in what happened that day. She never walked in on a party she didn't join, and she never spoke a word about what she saw or heard. We confided in Merce about everything, cried on her shoulder, and included her in all our escapades. Sister Mercita was our bluebird of happiness, and I never forgot that. Thirty years later, when her eyesight began to fail and she could no longer drive, it nearly killed her. On the day her car keys were taken away, she called me midafternoon in New York City from her room in the convent infirmary.

"They cut my legs off," she cried.

All I could say was how sorry I felt, and while her swollen legs did bother her, both were still intact. Then we laughed over the holy card she once gave me, part of which I quoted: "God forgive me when I whine, I've got two legs, the world is mine."

The laugh blew a little wind under Merce's wings, lifting her sad soul; but even receiving the finest of motorized wheelchairs in the convent infirmary offered no comfort. In Merce's life those wheels were a poor substitute for a car. Though I lived a thousand miles away at the time, I made sure Johnnie Walker Red (and flowers in the spring) kept her company until the day she died. After a lifetime of such sweet sisterly friendship, that was the least I could do.

We became full-time college students in the juniorate, and with the exception of dating and a wild night life, we pretty much lived like them. We carried heavy course loads and spent most of our days either in class or in the library, and our main focus became completing the re-

Sister Karol Jackowski

quirements for a degree and preparing ourselves "for apostolic works in the Congregation." Even though the vocational counselor, Sister Justin, told me that social work was not an available ministry for the Sisters of the Holy Cross, I studied sociology with her blessing and my hope of being among the first. If the Sisters of the Holy Cross didn't do social work, I believed that too, needed to change. After all, that's what the missionary sisters did in Africa, Brazil, and Bangladesh. Given the call of Vatican II to become involved directly in neighborhood life with the poor and needy, I felt it was only a matter of time before we'd be called to social work.

In and out of the classroom we immersed ourselves in college life. Classmates invited us to their dorm rooms, where we talked, watched TV, sometimes smoked and drank while discussing our lives. Being the same age, they marveled at the road we had chosen to follow, and always wanted to know why. I didn't tell them about the bet I lost with the Infant of Prague. What I did tell them was that "I got picked," and having been born and raised Catholic, they understood.

One night, late in the spring of 1968, a few of us slipped out to see the Beatles' movie *Yellow Submarine* in the college's O'Laughlin Auditorium. By the time we arrived and took our seats in the balcony, the auditorium reeked of marijuana; such was college life among baby boomers in the 1960s, even at the conservative and Catholic Saint Mary's College. Through the intoxicating fog we could barely see the security guard on stage making the feeble announcement, "Indiana state law prohibits smoking in the auditorium." The audience of Notre Dame and Saint Mary's students responded with wild hoots, hollers, and applause. We sat back, relaxed, and breathed deep. The air alone took us on a trip in the Yellow Submarine, and for weeks after we joked of dreaming nightly about living with the Beatles in a Yellow Sub fighting off Blue Meanies.

Our personal life changed dramatically in the juniorate, with similar changes happening in convents across the country. The first and most radical change occurred with the schedule of the day, the *horarium*. According to the documents of Vatican II on the Renewal of Religious Life, the sisterhood was called to adapt the order of the day to the situation in which sisters lived and worked. In other words, the 5:00 A.M. rising and 9:00 P.M. lights-out might not be best for everyone, especially those who worked long days. In communities dedicated to a variety of works such as teaching, nursing, and administration,

> *it will often happen that the order of the day cannot be identical in all houses, not even sometimes within the same house for all religious. But in all cases, the order of the day must be arranged in such a way as to provide for the religious, besides the time given to spiritual exercises and apostolic activities, a little free time for themselves and sufficient time also for legitimate recreation.* *

As a result, flexibility became the order of our day—for me, one of the most divine words in the English vocabulary.

Because of our various class schedules, we no longer needed to rise at 5:00 A.M., be in the Church of Loretto at 5:30 A.M. for meditation, morning prayer, and mass, then gather together for breakfast in the refectory; though superiors believed that we'd do so anyhow, having internalized the hundred-year-old sacred order of the day. Much to their shocked dismay, that didn't happen. Most of us rose an hour or two before our first class, grabbed a light breakfast down in the juniorate kitchen, where cereal, coffee, juice, fruit, and toast were available, and later in the day attended one of the masses in the college residence

*Vatican Council II: The Conciliar and Post Conciliar Documents, p. 629.

halls. Some didn't go to mass every day, while others walked across the street to the University of Notre Dame for the 5:00 P.M. mass at Sacred Heart Church.

With a half-empty church all of a sudden and only a few showing up in the dining room for a hot breakfast, superiors were stunned. That was one change no one anticipated or prepared for, especially the convent kitchen, which cooked enough food for a full house. As a result of that culinary disaster, they posted sign-up sheets to indicate what meals we'd take in the dining room. We also placed weekly orders with the convent kitchen, for lunch meat, cheese, eggs, bread, canned soup, fruit, cookies, and anything else needed for a quick lunch in the juniorate. Stuffing a genie back in the bottle would have been easier than trying to get us back into the old way of life. No way was that about to happen, especially since the Vatican recommended the change, and we readily reiterated that fact.

Eventually, a new order rose from our life as college students. Small groups with similar schedules met for morning prayer and made breakfast together at home before class. If convenient, we lunched in the juniorate dining room or ate at the college dining hall as a guest of our classmates. Most of us didn't see one another during the day and looked forward to meeting for dinner. After three years of spending every minute together, being on our own suddenly made community time far more precious. Within months, our suggestion for a 5:00 P.M. mass in the juniorate chapel was accepted, followed by vespers and dinner together in the dining room. That turned into our new schedule.

Being a night person, I tried to schedule no classes before 10:00 A.M., which allowed me to sleep until 8:30. Some days I rolled out of bed at 9:30 and made it to class just in time. Even if I walked in late or cut class, no professor ever questioned a nun's tardiness or absence— assuming, I suppose, that we prayed overtime. At night I worked as late as I wanted, even pulling all-nighters if necessary. I discovered I could write twenty-five- and fifty-page term papers in seventy-two hours, which made me the envy of all. I saw many sunrises fill my room with a closing paragraph and began to see myself as a good writer; especially when the papers received A's and B's with glowing comments that would make you think I spent months researching and writing. I did spend months brooding on a topic, but the writing usually happened three days before due date.

As a result of our new freedom, I saw more clearly the need to find time for solitude, prayer, play, study, visiting Concil, and socializing with my sisters. I liked being given the responsibility to work out the order of my day and loved that our religious life began returning to normal, even though superiors felt we were out of control.

I know Sister Leo Anthony felt that way, especially when she posted a list to sign up for spiritual direction and no one did. Occasionally one of us would volunteer just to help her feel better. Believing that the best defense is always a good offense, I signed up a couple of times, as did Diana Cundiff, a very funny sister in the group ahead of us. In response to Sister Leo Anthony's question about her satisfaction with religious life, Diana mentioned casually that she could probably spend more time folding convent laundry. As a result, Sister Leo Anthony noted in Diana's file that she didn't contribute enough to community life.

The reason for not signing up wasn't that we didn't need spiritual direction; we just didn't need that kind. Even then we knew spiritual directors needed to be chosen, not assigned as mandatory. Consequently, many of us found our own direction elsewhere, turning to other sisters at the college or priests who served as our chaplains. For example, Sister Kathy Reichert taught us theology. Kathy graduated from Saint Mary's before entering the sisterhood, so she understood both worlds in which we lived. Several of us met with her weekly for direction, three times more often than the monthly recommendation.

As part of my spiritual direction, Kathy Reichert introduced me to the writings of the Spanish mystics John of the Cross and Teresa of Ávila. This sparked a lifetime interest in mysticism, and the studies have continually changed my life. Kathy also played the trumpet and lived a fun-loving, active life that superiors found endearing. While her death from cancer on April 21, 1985, was untimely, I believed Kathy lived her life so fully in fifty-two years that eternity was the next step.

I suppose our superiors thought we were out of control in that we made our own decisions for the first time in three years, even the decision not to comply with some requests of the superior. But our lives were no less spiritual. We were discovering new ways of living a religious life. Our personal lives as sisters changed dramatically that way, but the transformation didn't stop there. Once the order of the day changed, it was only a matter of time before the same holy spirits renewed our communal life as well.

If certain religious give the impression of having allowed themselves to be crushed by community life, which ought instead to have made them expand and develop, does this perhaps happen because this community life lacks that understanding cordiality which nourishes hope?

From this point of view there are emerging tendencies aiming at the establishment of smaller communities. . . . Such smaller communities can favor the development of closer relationships between the religious and a shared and more fraternal understanding of responsibility. . . . Nevertheless, small communities, instead of offering an easier form of life, prove on the contrary to make greater demands on their members.*

*Vatican Council II: The Conciliar and Post Conciliar Documents, pp. 698–699.

The real issue of renewal, we soon found out, had little to do with clothes, names, or schedules, and everything to do with how we lived in community and how well we loved one another. The old way of life succeeded in providing the illusion of one big happy sisterhood. While constant togetherness defined and ruled religious life for years, it didn't take long for us to discover that physical proximity alone does not create community. Once we opened convent doors and our lives, it became painfully clear that we nuns were not the community-living experts we appeared to be. I experienced that the day we changed the habit and half the community couldn't even bear to look at us, and that happened in the House of God on Easter Sunday, the holiest day of the year for Christians.

As religious life began to change, the image of one big happy sisterhood faded when many nuns found the divisiveness within community life intolerable. Some sisters left because they couldn't bear the changes taking place, while others left because of the community's resistance to change. Ironically, both groups of women experienced the soulful anguish of feeling crushed by community life.

The truth we saw then is the divine truth that binds us together now. What unites and holds us together as sisters is far more a matter of spirit and shared beliefs than regulated ways of living and thinking. Depending on the quality of life among those living together, religious communities, like all families, can become just as dysfunctional, abusive, mean-spirited, and destructive as they can be life-giving, loving, trusting, and supportive. It's the enduring bonds of trust, friendship, and reverence for the diversity that creates, nourishes, and sustains community life. Nothing divides and destroys community life more than the presence of sisters who refuse to listen and revere as sacred the inspired voices of one another, especially those whose voice differs from their own or that of authority. For many sisters, that's the truth that still hurts.

Once we began to focus on the way we lived together, all hell broke loose. After one hundred years of being told what to believe, how to feel, and what to do, sisters were called on to begin thinking for themselves—something they hadn't done since entering the convent, if even then. When asked to voice their thinking about the changes taking place, many sisters felt embarrassed that they had nothing to say, having silenced their inner voice decades ago. While some of us needed no encouragement to speak up about how we felt and what we believed, other sisters suffered in silence—the kind of silence that no longer offered divine comfort. It pained them to speak in a group of their own sisters, the saddest testimonial of all to the kind of crushing community life so many nuns endured for so many years.

Far more difficult and essential than the change of clothes and schedules was the transformation of hearts and minds. Small groups and small group living appeared as one of the ways to open hearts and minds; the belief was that sisters would feel safer speaking in small groups and freer to talk about how they felt and what they believed. For example, large convents of fifty or sixty sisters—like the college convent—divided into groups of ten according to the floor on which you lived. The largest room on each floor was turned into a community room, with TV and lounge furniture. For house meetings, groups of six formed for discussion, with each group designating a leader and a recorder. After discussing the agenda, group recorders reported the results of the discussion to the large group.

That didn't happen as quickly or as simply as hoped. Some silences are not so easily broken. Older sisters had lived in large groups for decades, blindly and obediently following the leader, suffering desperation if they disagreed silently and emotional torment if they disagreed publicly. Since personal opinions never mattered, many sisters simply agreed with the superior. They didn't know what they thought. Living safely in the anonymity of a large group invariably resulted in the loss of self, making small group activities unbearable. Some sisters even became physically ill as a result, especially if conflict of any kind erupted.

What no one saw during the years of change in religious life was the soulful pain and suffering sisters endured. No one anticipated the deeply personal difficulties involved in changing the hearts and minds of sisters, who had obeyed in good faith for decades with the hope and prayer that nothing would ever change. That kind of soulful suffering was hidden in silence behind convent doors and, I suspect, in many places it still is.

Small group experiences swept through community life in 1967. Area meetings with mandatory attendance were planned throughout the country, with sisters assigned to small groups. Each sister was given questions for discussion, and group responses were shared and then summarized at the end of the day. And in large convents of ten or more, small groups began discussing household matters formerly decided upon by the superior. Sales of paper, flip charts, and felt-tip markers must have skyrocketed as a result, as did the growing weariness sisters felt about discussing every little detail of life (such as the length of time for signing out convent cars: one hour? two hours? impose a time limit?). Even I got to the point of asking for someone, anyone, to just make a decision. Eventually we found a comfortable middle ground of what did and didn't need to be decided by everyone, but in the beginning we hadn't yet arrived at that group wisdom.

Life in the juniorate also changed as a result of the small group movement: we formed cooking groups. Most of us had already formed small lifesaving groups in the novitiate. Those who cherished blind obedience and conformity formed a separate group from those who struggled for independence. Living side by side, we gravitated toward our own kind for recreation and moral support, but around the dining room table we were sisters. Accordingly, groups were mixed for the purpose of cooking and dining together. Each group of six was given $125 for a week of meal planning, grocery shopping, and cooking in the lower recreation room kitchen.

The thinking behind cooking groups was to provide an alternative to the large group dining experience, as well as the opportunity to learn how to cook. I suppose we were also being groomed to help assume cooking responsibilities when we moved into convents after graduation, even though nearly every convent I lived in employed full-time cooks or were blessed with excellent sister-cooks. Whatever the reason, I cheered the idea of cooking groups, immediately envisioning pasta dinners with wine, pizza, and beer, and a week of favorite foods. Volunteering to cook the first meal for my group, I planned a menu of cheeseburgers, fries, salad, and chocolate malts. In a Christmas card to Vern, dated December 18, 1967, I described the humiliating experience:

> You should have been here last Sunday—I cooked supper for seven of us and we were having cheeseburgers, French fries, tossed salad, and chocolate malts. I was a little embarrassed to say the least. The big juicy double cheeseburgers turned out like crispy little golden meatballs. We had three to a hamburger bun . . . so you know they were small. It was fun though . . . that's my specialty. We're cooking our own Christmas dinner too . . . all forty of us . . . turkey, baked potatoes, etc. They put me in charge of refreshments—so we're having wine. That took care of everything.

On my next turn to cook we voted for pizza and beer. Because no one trusted me making pizza, and none of the others volunteered, I suggested we take the night off and order pizza from Roma's, a local pizzeria highly recommended by my college friends. We decorated the table with a red-and-white-checkered tablecloth, and a Mateus wine bottle with wax-dripping candle. Merce drove to Don's Liquor for two six-packs of cheap beer and picked up paper plates from the 7-Eleven nearby. For some reason, we ate later than usual that night—because everyone was home when the pizza arrived. Under normal circumstances, that wouldn't have mattered, but that night it made all the difference in our world.

Little did we know that Roma's delivered in a big white van, illustrated with short mustachioed chefs holding large pizzas and equipped with a loudspeaker playing, "When the moon-a hits your eye like a big-a pizza pie, that's amore!" Pulling up in front of the juniorate, the driver made an even louder announcement of "ROOOOOOOOMAAAAAAAAAAA'S!" At that point everyone in the postulate and juniorate either looked out the window or gathered in the lobby where Sister Leo Anthony stood with arms folded and furrowed brow, an expression I hadn't seen since the novitiate. The sisters thought it was pretty funny until they saw the look on Leo Anthony's face, then scattered, leaving the two of us alone in a deadly silent lobby as the Roma's deliveryman drove off with the continuation of "That's Amore." Sister Leo Anthony wasn't at all amused.

"Would you like to join us?" I asked, while holding two large hot steaming pizzas (the Roma's Extravaganza with everything), hoping she'd see the humor and accept the invitation.

"This is *not* what we had in mind for the cooking groups," she said, maintaining her disapproving stance.

"I'm sorry, Sister," I said. "We just wanted pizza, and no one wanted to make it." Then in our defense I added a positive spin: "But we stayed within the budget."

Unimpressed and displeased, she turned and walked away in silence, shaking her bowed head, no doubt feeling confirmed in the belief that not only were we out of control but also the cooking group experiment was a complete failure. We, on the other hand, with Merce at our table, enjoyed the pizza dinner thoroughly with no regrets, becoming the envy of all the other cooking groups, who wished they'd thought of it first.

In retrospect, the error could not have been that egregious because six months later I was among eight nuns sent to Washington, D.C., to be part of another small group experiment. We were all sent out to work during the summer between our junior and senior years in college. The experiment that summer involved small groups of us living in convents, working, and receiving a stipend for our work. For the first time in four years, we'd be given money for personal use.

You hear rising up, more pressing than ever, from their personal distress and collective misery, "the cry of the poor." . . . How then will the cry of the poor find an echo in your lives? That cry must, first of all, bar you from whatever would be a compromise with any form of social injustice. It obliges you also to awaken consciences to the drama of misery and to the demands of social justice made by the Gospel and the Church. It leads some of you to join the poor in their situation and to share their bitter cares.*

In this country, the "cry of the poor" exploded violently in the summer of 1968 and resulted in thousands of sisters' feeling called to "join the poor in their situation and to share their bitter cares." It all began on April 3 at the Mason Temple in Memphis, Tennessee, with Martin Luther King, Jr., delivering the divinely inspired "I've Been to the Mountaintop" message:

**Vatican Council II: The Conciliar and Post Conciliar Documents, pp. 688–689.*

We've got some difficult days ahead, but it really doesn't matter with me now. Because I've been to the mountaintop. . . . I looked over, and I've seen the Promised Land.*

The following day, April 4, civil rights activist Andrew Young finally succeeded in lifting a federal injunction, to allow activists to march in support of Memphis sanitation workers. That evening Martin Luther King stepped out on the balcony of the Lorraine Motel in Memphis to celebrate the victory and was assassinated. In an unprecedented response of outrage, riots broke out in more than a hundred cities across the country, many burning neighborhoods to the ground. Two months after King's prophetic death, Senator Robert Kennedy, a civil rights movement ally and presidential candidate, was also assassinated. It was Senator Kennedy who told Martin Luther King to bring the poor people to Washington to protest, and in the violent aftermath of the death of both martyrs, that's exactly what happened.

Martin Luther King's successor, the Reverend Ralph Abernathy, initiated the Poor People's Campaign of 1968, calling on the poor from all over the country—black, white, Native American, and Hispanic—to travel in caravans to the nation's capital and live in shantytowns on the Mall in Washington, D.C. Prophetically named Resurrection City, the settlement was built as a tribute to the civil rights dream of Martin Luther King and Bobby Kennedy. From May 14 until June 24 more than three thousand of the nation's poorest demonstrated daily for decent jobs, good schools, and meaningful lives. Joining the thousands camped out in Resurrection City, another fifty thousand arrived for the Solidarity Day March to the Lincoln Memorial on June 19. I was one of them.

*The Estate of Martin Luther King, Jr., Papers Project Speeches: "I've Been to the Mountaintop," April 3, 1968, Memphis, Tennessee.

Eight of us were sent to Washington, D.C., that summer to volunteer at Resurrection City and take part in a summer enrichment program for twelve-to-fifteen-year-old inner-city girls. We became part of an experiment in that we'd work full-time and receive a stipend for personal use. It was a trial run to see what young nuns would do with jobs and money. I jumped at the opportunity. With the exception of long car trips to New Orleans to spend glorious summers on Lake Pontchartrain with my mom's family, I'd never been out of Indiana. The offer to spend a summer in Washington, D.C., felt like a vacation, and it was my first time on a plane (I barfed when landing). As a sociology major, the experience offered more than any class or research paper possibly could.

We were divided into two groups: Paj, Suzanne Shaffer, and Ellen Otte moved into Saint Patrick's Convent in D.C. I was assigned to Saint Peter's with Mary Sue Brennan, Mugs Gallagher, Helene Moynihan, and Ellen Gibson. With Saint Peter's located at 133 C Street S.E., we lived across the lawn from the Library of Congress and one block from the Capitol. Three true angels of God welcomed us to Saint Peter's: Sisters Maurice, Melathon, and Ann Shaw. Unlike the self-absorbed sisters at Saint Patrick's, who according to Paj, "settled into many La-Z-Boy chairs after supper in the community room," Maurice, Mel, and Ann wanted to hear our stories of what happened that day and how we felt. Every night we received their blessing in that way.

The day we arrived, unbearable heat and humidity blanketed the city, neighborhoods were still burning, and National Guardsmen stood on every corner enforcing the 6:00 P.M. curfew. At Saint Peter's Convent, the sisters lived in a four-story brownstone with three bedrooms. The laundry room and small air-conditioned chapel were on the first floor; air-conditioned community room, dining room, and kitchen on the second floor, and bedrooms on the third. We were given comfortable cots in the attic with a big fan, while our sisters at Saint Patrick's slept on cots in a hot, airless classroom. None of us complained about the camp-like accommodations; we were twenty-one-year-olds on the adventure of a lifetime.

At night the five of us angled our attic cots around the solitary fan, giving everyone a little breeze; but after we finally fell asleep, Ellen Gibson moved the fan directly in front of her bed for maximum coolness, leaving the rest of us to sweat through the night. Because Ellen endeared herself to us with an eccentric sense of humor, we rarely got angry. Often abandoning the nightly fight of the fan, the rest of us grabbed pillow and blanket and headed downstairs for the coolness of the carpeted community room floor. Even Ellen joined us several nights because there's only so much a fan can do with an attic full of the day's heat and humidity.

Every morning, like a blessing on our day, we prayed and ate breakfast together with Maurice, Mel, and Ann, then walked to work at Saint Patrick's under the protection of the National Guard. On an oversized, five-by-eight-inch, postcard of Mae West sent to Vern, dated July 2, 1968, I described what our workdays were like:

> well here I am in hot, humid D.C. . . . in the middle of all that's going on this is one of the few quiet moments I have to realize how much I love being here. we are living at saint peter's . . . right across the street from the capitol . . . although ironically the streets on this side of the fence are not so glorious. Life is terrible here . . . especially for the 12–15 year old girls we work with from 9–3, and then after school we visit their homes. The work is exhausting, somewhat frustrating, and very difficult, but I find myself loving every minute of it. it's not easy being called "whitey" and "nigger lover," but both are true. Along with the kids we've been working with the Poor People's Campaign and the SCLC [Southern Christian Leadership Conference] . . . the picture of how it

really is here isn't shown on TV, radio, or the press. You don't believe it
until you see it.

While others taught drama, reading, music, volleyball, and typing in
the cultural enrichment program, I taught art and creative writing. But
I learned as well. I remember sitting around and talking with the young
African-American girls about boyfriends and what had happened at
home the night before. In after-school home visits, a door opened into
their lives through which everything about them made sense. By the age
of twelve, many of them had skipped childhood and lived far beyond
their years. Referring to the Washington Monument as the "national
erection"—a monument to screwing poor people—they saw no hope for
a future other than the poor, violent life they knew. Most didn't expect
to live long enough for a future and they rarely smiled. But when they
did, as I wrote to Vern, "they shine inside and out."

Fascinated with our lives as young nuns, the girls couldn't believe we
lived without sex, but they loved the veil and silver heart. Looking at
the medallion's embossed image of Mary with seven swords piercing her
heart, one of them exclaimed, "Holy fuck. I didn't know Jesus' mother
got stabbed." In their eyes, that elevated Mary to being one of them—a
blessing on a manner of death they knew all too well. The girls in my
group took turns wearing the silver heart with my veil, pretending to
be a "nun for a day," but then returned both at 3:00 P.M. sharp because
they felt they might be cursed to a life without sex.

We also took all the groups to Camp Merryland for a day, the Sisters
of the Holy Cross vacation house on the shores of the Chesapeake Bay.
We grilled hot dogs, burgers, made Kool-Aid, and prepared the marsh-
mallows, graham crackers, and Hershey's candy bars for s'mores while
the girls swam and screamed over being swarmed and stung by jellyfish.
Most huddled in groups near the shore in ankle-deep water fearful of
being attacked. Some yelled "Rape!" when Father Steve Gibson, a great

Holy Cross priest from the retreat house at Notre Dame, tried picking them up and throwing them in deeper water. Steve was a young priest, almost seven feet tall, with a great voice and an even better sense of humor. He often came to our convent to celebrate mass, asking us to concelebrate with him, and even to give the homily. He was the chaplain for our summer program, and the girls loved him as much as we did.

We returned to the city that night exhausted and aching from laughter. I'm not sure whose lives were more enriched that summer, but I am quite certain that we succeeded in giving those wonderful troubled girls a healthy breakfast and lunch, some good laughs, and a six-hour breath of fresh air—all of which they accepted like a big prize for surviving.

Nothing could have been more divine that summer than coming home to Maurice, Mel, and Ann who couldn't wait to hear what happened that day. While at first we were upset that they wouldn't let us volunteer in Resurrection City, after seeing the living conditions there at the Solidarity Day March, we thanked them for sparing us the misery. Rain poured down for twenty-eight of the forty-two days of Resurrection City's duration, turning the grassy parkland into ankle-deep mud, with some puddles knee-high. Plywood homes were soaked from weeks of rain. Trash and rotting food sank into the mud, intensifying the hopelessness that drove many of Resurrection City's poor residents from across the country to join together. I'm sure they wondered in desperation, as we did, how much more they could be given to bear.

Disillusionment and despair filled Resurrection City, touching everyone who marched to the Lincoln Memorial on Solidarity Day. Being the first of the protests I attended, it remains the most memorable. Thousands of sisters and priests from different religious communities all over the country marched in protest and solidarity with the poor. Gathered before the Lincoln Memorial, my favorite monument in Washington, hanging on every powerfully chosen word, we listened to inspired messages from civil rights activists like Ralph Abernathy, Andrew Young, Hosea Williams, Marian Wright Edelman, and Jesse Jackson. Never before had I been surrounded by such profoundly devastating hopelessness, nor had I ever experienced such undying, heartfelt faith.

No new life rose from Resurrection City that summer, and all but three hundred of its residents left in despair after the Solidarity Day March on June 19. Historians record Resurrection City as a civil rights failure and a living nightmare, but I suspect mine was not the only life transformed that summer. Nor was I the only one who walked home from my first protest march with a lifetime commitment to do what I can to relieve someone's misery, even if it's simply a matter of giving a dollar to the disoriented young woman begging at the corner of East Houston Street and Avenue A in New York. I felt as if my soul had been branded that day with the gospel message "Whatsoever you do to the least among you, that you do unto me."

Sister Maurice was the superior at Saint Peter's Convent, but she treated us as equals, and she created community at its holiest best. Maurice made sure we ate a good breakfast every morning before work, and we came home to an even better dinner every night. Often she surprised us with some treat she knew we'd love. For example, if Maurice overheard us talking about oatmeal raisin cookies, a big plate of them awaited us when we got home that night. And if we sat around the community room at night watching TV, she appeared with big bowls of popcorn and soft drinks or beer. Maurice loved making people happy. She cherished her life as our sister so much that she couldn't stop from helping us love our lives as sisters too.

One night Maurice really surprised us with her favorite homemade dessert. At first we thought she made chocolate mousse, but a closer look revealed something none of us had ever seen before, much less eaten: prune whip—a mixture of stewed prunes and Cool Whip. The five of us collectively gagged, laughed at the thought of prunes for dessert, then spent the rest of Maurice's life apologizing for our thoughtless response. Prune whip became the joke of the summer, so much so that we even requested it for dessert at our last supper the night before we returned to Saint Mary's. An otherwise excellent cook who transformed every meal into Eucharist, Maurice also taught us the Dieter's Prayer, which we recited together before every meal:

> *Lovely Lady*
> *dressed in blue,*
> *make me tall*
> *and skinny*
> *just like you.*
> *Amen.*

Our other angel of God, Sister Melathon, known to all as Mel, spent her life in Washington's inner city as a social worker, community organizer, and civil rights activist, working side by side with Ralph Abernathy, Jesse Jackson, and Andrew Young. As a social worker, Mel lived the life I wanted but was told didn't exist within the Sisters of the Holy Cross. Seeing her live that life revived my hope that someday I could too. Injustice of any kind infuriated Mel. But unlike many who grow bitter and hardened by inner-city life, Mel turned kinder, gentler, and more persevering. Deeply spiritual in an extraordinarily ordinary way, she was mysteriously mystical and saintly: Joan of Arc, Saint Francis, and Julian of Norwich rolled into one nun. A free spirit in step to a drummer few hear, much less follow, Mel didn't suffer fools kindly, and all authoritarian superiors fell into that category.

For example, Mel, Maurice, and Ann surprised us one night with a plan to drive to Georgetown to see *The Graduate*, the hot movie of the summer, starring Anne Bancroft and Dustin Hoffman. We invited our sisters at Saint Pat's to come with us, but their superior wouldn't let them go because of the movie's nudity; nor did she want them out after dark. Even Maurice's personal appeal on their behalf failed. Mel was fit to be tied when she found out, threatening to go to Saint Pat's and kidnap Paj, Suzanne, and Ellen.

On another occasion, our Fourth of July picnic, Paj and the others had to leave in the middle of the afternoon to go back to Saint Pat's for confession to the "extraordinary confessor"—a traveling priest with allegedly extraordinary powers. We at Saint Peter's decided to forgo the exceptional opportunity, and it made Mel angry that our sisters weren't free to decide for themselves. Any display of a superior's authority like that evoked the wrath of Mel and equal displeasure from Maurice and Ann—sentiments we wholeheartedly admired and shared.

Ann Shaw, whose name at the time was Sister Philothea, completed the holy trinity of sisters with whom we lived. Ann envisioned education as a divine tool to fight injustice, and she worked with Mel and Maurice in their total commitment to civil rights activism. Being principal of Saint Peter's Grade School, Ann worked long days and many nights, but no matter how tired she was, she wallowed in the pleasure of our company, letting us know every day how much she loved living with us. If we wanted to talk, Ann sat with us until all manner of things were well. Possessing an unshakable inner strength, Ann grounded us even on the worst of days. And when Mary Sue and I joked about her nun name, Philothea, she responded in kind with humor, never making an issue of the fact that she cherished the name, which meant "love of God." I wanted to be like Ann in every way. We all did.

There was so much love in the convent at Saint Peter's that I wonder why that house didn't lift up and float to heaven. Not only did Maurice, Mel, and Ann give me the best summer of my life but they also wakened in me a social consciousness I never knew before, showing by example how to be the sister I felt called to be. I wanted the pure joy and boundless generosity of spirit that Maurice wrapped around us like a divine comforter. I wanted Mel's outrage for injustice, her love of the poor, her mystical spirit, and her refusal to accept irrational and abusive authority as the will of God. And I wanted to be a pillar of gentle strength like Ann in her love of God. I prayed to be able to listen to anyone in need until all was well, even responding with humor and understanding to those who unconsciously ridicule the religious life I love.

I still pray to be like Maurice, Mel, and Ann who in my life became sisters in the truest, most sacred sense of the word. Blessed be the divine power of those holy three.

How such a divine summer could end so sadly is something I still don't fully understand. Of the eight of us sent to Washington, D.C., only five returned to Saint Mary's for our second year in the juniorate. The first departure was that of Ellen Gibson. After receiving our last paycheck of $150, we walked back to Saint Peter's while Ellen went off "to run an errand." We jokingly told her not to blow her paycheck all at once without knowing what she had in mind, and never in our wildest imaginings could we have guessed.

To this day I haven't met anyone like Ellen Gibson. Despite her abuse of the attic fan, Ellen was hilariously funny in ways not even she understood. While we laughed hysterically at something she'd say, Ellen looked clueless, not seeing the humor at all. Even a complete explanation didn't help, which made the incident funnier. Only when Ellen didn't show up for dinner did Maurice begin to worry. She began to pace like a mother hen over a missing chick.

"Don't worry, Maurice," we assured her. "Nothing will happen to Ellen. She can take care of herself better than any of us."

As we were trying to soothe Maurice's nerves, the doorbell rang.

"I'll get it," I said, rising to answer the door while the others helped clear the table for dessert.

I opened the front door and nearly screamed. Walking past me up the stairs and into the dining room was Ellen Gibson in a pink and white polka-dot dress with matching purse and shoes. Grinning from ear to ear, she stood before us with outstretched arms, and announced with a squeal, "I'm going home!"

We stood there staring, openmouthed and speechless.

"You're what?' we asked.

"Sit down and talk," Maurice added, going to the kitchen to get Ellen's dinner, which had been kept warm in the oven.

Ellen sat down and talked, explaining that she decided to leave and that her parents had sent a one-way plane ticket to Pocatello, Idaho. Not wanting to fly home in the habit, she took her paycheck and bought a new outfit with matching purse and shoes.

"There's nothing you can do to change my mind," she said with complete confidence, adding, "so don't even try."

We didn't know whether to laugh or cry. True to form, the manner of departure was pure Ellen Gibson, and for weeks after we did laugh, as did our sisters when we returned to Saint Mary's and told the story.

Ellen left late that night, with Maurice and Mel driving her to National Airport. Ann stayed home with us, still spinning in shock over Ellen's sudden departure. Maurice and Mel returned with the makings for banana splits, which we devoured as we sat up talking. Though we were a sadder group without Ellen, Maurice was left with the dreaded responsibility of phoning Mother Octavia in the morning to report Ellen's departure.

Two days later and three days before we returned to Saint Mary's, Helene (the composer of "Let It Grow") received a letter from Mother Octavia informing her that "due to a dearth in personnel," she was being sent to a notoriously wretched convent in Virginia to teach fifth grade. Within minutes, Helene tore up the letter and decided she would leave rather than submit to guaranteed misery. Had it been any of us, we would have done the same. In fact, we all felt like leaving.

Unbeknown to us, Maurice called Mother Octavia that day with the hope of appealing the decision but received a stern reprimand in return for being so permissive with us. Apparently some sister at Saint Patrick's reported Maurice, Mel, and Ann for taking us to see *The Graduate* and allowing us to forgo the "extraordinary confessor" on the Fourth of July. When Maurice told us what Mother Octavia had said, we were fit to be tied; we were angry over Helene's leaving, some mean-spirited complaining nun at Saint Pat's, and Maurice's condemnation. We spent the day comforting one another, especially Helene and Maurice, who felt crushed by the Octavia letter and reprimand. Mel was so angry we thought she'd leave too, taking Ann and Maurice with her.

The final blow struck two days before returning to Saint Mary's. Mary Sue (of "Chicken Fat" fame) changed her plane ticket to leave a day early in order to visit her friend Blanca, a sister in the group behind us who had left the community that summer. Instead of returning with the group, Mary Sue planned to fly to Los Angeles to see Blanca, then return to Saint Mary's a day later. No one perceived the change of itinerary to be a problem, but Mother Octavia did. Somehow she received word of the plan and called to tell Mary Sue that if she didn't return with the group, she should not bother to return at all. That did it. Mother Octavia pushed Mary Sue over the edge. She left for California that day and never came back.

We were totally devastated. All of a sudden, without notice, at the end of the best summer of my life, three of our sisters left in one week. Maurice, Mel, and Ann mourned the loss as their own. I remember our last night together in D.C. as a holy night. Bound together that summer by the best and worst of times, we thanked those three angels for the extraordinary blessings that changed our lives. In the tender care of Maurice, Mel, and Ann Shaw, my social consciousness was born. I learned to see the face of God in everyone, and for that life-changing miracle, I'll thank them forever.

Our first year in the juniorate began with a liberating bang and ended with a crushing whimper. At the end I was not the sister I had been at the beginning. In one year life returned to normal, and I woke up in ways that I could never have imagined, much less prayed for. I had no idea how socially unconscious I was until I spent the summer in Washington and started to become uncompromising with any form of injustice in myself. If I wanted to fight discrimination and inequality, I knew I needed to begin with me. I had to look at my enemies and see the face of God. There's nothing worse in humanity than being the first to cast stones. "No stone throwing allowed" is what I learned in Washington, D.C. In the fight for justice and equality, I discovered with the followers of Martin Luther King (and Jesus) the least traveled path of nonviolence. The whole world knows how to hate and make war, but no one yet has led this world in the divine path of loving enemies and making peace. When I left Saint Peter's so full of outrageous anger, Mel gave me Saint Francis's "Prayer for Peace."

Lord, make me a channel of your peace.
Where there is hatred,
let me sow love.
Where there is injury, pardon;
Where there is doubt, faith;
Where there is despair, hope;
Where there is darkness, light;
Where there is sadness, joy.

O Divine One, grant that I may seek not so much
To be consoled
as to console;
To be understood as to understand;
To be loved as to love;
For it is giving that we receive;
It is in pardoning that we are pardoned,
It is in dying that we are born to eternal life.

"Don't let your anger consume you," she told me. "We need peacemakers."

While I wasn't in the mood for making peace when we returned to Saint Mary's, I knew Mel was right. I came of age that summer in being led to take seriously the gospel message of loving enemies and doing something every day to relieve the suffering of the miserable, regardless of how I feel. That's what I brought back to Saint Mary's in beginning the second year in the juniorate and my senior year in college. Feeling soulfully devastated and beat-up over the unjust loss of Helene and Mary Sue, I didn't know what to expect.

Being the only two returning from "permissive" Saint Peter's, Mugs and I felt we too could be sent home as part of Mother Octavia's plan to teach us a lesson. Given that we were midwesterners, being sent home from South Bend made sense since we had to fly back anyway. Once again, we faced another leap into the unknown.

Meeting us at the South Bend airport where Gates 1 through 7 all open and exit through the same door were our new superiors, Sister Gertrude and Sister Vincent Clare, and our sister Nancy Gros de Mange, who returned the day before from a similar summer program in San Francisco. After what happened in D.C., it was a tearful arrival, but it felt as though Sister Gertrude waved a magic calming wand when she embraced us with a warmhearted sisterly greeting of "Welcome home."

None of us knew Sister Gertrude or Sister Vincent Clare—except for the fact that Sister Vincent Clare was the sibling of Beth Mulvaney, a sister in our class. But as we climbed into the convent van for the fifteen-minute ride back to Saint Mary's, they turned on the radio to a pop music station. Simon and Garfunkel's soulful song played, "Hello darkness, my old friend." Our new year began with "The Sound of Silence" and a tearful homecoming.

chapter six

convent life unveiled

A Solemn thing within the Soul
To feel itself get ripe—

—EMILY DICKINSON, #483

In beginning the second year in the juniorate and our senior year in college, I did so with a Solemn Soul ripened by my experiences in Washington, D.C. News of the sudden departure of Ellen, Helene, and Mary Sue spread throughout the Motherhouse in South Bend, turning Mugs and me into prodigal sisters. Even Concil wanted "the truth" about what went on at Saint Peter's, as though we had spent the summer in dissolute living, wallowing in sex, drugs, and rock 'n' roll. Along with the silver heart, a scarlet S hung around our necks when we returned to Saint Mary's. The bad sisters arrived with music just waiting to face us.

Needless to say, we weren't welcomed home like the prodigal son, with a party celebrating our safe return. On top of being met by scornful looks of "Shame on you," our new superior, Sister Gertrude, asked to see Mugs, Paj, Suzanne, Ellen, and me in her office before we got settled. My already devastated heart sank deeper.

What did we do now? I immediately wondered: *Maybe this is when we get sent home.*

The five of us walked into Sister Gertrude's office together. With only one chair in front of the desk, I knew that what we were in for would happen quickly, and we'd have to take it standing. We stood in a row before Sister Gertrude, pale-faced and nervous. Even she appeared apprehensive and anxious—rarely, if ever, a good sign, especially in a superior.

"Tomorrow morning after breakfast," she said with a soft voice, "Mother Octavia wants to see those who are left from Washington, D.C."

"Those who are left?" I blurted out, adding, "That sounds ominous. Should we even unpack?"

Sister Gertrude tried to calm our fears about being sent home, assuring us that Mother Octavia had no such intention.

Easy for you to say, I thought, but I kept quiet. We saw those intentions in action the week before. They had a life of their own.

"Brace yourselves, sisters," I said as we left the meeting with Sister Gertrude. "I think we're in for a bumpy ride."

Paj, Mugs, and I sat around that night, trying to envision what would happen with Mother Octavia. Only the grimmest scenarios came to mind, filling us with fear. We felt doomed to endure an intensely blistering reprimand, if not sudden dismissal.

"Woe is me . . ." Paj moaned.

Followed by Mug's, "Woe is me too . . ."

And me, "Woe is we three."

Given my already contentious relationship with Mother Octavia, I wasn't sure what possessed me to offer a positive spin on the situation, but I did.

"Maybe she just wants to hear about our summer," I said, trying to add a little levity to the bleakness. "You know, like how the program was, the Solidarity Day March, Resurrection City . . ."

"What are you, nuts?" Paj asked in disbelief. "You think Mother Octavia wants to sit around and chat about what we did on our summer vacation?"

"I don't think so, Kare," Mugs added, shaking her head.

"Well, I'm bringing the photo album anyhow," I declared with blind unflagging optimism. "Maybe if we start showing photos of the kids, it'll take the edge off. You know, like the best . . ."

"I know, I know," Paj interrupted, "you think the best defense is a good offense. Bull."

They really thought I was crazy, and I was. But I brought the photo album anyhow when we gathered the following morning after breakfast. I was determined to make my pointless point. Paj took one look at me and the photo album and spoke two words, "You're nuts."

"So what?" are the two words I gave her in return.

Sister Gertrude asked to see us in her office before we left for the Mother Octavia meeting.

When I jokingly said she probably wanted one last look, no one laughed—a very bad sign. We were sinking fast and hadn't even left the house.

"We'll be praying for you," Gertrude told us with a blessing of divine comfort.

Without publicly taking sides, I felt Sister Gertrude was mysteriously and secretly on our side. She looked equally nervous, feeling our anxiety as her own while hugging us as we left.

"Don't worry," she added to each hug, "it'll be fine."

"Thank you, sister," we said faintly, "we hope so."

"Okay now" I said as we walked to the generalate. "When Mother Octavia enters the room, I'll hand her the album and ask if she'd like to see photos of the program."

Mugs and Paj shook their heads, laughing in everlasting disbelief, but they went along with the plan anyhow, as did Suzi and Ellen, as if they had an alternative.

"When I have a plan, I will not be denied," I declared, like a battle cry, photo album proudly in hand.

"Yeah, right," Paj said. "You'll see what 'denied' feels like in about ten minutes."

The room where we met Mother Octavia was the same Temple of Doom in which we waited in agony to see Mother Katrina about receiving the habit, and a year earlier to see Mother Octavia about accepting us for profession. The room was permanently charged with generations of high anxiety, and our edgy presence only raised the intensity level. At any moment something explosive could have happened, which was a compelling reason to sit still.

While teetering on the brink of bursting with nervous laughter or anxious tears, we prayed for strength to remain calm and collected. We sat in silence as we waited. No one spoke. We didn't dare. At the sound of the bead-rattling and footsteps of Mother Octavia approaching, we froze.

"Good morning, Mother," we chimed in unison (while secretly calling all angels). Then the freeze broke as we rose and smiled when she entered the room.

"Good morning, sisters," she said, with a firm voice. Taking her seat in the thronelike chair positioned before us, she looked like a judge facing the accused. She added a terse "Be seated."

Holding our photo album like a holy grail, I stepped forward and handed it to Mother Octavia. The others held their breath.

"We brought photos of kids we worked with and the Solidarity Day March," I said, smiling. "We thought you'd like to see them and hear about the work we did this summer."

Without changing her expression, Mother Octavia took the photo album like a piece of debris, setting it on the floor beneath her chair. Ignoring my pointless plan completely, she proceeded with her own. That did it. So much for blind optimism. Paj and Mugs were right all along, but even they sympathized with me in my crushing defeat.

I turned away from Mother Octavia, bowed low but not broken, and took my seat. The grimmest of scenarios envisioned the night before was about to materialize. At that point, everything floated beyond control, leaving us at the mercy of our patron, Mary, the Mother of Sorrows. Holding on to the silver heart with its multistabbed Mary, I prayed for divine protection. Bracing for the worst, I commended our terrified spirits into the hands of God, just as we did every night before the lights went out.

For nearly an hour, Mother Octavia expressed in no uncertain terms how displeased she was with our behavior in Washington, D.C., and how miserably our "small group experiment" had failed. Irresponsible, negligent, immature, untrustworthy, and defiant of authority were some of the adjectives used to describe us, but most frightening of all was the final mysterious warning before letting us go.

"Sisters," she said, with heightened seriousness, "in the next three years, you will be watched very closely. You will never know who, when, or where, but you will be observed carefully."

We sat as though suspended in midair, listening to Mother Octavia explain that we were on probation with no room for the slightest deviation or error. Even though we grasped the point quickly, she went on about our glaring need for close supervision and her divinely appointed responsibility to see that we got it. Obviously other superiors failed. Then pausing to stare each of us in the eye, Mother Octavia announced the ultimate threat—the "triple-dog dare."

Sister Karol Jackowski

"For the next three years," she proclaimed, as if announcing the eleventh commandment, "you will be in the Eye of the Beholder."

After pausing again for reflection, she repeated, "The Eye of the Beholder," while nodding her head in affirmation.

God glued our eyes to Mother Octavia's face. We didn't dare look at one another. After my introductory offer of the photo album had failed so miserably, none of us spoke a word. Clearly, it was time to listen, because nothing we had to say mattered. We were trapped gadflies braced for the Big Swat.

Mother Octavia repeated "The Eye of the Beholder" five times with greater and greater gravity, looking at each of us with every repetition. Being the last in line, I received the greatest gravity with a look that could kill. I wanted desperately to get up and run home to Mommy and Daddy in East Chicago, but I felt nailed to the chair by the Octavia stare.

"Are there questions?" she asked, leaning back, looking pleased, as if daring us to speak.

Well. I was dying to ask, "Who's the Beholder?" but for the grace of God I didn't. "Who's the Beholder?" was the only question we all had but didn't dare ask out loud. Inspired by the Holy Spirit, we sat upright in silence, holding our tongues.

"Very well," Mother said, rising from the throne, looking well pleased, "you may go."

Without taking the photo album or welcoming us home, Mother Octavia turned around and walked away, fading into the darkness at the end of the hall where her office was. Only when we heard the door close did we feel safe to leave. One by one, we filed out of the generalate in silence. I was last in line. Not wanting to leave trash behind, I took the photo album with me.

Once we were out of sight of the generalate, we burst out laughing. We didn't know who the Beholder was, and began naming every nun we knew who fit that description. The Photo Album Plan—later called the

PAP Smear—became a joke of cosmic proportions, and to this day we still laugh about being in the Eye of the Beholder.

After our life-threatening encounter with "The Eye," we came home to a surprise party rivaling that of the prodigal son. Waiting on pins and needles, Sisters Gertrude, Vincent Clare, and all our sisters welcomed us back with the great news that we were packing up immediately and going to Lakeside (the Sisters of the Holy Cross vacation house on Lake Michigan). Zapped with the rapture of being snatched into heaven by angels, it felt like a glorious miracle. We weren't going to Disneyland with Olympic gold medal winners, but we were headed to our ocean for a week. *Wahootie.* What could our Jesus do more?

Sister Gertrude didn't know us at all, except by bad reputation, but she did know that what we needed most before our year began was time alone and time together. Somehow she knew that our newly ripened Solemn Souls needed a big shot of fun in the sun, far far away from the glaring Eye of the Beholder. Just when we expected fully to be punished with the strictest superiors in the community, Gertrude and Vincent Clare entered our lives as surprisingly angelic. They were divine intervention at its best.

The Sisters of the Holy Cross own two large cabinlike houses on the shores of Lake Michigan, about forty-five minutes north of South Bend. Built on a hill overlooking the lake, both are equipped with kitchens, dining rooms, living rooms full of quilted rocking chairs and soft stuffed sofas, wood-burning fireplaces, screened-in porches, and eight bedrooms between them: five accommodating two to four sisters and three small singles reserved for "superiors or the sick."

Paj, Mugs, Nancy, and I shared a room in the front house with lake views, while Sister Gertrude took the tiniest "superiors only" single in the house with us.

"I hope we don't keep you up tonight," I said to Gertrude in jest.

"I hope you don't either," she responded, not entirely in jest. "You can do whatever you want after midnight as long as you keep it quiet or take it outside. Get it?" Gertrude added, making sure the point was clear.

"Got it," I answered, nodding my head to seal the understanding. "Keep it down after midnight. Not a problem."

"Very good," she said, smiling. "End of subject."

This is very good indeed, I thought on my way down to the beach with Gertrude. *She's clear and funny.* Two of my favorite virtues.

Step out the back door, down the pine wood stairs, and there's the beach fully embraced by pale blue skies and a giant freshwater lake full of welcoming waves.

"Listen to the water," Gertrude said, stopping me, "come on in . . . come on in . . . come on in."

Without a shore in sight from where we stood, Lake Michigan spread before us—so big and so everybody's—for as far as the eye could see. On a clear day the Chicago skyline appears on the horizon like the Emerald City; and on a clear night every constellation in the galaxy illuminates the pitch-black sky. Lake Michigan was our ocean. Indiana's paradise. One look is all it took to grant me peace. My soul swims to the top whenever I see water and sky, and Sister Gertrude was right. That's exactly what we needed. In a year of living in the Eye of the Beholder, we were suddenly blessed with angels of God, guardians dear. After such a great summer with such a stunningly awful ending, I felt safe and a little invincible, as if no harm would come to us that year.

In a blessing from Gertrude and Vincent Clare, we were given one week of free-spirited days, without which even paradise can be hell on earth. Morning prayer happened on the beach after everyone awakened and breakfast was served. Our D.C. chaplain, Father Steve Gibson, joined us daily to celebrate Eucharist on the beach at sunset. Every night around a campfire, under moon and stars, we gathered for night prayer. Heaven and nature prayed with us every day.

We all took long walks on the beach, first with Gertrude, then with Vincent Clare, each wanting to know about our summer experiences. They felt soulfully ripened by my story as much as I was, and they thanked me for sharing what I learned.

They thanked me.

Mercy.

Every day held a wonderful surprise, and one of those days Gertrude suggested we go blueberry picking, stopping on the way home for fresh corn, frozen custard, and beer—all of which we welcomed. Our new superiors, we were discovering, were fun to be with. From the day we met, and every day thereafter, Gertrude and Vincent Clare became our older and wiser sisters, not religious superiors; and while we lived in the Eye of the Beholder, that made all the difference in our world.

When we got back to the house after the berry-picking field trip, the others went down to the beach, and I decided to bake. With every blueberry I picked, I dreamed of fresh-baked muffins, and by the time we got home, the vision became a mission. I preheated the oven, whipped up the batter with fresh eggs and sweet farmer's butter, folded in big handfuls of berries, and greased two muffin pans, spooning the mix evenly into each, then shaking the pans to level the batter. Opening the oven door, I slid the pans onto the middle rack, only to realize the pilot light wasn't lit. Grabbing the big blue-tipped stovetop matches, I struck one and BOOM!

As everyone says it does, my life flashed before me. While dishes flew out of the cupboard over the stove, the explosion knocked me back against the kitchen wall, covering me in batter with empty muffin tins in my lap. The sisters raced up from the beach, expecting to discover me dead and blown to bits. Finding me blasted against the wall, covered in blueberries and muffin mix, was a miraculous relief for them as well as me. I was still here.

"My God, Kare, are you all right?" Sister Gertrude cried with a look of terror (her first day on the job and one of us dies!) while turning off the gas.

The others stood around open-mouthed and pale-faced, waiting for me to speak; some frantically opened all the doors and windows, gasping dramatically for fresh air.

"I'm okay, but the muffins are dead," I said, dazed and confused, wiping batter and blueberries from my face.

A collective burst of relieved laughter turned quickly into a firing squad of questions; all asked how I could be so stupid as to light a match in an oven full of gas. The hair on my arms was singed, and had my face not been protected by batter and blueberries, my eyebrows and hair probably would have disintegrated also. Miracle of miracles, within an hour, everything had been cleaned up and I was walking on the beach. Banned from using the oven, I made blueberry pancakes for breakfast the following morning instead, which Paj described as "dynamite, pun intended."

The ripening of our Solemn Souls continued. Like Maurice, Mel, and Ann, our new superiors made it clear how much they looked forward to the year ahead. Me too. Being free to do whatever we wanted was the greatest blessing Gertrude and Vincent Clare could have given us on our sad return, and it didn't stop after that week at Lakeside. The best and blessed of times we shared as our year began continued, even under the mysterious Eye of the Beholder. In 1968, while our classmates smoked pot, Lakeside became our drug of choice. If tensions ran high, Gertrude packed us up and took us to Lake Michigan. When she and Vincent Clare felt our spirits sinking, they set us before sky and water where souls swim to the top to be anointed with the sweet balm of sisterhood. Blessed be we.

In returning to Saint Mary's, we moved back into the old novitiate building, newly named Augusta Hall. With an increasing decline in postulants, the loss of sisters in our group, and growing enrollment at the college, Saint Mary's students moved into the postulate–juniorate building in the fall of 1968, renaming it Regina Hall: North and South. Jokes spread around the college about Mary's girls moving into a convent, but once they had, they met the magic. How the rooms held TVs, stereos, radios, boom boxes, trunks full of clothes, shoes, books, and miscellaneous treasures was truly miraculous. And the miracle continues today.

We moved back across the street into Augusta Hall with the group of newly professed sisters one year behind us, but not into the dorms we lived in before. While we were away for the summer, the dormitories had been renovated into single and double rooms, bathrooms were modernized, and the incubator feeling of solitary confinement was noticeably gone. When we entered the building, my stomach didn't turn. It felt as though everything old was made new again, and all earthbound ghosts of novices past were suddenly set free, including ours.

"This is great," I said to Sister Gertrude, walking up the Guardian Angel stairs to my new room, excited over the renovation. "The spooks and heebie-jeebies are gone."

"Well, that's the least we could do," she replied, though I wondered if she really knew what I meant.

In what was formerly the third-floor Saint Joseph dorm, where twelve of us had slept as novices, I was given a spacious single room on the northeast corner of the building with not one but three big windows, and Paj, Mugs, Nancy, and Jane were neighbors. Equipped with a new bed, desk, crucifix, bookcase, and lounge chair, our rooms were bigger and brighter than that of our college classmates and far better than the two small single rooms I loved in the juniorate. This really was heaven.

I could lie in bed and watch the moon rise in all three windows. I could also lie in bed and behold a triple view of the sunrise, but I never did.

Before classes began, Sister Gertrude encouraged us to make ourselves at home. Not only could we decorate the rooms with posters and family photos, but we were allowed to have radios and electric typewriters. My family sent both and I tuned in once again, as I had as a high school student, to WLS in Chicago. I fell asleep with Casey Kasem playing top hits through the night, making up for years of daily news and pop music deprivation. I binged on radio. Every return to a normal life made me giddy as a five-year-old getting everything she wants for Christmas. In my life God's manner is ordinary, and normal equals divine. As such, the radio once again became the sacrament that kept me in touch with the holy spirits of the day.

The next surprise came with news that we could make our own bedroom curtains, even select whatever material we wanted, within a budget of twenty dollars each. Every bit of individuality crushed in the first three years, all of a sudden began to rise from the dead. A group of us drove to University Park Mall in Mishawaka for the fabric fiesta. Some chose big daisy floral prints, polka dots, shooting stars, geometric and space age designs, and gingham checks—all in the brightest colors. I picked narrow vertical stripes of maroon, yellow-gold, and navy. We kept the choices secret, wanting to surprise Gertrude and Vincent Clare with our newly crafted creations, and, boy, were they surprised.

On the day of the drapery hanging, we invited Gertrude and Vincent Clare to an open house—a first look at our fully decorated rooms. In the hallway, under the statue of Mary, punch and chocolate chip cookies were self-served. My room was first on the tour. I hung posters of Joan Baez, Martin Luther King (with his "I Have a Dream" speech), Sister Corita's "Damn Everything but the Circus," and a bright yellow sign illustrated with an empty chair and the saying "Sometimes I sits and thinks and sometimes I just sits." In addition to the shiny gold crucifix already mounted above the desk, all four walls displayed my first art collection.

Driftwood and painted rocks covered my windowsills, and the radio played WLS's top hits of the 1960s. I put statues of Mary and Joseph on the bookcase surrounded by freshly picked black-eyed Susans. Lined up on the desk, like an exhibit, were framed snapshots of family and friends. Over the desk hung (under the crucifix) a wood-framed bulletin board littered with "To Do" lists, favorite quotes, a calendar with special dates highlighted, and recent school photos of nieces and nephews. If prizes were given for the best-decorated room, I would have won. We all felt like winners, with rooms that for the first time in four years were truly our own.

As we escorted Gertrude and Vincent Clare from room to room, they looked as though they had no idea what they had done in telling us to make ourselves at home. While grinning fragilely from ear to ear, Gertrude repeated the same refrain: "Oh, how nice," she said, room by room, with the weakening voice of someone about to faint.

Vincent Clare followed with an equally frozen smile, saying nothing. Words clearly failed her.

Regardless of how they felt, neither one disapproved of what we did or made us change; nor did they express even the slightest wish that we'd tone things down a bit, except for the volume on my radio. I loved that about them. They let us be. They even joked about the wildness and craziness of our choices, noting in mine a Freudian slip with a certain prisonlike theme.

The peaceful palace created at the open house lasted less than twenty-four hours. While we slept in heavenly peace, out of the night with the moon burning bright, the Eye of the Beholder appeared. No one saw it coming.

"May I have your attention," Gertrude asked after lunch, ringing the bell to stop the chatter. "I have an announcement."

Like Pavlov's nuns, conversation stopped at the sound of the bell and all eyes turned to Gertrude.

"Sisters," she said with a shaky voice, "there will be a meeting tonight after dinner in the recreation room. Please be there."

We ached to know what was going on, but no one asked. Part of me never wants to know anything in advance. But something was up, and it didn't look good. Gertrude appeared uncharacteristically nervous in making the announcement, while Vincent Clare struggled to avoid eye contact. Both appeared to have had a close encounter with The Eye.

As instructed, we gathered in the recreation room after supper, dreading the worst (almost forgetting what that kind of dread felt like). After taking our seats in the newly traditional circle, Gertrude and Vincent Clare joined us.

"Sisters, we need to talk about the curtains," Gertrude said, still uncharacteristically nervous. "Mother Octavia wants them replaced with something plain and uniform."

"*Why?*" several of us blurted out, as though a light switch flipped on sleeping fury. "What's wrong with our curtains?"

"Mother thinks they make this look like a college dorm," she said, trying to minimize the issue.

"Well, this is a college dorm," I answered with rising anger. "We're college students and we live here."

"I know, I know, Kare," Gertrude said, trying to calm us down. "But this is also a convent building."

"Yes," I shot back. "A convent full of college students. If Mother doesn't like it, tell her not to look. You and Vincent don't mind. What's her problem?"

I apologized immediately for yelling at Gertrude and blasting the messenger, but I hated seeing her tormented that way by Mother Octavia on our behalf. After wrangling back and forth over not removing our curtains, we finally reached a workable compromise. We'd line the curtains with white fabric and turn them inside out. That way only we would have to live with the selection of colors and patterns we chose. Fair enough.

After all was said and done, I still felt the Eye of the Beholder had overstepped rightful authority personally by imposing the curtain rule and making Gertrude enforce it. Gertrude and Vincent Clare didn't say so, but we knew they agreed with us; in the end, that mattered most of all.

Once classes began, we returned to life as full-time college students; our senior year. We looked far less puritan in 1968. While still wearing shorter, more hair-revealing veils, we began wearing store-bought suits, and our hemlines rose from midcalf to two inches below the knee. We didn't look that bad in manufactured clothes. Although it was still easy to spot a nun in a crowd—without the veil and in our very best, we could be mistaken for flight attendants.

Either way, our appearance inched year by year toward normal and was becoming less and less of an issue. Even nuns who swore over their dead bodies that they'd never change the habit did so peacefully without immediately dropping dead. I never thought I'd live to see that miracle, but I did—over and over again. Changing hearts, minds, and bad habits is the miracle that keeps the sisterhood alive.

Carrying full course loads, many of us spent part of the week with internships as student teachers or nurses. I was the only one with an internship in social work, traveling to a public middle school in Goshen, Indiana, where I counseled troubled sixth-graders. As required by the school district, I worked without a veil and was called Miss Jackowski. The public school system was a good fit for me, given my discomfort with titles and formalities. Senior-year anxiety set in with us just as much as it did our classmates, even though we didn't share the worry about finding jobs, getting the "Mrs." degree (marrying a Notre Dame guy—as it was still all male then), or being accepted into graduate school. After graduation we'd be given work somewhere. Our anxiety focused on where.

Even with senior jitters about life after college, our second year in the juniorate with Gertrude and Vincent Clare was wonderful. In a superior effort to involve us in everything, they set up a house council of elected sisters to help decide community issues, such as housekeeping, schedules, feast day and birthday celebrations, holiday plans, etc. We voted for Nancy as president. Nance had the organizational skills and temperament for the job, as well as our unconditional respect and that of our superiors, including Mother Octavia. No one else qualified in that way, especially the semiprecious ones in the Eye of the Beholder.

Gertrude ensured that we decided everything together, showing us daily how important it is in community that sisters be involved in the decisions that affect their lives. For example, we weren't told what we'd be doing on holidays and college breaks, we were asked what we'd like to do. They even accepted our suggestion for occasional sleep-ins on Saturdays and holidays, and let us watch favorite TV shows, like *Mission: Impossible* and the Academy Awards. We learned to listen to differences of opinion and discern the truths we held in common—no small achievement. Gertrude and Vincent Clare anointed us daily with the holy spirit of obedience, the spiritual work of listening to one another in the way we did at Saint Peter's. Once again we experienced how sweet it is to live in community, where all voices are sacred.

More often than not, Gertrude didn't agree personally with what I believed or what we did, but she never withheld her support. That mystified me.

"How can you support someone you don't agree with?" I asked Gertrude during a long lakeside walk. "Without losing your soul?"

She took a few steps, then stopped and turned toward me.

"Because I look at all of you and see nothing but love in your eyes," she said in words I couldn't forget. "What you do comes from such a good, God-like place . . . I could never withhold my blessing."

"But what if someone is basically mean-spirited, not good at all?" I asked, looking for that exemption. "I should support that?"

"All the more reason to," Gertrude said, sharpening the whole point. "What have you got to lose, Kare? What could you possibly have to lose?"

Gulp.

Later that week Gertrude gave me a slip of paper with a handwritten quote from the sixteenth-century Spanish mystic John of the Cross: "If you put love where there is none, then love is there."

That lakeside chat was a five-minute course in loving. Every day served as a divine reminder to see good in everyone, which in itself is a blessing. In teaching us the spiritual work of seeing goodness, Gertrude and Vincent Clare showed how to love our enemies. It's an invaluable survival skill in community life, as well as the magic ingredient for peace on earth.

As I began my senior year of college, I also became executive director of Concil's Poodle Club, serving as prime accessory to the C.C. escapades. One of our jobs as college seniors included driving the elderly sisters to and from doctor's appointments. We drove a big beige Checker cab, with an American flag waving from the antenna, and we operated a two-way radio communicating with the dispatch office in the convent. Two of us rode in the front seat, the driver and the radio operator. Jane Calabria usually drove because I fought for the radio.

"KGX912, mobile unit to base," I'd call in, like Wonder Woman, with a dramatically serious voice, "come in, base."

"This is base, KGX912," Sister Charity, the cheerful dispatcher, responded. "Sister Cresentia is ready to be picked up at the south entrance of Saint Joseph's Clinic. Needs assistance. KGX912, do you copy?"

"This is KGX912," I said, "copy on Sister Cresentia at Saint Joe's Clinic, south entrance. Needs help. Is that all? Over to base."

"This is base, KGX912. Waiting on a pickup of Sister Concilio at Dr. Toothaker's," she'd say, "check back in ten, KGX912. Copy?"

"Copy, base. Check back in ten for pickup at Toothaker's," I'd respond, often chuckling over the Concil pickup, knowing she was waiting to be last in order to stop at Don's Liquor Store for a refill.

"This is KGX912, mobile unit to base." I said with the sign-off voice, "over and out."

I loved working the radio and driving around town in that tank of a car. When packed with nuns, it felt like a cartoon, and the students dubbed it the Nunmobile. Between pickups we'd occasionally stop at the Dairy Queen for a chocolate shake, a butterscotch sundae, or the best chili dog in northern Indiana. Or if the soul needed a swim, we'd pull over, park, and sit along the shore of the Saint Joseph River; especially in the spring when the river thaws and South Bend explodes with wildflowers, or in autumn when it showers endless beauty with falling leaves.

Turning the two-way radio off was risky on our pit stops, but Sister Charity believed me when I explained that there must have been a short circuit because her call didn't come through. Needless to say, the convent mechanic never found the faulty wire and the problem persisted. We weren't supposed to play the car radio while driving around either, but we did, and none of the sisters I knew disapproved. Even when we'd crank the volume up and open all the windows, they'd squeal with delight, holding veils and headgear in place. I looked at those times as mobile unit therapy. All our sick and elderly passengers looked more alive after a good scream, and they told us they felt better too. God blessed them.

Sister Charity couldn't understand why some sisters requested certain drivers, and we never offered any explanation. We attributed our popularity to timely arrivals and pickups, accompanied by cheerful dispositions—both of which were true. Driving the Checker cab was the best part-time convent job of all. It was the closest we'd be to having our own car, so it was a college senior's dream come true.

Sister Gertrude became the mother of my soul that year. Just as Merce did the year before, she walked the halls at night, visiting and checking our well-being. On more than one occasion she came in to ask me to turn down the radio because she could hear it in her room at the end of the hall.

"Sorry," I'd say, sincerely. "I like to feel the music."

"Sorry," she'd respond with the charitable smile of one pushed to the edge, "I don't."

Attentive to every one of us, Gertrude knew when we were bothered by something, upset, or depressed. There was no need to post lists for spiritual direction because we lined up on our own. While she cared that we did well academically, Gertrude's primary concern was the life of our soul: how we prayed, what we read, where we found divine life, and what bothered us. She wanted to know what spiritual work we were doing.

Though our days were consumed with academic life and our nights with studying and writing papers, Gertrude kept us focused on the experience of God. She wanted us to be just as conscious of our spiritual lives as we were of our academic ones, concentrating on what's happening inside and living in accord with the truth we found. In showing us how to let conscience be our guide, Gertrude gave us a key to heaven on earth. She taught us to live inside out.

I don't know whether she believed in reincarnation as I do, but

Gertrude talked as though she understood fully that we are old souls born with a divine purpose that needed to be fulfilled, that it was our job in this life to discover the call, our mission, and follow the sacred path wherever it leads. She talked about misery and suffering as the pain of new life breaking through parts of us that we've outgrown. Even when commiserating with us, Gertrude radiated an inexplicably peaceful happiness.

"You're being touched by God," she'd tell us in our bad moods, looking disappointed when we didn't jump with joy at the thought alone.

I'm sure I looked at her as if she was nuts, but inside I knew she was right about that mystery of life. Appearances are not reality, and there's far more going on in our lives than we ever can see. Whenever I'd fly off the handle, or distance myself, or become uncharacteristically silent, Gertrude pulled me back to the center. She taught me to keep still when I wanted to run, to remain calm when I'm moved by anger, and to wrap myself in solitude when I can't sit still. While I focused on becoming an excellent social worker, Gertrude kept my twenty-one-year-old life focused on becoming an excellent sister, because, as she'd tell me, if I became a good sister, "you'll shine in everything you do."

In the first four years we learned to value as divine formal prayer and communal prayer, but in our year with Gertrude and Vincent Clare, I learned to treasure personal prayer as the air my soul breathes. In the beginning we prayed with the head, gradually learning to pray with the heart. Our ripened Solemn Souls took a flying leap inward that year, sinking into the depths of whom-we-knew-as-God, grounding us like a rock.

I felt drawn to a different kind of solitude, discovering the inner world of contemplative activity. Leisure, the finest art of doing nothing, became my new best friend. All you need to do is keep calm, make no noise, and don't go looking for words. Don't go doing anything. Just *sit* and listen. In the soul's "Temple of O My God," a door opened into an unknown world, wherein I felt welcomed by an old friend I hadn't seen in two hundred years. It was then that I began to hear a distinct call to contemplative life; though I didn't hear or see it clearly until years later. More than anything else, I simply loved being alone.

What a divine coincidence it was that we began exploring the depths of personal prayer at the same time the Catholic Church began changing and personalizing its medieval liturgy. In the American Catholic Church, English replaced Latin in the language of common prayer, and the physical structure of churches changed to bring priest and people together, removing centuries of physical and spiritual distance. While previously we sisters had nothing to do with church services, other than setting up and cleaning up, now we became part of everything. We began to realize the divine inspiration of Vatican II in revealing that the Church is not exclusively the ordained priesthood but the "people of God." In other words, you and me, we are the Church.

In becoming the Church, we renovated the juniorate chapel by moving the altar down and forward to the center, surrounded by a semicircle of pews. We also began practicing priesthood in planning and preparing our masses and prayer services. While working closely with our chaplain, Father Bill Toohey, a Holy Cross priest at Notre Dame, to plan the music and readings for daily mass, we also prepared prayer services for special occasions with Gertrude and Vincent Clare. Prior to Vatican II, we knew no such thing as prayer services outside mass, but we welcomed the opportunity wholeheartedly.

Encouraged by Gertrude to choose music meaningful to us in prayer, we sang "Blowin' in the Wind" and "If I Had a Hammer," Joan Baez's "All My Trials," Leonard Cohen's "Sisters of Mercy" and "Suzanne," and

Simon and Garfunkel's "The Sound of Silence." In 1968 we began praying with the greatest hits.

In our choice of readings, we reflected on the poetry of T. S. Eliot, e. e. cummings, Kahlil Gibran, Charles Péguy, Lawrence Ferlinghetti, Saint-Exupéry's *The Little Prince*, and my favorite, Robert Lax's *Circus of the Sun*. Our prayer services and masses became so popular that other sisters on campus joined us, as did Saint Mary's students. Even the Eyes of the Beholder—Mother Octavia and her council— attended on occasion. When they did, I always smelled trouble—and I was right.

Once, after singing a heartfelt round of Bob Dylan's "The Times They Are A-Changin' " at a mass in honor of Martin Luther King, the song was banned. There was one verse that caused Mother Octavia to get up and leave the chapel. *"Come mothers and fathers, throughout the land . . ."* we sang, then proceeded to proclaim that we were beyond her control and there was nothing she could do about it. Some sisters felt that we gave a little too much vocal emphasis to "mothers," and Octavia felt it personally. That wasn't our intention. We planned the liturgy to honor Martin Luther King on the first anniversary of his assassination; we never thought of Mother Octavia. Even so, Sister Gertrude took a bullet for that incident. She never admitted being reprimanded by Mother Octavia for allowing us to sing secular songs at mass, but we felt that must have happened.

Something unpleasant was up. We felt the imminent aftermath of The Eye about to crush us. As suspected, the next day Sister Gertrude told us to choose only church music for mass or songs approved by her and the General Council. We could sing whatever we wanted in our prayer services but not at mass. That's when we knew that she had been taken to task. We agreed to the new "liturgical guidelines" without question. In the holy spirit of sisterhood, it was our duty to lay down our lives for our sisters, and our turn to protect Gertrude and Vincent Clare from the Eye of the Beholder.

On another occasion, we planned a special Mother's Day celebration—mass and steak supper—for Mother Octavia and her council. It was a sincere attempt to offer an olive branch of peace and make nice. Our selection of music was approved well in advance, and Father Toohey worked closely with us in preparing the liturgy, urging Paj and me to bake bread for the Eucharist. While receiving Holy Communion in the hand was sanctioned by Vatican II, it was not yet common practice at the Church of Loretto; nor was the use of homemade bread. But both were part of the ritual preparation for Eucharist in our chapel, and part of what we wanted to share with Mother Octavia and the council at the Mother's Day celebration.

A priest in the most sacred sense, Bill Toohey felt strongly about involving the community in the celebration of mass. Calling us to exercise our priesthood, he invited sisters to assist him at the altar. He asked that we share our thoughts on the day's Scripture reading at the homily; and at the blessing of the bread and blessing of the wine, he called the community to pray the words of consecration with him.

Extending our right hand in blessing over the bread, we prayed, "Take and eat, this is my body," and in blessing the wine, "Take and drink, this is my blood." In consecrating the "food and drink of everlasting life," we repeated the gospel words of Jesus at the Last Supper, "Do this in memory of me."

Step by step, Mother Octavia and the Council appeared more and more uncomfortable, while Vincent Clare and Gertrude stood proudly on my right in full support. Mugs stood at my left.

"Check out Octavia," I whispered to Mugs with the slightly moving lips of a bad ventriloquist.

"I can't look," Mugs responded, tight-lipped, "I'll faint."

We all looked faint, but Father Toohey remained calm.

When the time came for Holy Communion, he took the two baskets of homemade bread and asked that we give communion to one another. Passing the basket, we broke the bread to be given to the person beside us.

"This is the Body of Christ," we said, while giving one another communion.

In response, we prayed, "Amen."

As the basket neared Mother Octavia, she stepped out of the pew and left the chapel, followed in single file by the members of the Council. It was a total corporate boycott. They refused Holy Communion with us. Gertrude and Vincent Clare looked ill, but they didn't leave. Father Toohey called on us to bow our heads in a prayer of blessing for our sisters who "left the table." What I heard were audible deep breaths, soulful sighs of relief, as though holy spirits surrounded us with fluttering breathtaking wings, blessing us, everyone.

After mass, following Bill Toohey's blessing to "go in peace," Gertrude went to the generalate to salvage what she could of the olive branch with Mother Octavia, while Vincent Clare stayed with us. From the chapel, we recessed to the dining room for the special Mother's Day supper, in a daze and without the guests of honor. It felt like a death with no crime scene or body.

"What did we do?" I asked Vincent Clare as we walked down the Guardian Angel stairs to the dining room. "What happened?"

"I'm not sure, Kare," she said, shaking her head. "I'm not sure."

We waited for Gertrude to return. Every table buzzed with great speculation over what we imagined happening; naturally, we feared the worst. We knew how awful The Eye could be, because we'd been there.

"Woe is Gertrude," Paj moaned in sympathy.

About half an hour later Gertrude appeared, smiling, teary-eyed, and pale, as though she had seen a ghost and it wasn't friendly. A heartfelt round of "She's a Jolly Good Sister" moved her to laugh, after which she did the unforgettable.

"I want to thank all of you and each of you for being so free-spirited and brave," she said tearfully in words I never forgot.

She thanked us.

Mercy.

"What happened?" several of asked out loud, dying to know and hoping to hear.

Gertrude simply smiled and said, "Don't worry. Everything is fine. Let's eat!"

All we could do was applaud Gertrude with a tearful standing ovation, then sit down and enjoy the special steak dinner with surprisingly fine red wine. We never knew what took place between Gertrude and Mother Octavia that day, but it felt serious. I think she stood up for us and got blasted. Whatever happened between them, Mother's Day became a powerful turning point between us. Gertrude and Vincent Clare became our guests of honor that night. We toasted them as the "Mothers of our Soul." The bonds between us deepened and became the Holiest Communion of all.

I never understood clearly how Gertrude supported us and Mother Octavia at the same time, but the year was full of daily examples, as though that's what we needed to learn most before we graduated. In order to earn our "degree in sisterhood," we needed to understand how to live in community, especially with those we saw as enemies. Gertrude and Vincent Clare exemplified perseverance in teaching community life, while we provided ample "educable" opportunities.

A case in point: "Two Blind Mice."

As an emergency favor to a biology class lab partner, Paj came home one day with two white mice, housed in a pinewood box three feet square, covered with a mesh screen barely held in place with rocks and tennis shoes. An unexpected opportunity to study abroad for the spring semester had left the classmate looking frantically for someone to take care of her "mouse project." Paj volunteered.

"How could I say no?" Paj pleaded to Gertrude on behalf of two orphaned white mice. "Look at them."

Even though we helped Paj assure Gertrude and Vincent Clare that both mice were female—avoiding reproduction—you could tell they weren't as convinced as we were that there'd be no problem. They smelled big trouble in the beginning, but for as hard as they tried, they found no good reason to object. Paj's grand finale sealed the deal.

"Pleeeeeeeeeeeease," Paj begged, adding pathetically, "they have no one but me."

"Just keep them in the box," Gertrude warned, while grudgingly giving her approval. "Don't let them out. I want them kept in that box. Understand?"

"Understood," Paj said seriously, adding a bonus, "we'll keep them sealed in the box with the laundry room door closed." As if that would increase security.

The mice became our new friends. Only behind a closed laundry room door did we let them out of the box, feeding them Frosted Flakes and Cheerios, cheese, bread, and lettuce. With no success whatsoever, we even tried teaching them tricks. Within two weeks the laundry room turned into Disneyland with Minnie and Minnie, both of whom packed on the ounces from our smorgasbord of treats—so much so that we joked about Minnie virgin births. Well, *hardy-har-har*, the joke was on us.

I was with Paj the morning she checked on the mice and screamed.

"Kare, look!" she gasped, staring into the mouse house. "What are those little pink erasers?"

I looked into the box, leaning up close. "Oh my God, Paj," I said, "those little pink erasers are moving. They're babies!"

"They can't be," Paj moaned with a face full of disbelief. "They're girls."

"Well, one of them ain't," I said, laughing. "It's a miracle!"

We stared in disbelief at twelve tiny pink mice with big ears and long tails.

"Think I should tell Gertrude now?" Paj asked faintly. "Or do you want to?"

"I'll stay here and you go get her," I decided. "We'll break the news together."

A little crowd gathered by the time Gertrude and Paj arrived, with everyone oohing and aahhhing over the laundry room nativity. At the sound of Gertrude's unmistakably angry footsteps, the excitement stopped suddenly. Silence reigned when Gertrude entered the room and the crowd parted, allowing her access to the nursery. Paj followed as if in trance.

Before Gertrude had the chance to look in the box, we stood eye to eye as I announced softly, "We got babies."

She closed her eyes momentarily, collecting herself, as if to pray, "Don't let it be true."

"It's okay," I said mindlessly. "It'll all be okay."

Opening her eyes slowly, Gertrude leaned over the pine box and looked down at twelve squeaking baby mice.

"I don't believe it," Gertrude whispered to herself. Then, turning to us, she asked, "How did this happen?"

"One of the Minnie's was a Mickey," I said, grinning desperately. "It's a miracle!"

Gertrude didn't laugh. We braced for the worst and got a true miracle.

"Keep them in the box, and I mean it this time," Gertrude said with a proverbial slap on the wrist. "And you better make sure they can't get out . . ."

"I will," Paj said, feeling heartfully sorry, even though it wasn't anyone's fault. "I will. I will. I will." Paj kept repeating "I will," as if stuck in a bad dream that won't end. "I will . . . I will . . . I will . . ."

Everyone took an active role in the care and feeding of the "Two Blind Mice" family: cleaning the box, freshening the water, preparing meals, and supervising the exercise wheel to ensure that every mouse got a turn. Hearing of the miraculous multiple births, one of the convent maintenance men built a bigger box, supplying fresh wood shavings daily and a more secure screen cover. All manner of things went well in the mouse house as we watched the little ones grow. And once again, I was with Paj the morning she checked on the mice and screamed. I jumped.

"What!" I asked, startled. "You scared me."

At first I feared more babies because we may have left the males and females in the same box too long, but the look on Paj's face indicated something far more serious.

"Look," Paj said faintly, pointing first to the tennis shoe on the floor and then the lifted corner of the screen. "They're gone!"

"Gone?" I asked in mindless disbelief.

"All gone," Paj replied with dead certainty.

I looked in the ominously quiet box and whispered, "Fuck," the word we always feared would strike us dead and level the building but didn't.

The box was empty. Before a thought could come to mind, we heard angry footsteps approaching—unmistakably Gertrude's.

"She knows," I said, looking at Paj in terror, bracing for all hell to break loose.

Following Gertrude were the footsteps of all the other sisters in the vicinity, gathering outside the laundry room like bystanders after an accident.

"Sister Agnes Anne called," Gertrude yelled even before she saw us, eyes glazed and arms folded, as she tried to remain calm.

"There. Are. Mice. Running. All. Over. The. Kitchen," Gertrude announced slowly with fury, each word a complete sentence.

"Sorry—" we started to say, but got swiftly cut off.

"Wait!" Gertrude interrupted, with hands held up as if to stop us from speaking at all. "That's not the end of it."

Taking a deep breath, she continued in a voice cracking with anger.

"Sister Lillian called," she continued. "There are mice. In the convent infirmary. Sisters are screaming."

For fear of laughing out loud, I couldn't linger on the image of mice in the kitchen and old nuns screaming. I still have the tendency to laugh in the face of harmless disaster.

"Sorry . . ." we tried to say again, but she wouldn't hear it.

"They're wondering what's going on here!" Gertrude continued with mounting anger. "What do I say? What do you want me to tell them?"

Dead silence.

"That it'll never happen again?" Paj whispered sincerely, but it made us laugh.

"This is no laughing matter!" Gertrude shot back. "I told you to keep them in the box and you didn't. I want all of you to get over to the kitchen and the convent right now and apologize to Sister Agnes Anne, Sister Lillian, and the sisters. Then find the mice."

Dead silence.

"Find the mice?" I asked, thinking she couldn't be serious, "Really?"

"Every one of them!" Gertrude yelled with unmistakable serious-ness. "Every single one!"

There was no way I was going to argue the impossibilities of catch-ing fourteen white mice in a six-story building three city blocks wide, with a campus-wide tunnel system to boot. We stood there looking sorry, wanting to be forgiven, but Gertrude was having none of it. Brush-ing us out of the way with a sweep of her hand, she said, "Just go! Get out of here!"

With head bowed low, Gertrude walked back to her office and closed the door. She wanted us out of sight. Never before had we seen her that angry, and "Sorry" would never cut it.

"This is *B-I-G*," I said to the group, after hearing the office door slam. We stood stunned and stupid.

"Let's go," Paj said, snapping us out of it. "We got some 'Sorrys' to say."

About twenty of us marched to the kitchen, apologizing one by one to Sister Agnes Anne and the kitchen staff, then to Sister Lillian, the sisters, and the nurses in the convent infirmary. Regardless of the reprimand, nothing altered our consciousness over how funny the day really was. Stifling laughter was the hardest part of having to say "I'm sorry" with a serious face.

In a parade of sorry after sorry after sorry, we wandered the kitchen and convent pretending to look for mice and not finding any. Every now and then we'd hear a distant scream and burst out laughing over a mouse sighting, but as far as I know none were caught, thank God. We couldn't bear the thought of our semiprecious pets' being snapped to death in a trap or mercilessly poisoned. They weren't that kind of mouse.

Day after day we were given good reason to believe that all fourteen mice lived long happy lives. Random screams in the kitchen and convent erupted for months, with waves of disapproval washing over us with each sighting. Even though we cheered every live-mouse report, especially from the college (we speculated they returned to the bio lab to visit relatives), we paid dearly for that mistake.

"In community life, what you do affects more than you," Gertrude told us over and over. "You need to see that. This life is not about you. It's about all of us."

Those words were burned into our hearts by Sister Gertrude at an age when life is always about us. If we were to survive as sisters, we needed to live differently. We needed to see ourselves connected to every sister in the community, and "Two Blind Mice" lived on as a constant reminder. I did feel sorry for the sisters (and mice) whose lives were rudely disrupted for months. but I still think that unbeknown to us and behind closed doors, everyone surely must have laughed over how funny that day really was.

Years later, on a lakeside walk with Gertrude, I asked about the great mouse escapade.

"Truth be told," I said, recalling the incident, "didn't you really find the mice escape hysterically funny?"

Gertrude stopped and stared down at the sand in silence.

"Come on," I urged, "the squeals in the kitchen . . . the old nuns screaming . . . white mice sightings months later . . ."

Gertrude looked up at the sky, then out over Lake Michigan, then at me. She laughed. She never said yes or no, just laughed as though reliving every moment. That's the answer I longed to hear.

Two months before graduation we received news of where we'd be sent to work in September. The time had come in our "sister formation" to be sent to work in the proverbial vineyard; it was time for the young sisters to start making money. All year we hoped and prayed for jobs we knew how to do. Haunted by my past with Mother Octavia, I harbored hidden fears that I'd be sent to Flint, Michigan, to teach high school chemistry. An ominous cloud of fear hovered around all sisters of the Holy Cross on March 25, the Feast of the Annunciation—the day the Angel Gabriel announced to Mary that she was to be the Mother of God. For us, it was also Obedience Day.

We were supposed to find it supernaturally fitting for the Annunciation to coincide with Obedience Day, the date job assignments were announced for the upcoming year. Jobs were called "obediences" because of the expectation that we were to accept them on that day and every day thereafter (without whining) as the will of God, whether we liked it or not, just as Mary had accepted God's will. I dreaded my first Obedience Day with growing suspense, as the springtime date and college commencement drew near. Every day, over and over, I practiced the line "Let it be done unto me according to thy Word," praying to be Mary-like when the angel arrived with good or bad news about my first job. It's so easy to slip and say, "Let it be done unto me according to *my* Word.

That evening, March 25, we gathered in the recreation room for a special ceremony created by Gertrude and Vincent Clare. In the seriously funny spirit of a *Mission: Impossible* gathering, we took our weekly seats while Gertrude and Vincent took to their rockers. A table already set with wine, beer, cheese, crackers, and dip awaited the celebration to come. Only after a meditative reading of the gospel's "Beatitudes" did we receive our obediences; reminding us of the most important spiritual works—the divine attitudes we're called to embrace:

Blessed be the poor in spirit; everlasting life is theirs.
Blessed be the sorrowing; they shall find comfort.
Blessed be the lowly; they shall inherit the earth.
Blessed be those who hunger and thirst for justice;
they shall be satisfied.
Blessed be those who show mercy; mercy shall be theirs.
Blessed be the single-hearted for they shall see God.
Blessed be the peacemakers;
they shall be called "friends of God."
Blessed be those who suffer persecution for the sake of goodness;
heaven on earth is theirs.

The *Mission: Impossible* theme song played softly in the background on a poorly recorded cassette tape. Gertrude called us forward, one by one, announcing our "impossible mission" (should we decide to accept it). She and Vincent Clare sat before us with the radiant loving faces of guardian angels sending trainees to their first divinely appointed mission, as if giving us our wings.

"Sister Margaret Gallagher," Gertrude said, smiling while calling on Mugs, "your mission, should you accept it, is teaching history at Marian High School in Park Heights, Illinois."

"Thank you, Sister," Mugs said, accepting the letter formalizing the appointment and returning to her seat. "I accept."

"Sister Nancy Gros de Mange," Gertrude announced, as we applauded our house council president. "Your mission, should you accept it, is teaching fifth grade at Saint Charles in San Francisco."

That made Nance happy, since her family lived near.

"Sister Mary Ann Pajakowski," Gertrude called next. "Your mission, should you accept it, is teaching English and religion at Saint Mary's High School in Danville, Illinois."

One after another, my sisters were missioned near and far: California, Idaho, Utah, Virginia, and Maryland. All I cared about was going far away from Saint Mary's.

"Sister Karol Jackowski," Gertrude said, smiling warmly.

I stepped forward, trying not to burst into nervous laughter.

"Your mission, should you accept it, is teaching junior and senior religion and counseling freshmen at Saint Joseph High School, South Bend, Indiana."

"I'm going to the corner?" I blurted in shock, inciting laughter. "Everyone gets to leave and I'm going to the corner?"

Only I wasn't laughing. Saint Joseph High School was a six-block walk down the railroad tracks from Saint Mary's—really on the corner. I felt as if I wasn't going anywhere. While laughter continued for several minutes over my being "sent to the corner," I took my letter, sat down, and didn't say anything. I couldn't believe it. The job sounded great, but I knew nothing about Saint Joseph High School convent except that it was not much farther away than across the street. The excitement of travel was not destined to be part of my deal. I was still well within range of the Eye of the Beholder. Being "sent to the corner" ranked as one of the worst parts of my year.

I don't know how it happened exactly, but when I graduated from Saint Mary's College on May 31, 1969, with a B.A. in sociology, I felt ready to go, even if it was just to the corner. After five years of relative confinement at Saint Mary's, I wanted out. I wanted to see the world. I wanted new faces and new places away from the Eye of the Beholder. While the summer of 1968 began to ripen my Solemn Soul, the summer of 1969 completed it, making me exceedingly ready to move on.

Gertrude and I nearly came to blows and parted ways at the end of the year, which ripened my Solemn Soul considerably.

"I want to go to Woodstock this summer," I told Gertrude in spiritual direction.

"The retreat house?" she asked, referring to someplace I didn't know.

"No, no, no," I said, "the rock music festival . . . in upstate New York." She looked at me as if I were telling a joke.

"I'm serious," I said, prepared with a few fascinating facts. "This is a cultural event of the century. Last summer the place to be was Resurrection City. This summer it's Woodstock. I have to go. We need to be there."

"We do?" she said, hardly believing what she was hearing.

"I do," I said, as if seized with zeal. "What more suitable place for nuns to be than Woodstock? Thousands of young people . . ."

"Wait a minute," Gertrude interrupted in an effort to get real, asking, "what would you do there?"

"Volunteer!" I cheered, nearly jumping out of the chair. "They need people to cook, take care of children, serve meals—it's the opportunity of a lifetime. I have to go."

As a last resort, I preached about Jesus traveling to Woodstock alone because no nuns were allowed to go with him. Did she want that on her conscience?

"O Kare, Kare, Kare," Gertrude said delicately, not wanting to incite my hope or anger, "I don't think so . . ."

Triple "Kares" usually didn't bode well, especially given the circumstance.

"Oh, please, think about it a little," I said, begging. "Think about how maybe, just maybe, God's calling me there. Jesus wants company. At least think about it . . ."

"Okay, I will think about it," Gertrude said, patting my hand. "I'll pray about it. But remember, it's not me who makes the decision. Mother Octavia approves . . ."

"Oh well then, forget it!" I said, with instant anger. "There's no way that's going to happen."

"Let's pray over it anyhow," Gertrude suggested with a parting blessing. "Let's really pray."

Well, I did really pray and the answer I got was a big fat no. Gertrude expected me to pitch a fit and scream so she delivered the bad news on a nature trail walk in the middle of nowhere.

"Kare, you can't go to Woodstock," she said, giving it to me cold.

Not surprised but still disappointed, I suspected the Octavia curse.

"The Eye?" I asked, trying to remain calm.

"It's not only Mother Octavia," she said, trying to help me understand. "Though you're right, she'd never approve. It's me too, Kare. I don't think it's a safe place for you to be."

"Don't pay attention to all that news about drugs and sex," I said, wanting to defuse any argument. "I can take care of myself."

"It's much bigger than that," Gertrude explained. "I fear for your safety. I can't let you go."

Period.

I didn't go to Woodstock, and I was furious. For weeks I avoided Gertrude, refusing to speak to her. I don't recall what broke the ice, but by the end of the summer I thanked God she hadn't let me go. Pounded by weeks of rain, living conditions at Woodstock rivaled those of Resurrection City, and I would have died of misery. She spared me a once-in-a-lifetime horrendous experience. I still listen to and love the music of Woodstock, but every time I watch the documentary of the concert, I thank Gertrude out loud for not letting me go. She saved my life.

With Woodstock out of the summer plan, I envisioned a leisurely three months at Saint Mary's. I'd be packing up to move to the corner while sisters from all over the country came home for the summer. There'd be a lot of new faces and, in those days, a variety of remarkable outfits. Every summer after changing the habit I looked forward to the annual fashion faux pas show of "nuns on parade."

"You think they're going to let us loaf all summer?" Paj asked upon hearing of my free-floating plan.

"Well, I volunteered for Woodstock," I said, as though that were a case in point, "and they won't let me go."

"Well, duh," Paj said, "you didn't really think . . . ?"

"Let's not discuss it," I interrupted. "It's a sore subject."

Once again Paj was right. Of course I wouldn't be left on my own all summer. Shortly after graduation, Gertrude called an important meeting, and I knew then that the summer was over. We gathered in the recreation room, seated in our now sacred circle. Gertrude looked nervous-happy, as though she knew in advance what our reaction would be but had to remain positive anyhow, for all our sakes.

"Since many of you expressed a desire to volunteer again this summer," Gertrude said, holding a typewritten list in her hand. "Mother Octavia has found some wonderful opportunities."

My heart sank. Not only did The Eye put a curse on Woodstock, but now I'd be sent to Siberia for the summer. I felt bad news coming like an approaching tsunami, and Gertrude made it sound as if I'd asked for it.

Gertrude, God love her, read our names and assignments like awards being given for some unknown excellence.

"Mary Ann Pajakowski," Gertrude announced with a smile, "Lake Leelanau, Michigan, working with migrant workers."

"Margaret Gallagher and Karol Jackowski," Gertrude continued, as if delivering even greater news, "Anderson, Indiana, Saint John's Hospital. Mugs will supervise candy-stripers, and Kare will microfilm medical records."

"That's not a wonderful opportunity," I blurted out, "that's punishment."

Everyone laughed but me. I didn't go on as I wanted to, but Mother Octavia was making sure that "those who were left" from Washington, D.C., paid more dues for the summer sins of 1968. Paj was exiled to northern Michigan to pick cherries with migrants at Camp Leelanau (which, by the way, she loved), while Mugs and I were banished to Anderson, Indiana.

"Candy-stripers, migrants, and microfilm is all I remember," I told Mugs and Paj after the meeting, feeling slightly sick.

"Well, pack your bags," Mugs said, looking equally ill, "we're going to Anderson."

"Why do I feel like we're being sentenced to prison work camp?" I asked.

"Because we are," Paj said, hopelessly. "We are."

The convent at Saint John's in Anderson is attached to the hospital, and every nun in the convent worked there. Saint John's was not a happy home, though Sister Felicia was a kind and excellent cook, and Sister Dorothy Marie, the hospital and convent accountant, welcomed us. She held the purse strings, gave us spending money, and was the only sister to pay attention to us. Every day I'd go to the kitchen for coffee, say "Good Morning" to whoever was there, and be looked at like someone who broke in to steal their food. I started every day feeling like a thief.

Mugs and I were the youngest by at least thirty years, and neither one of us hit it off with any of the sisters in the convent (except Dorothy). Our superior, Sister Angela, was president of the hospital and our job supervisor. Mugs and I felt she was the designated Eye of the Beholder for the summer. Angela had the judgmental taskmaster look we had come to know as The Eye, and in her presence it was fear at first sight.

Before starting our new jobs, we met in the office of the president. Mugs and I sat before an enormously cluttered administrator's desk, smiling at Sister Angela with the appearance of two eager young sisters reporting for duty.

"Well, let's see," she said, looking through yet another personal file. "One of you is Margaret Gallagher and the other Karol Jackowski. Is that correct?"

"Yes, sister," Mugs and I responded.

"And?" she asked, looking up, as if we were stupid.

"Oh," Mugs said, "I'm Margaret Gallagher."

"And I'm the other one," I said, urging a little laughter; then added quickly, "I'm Karol Jackowski."

Sister Angela didn't even crack a smile. After continuing to record educational information and social security numbers, she reached the final question.

"And you are how old?" she asked, looking at me.

"Twenty-four," I said proudly, as if I finally got one right.

"You are not!" Mugs blurted out.

"I am too!" I shot back, as if she was nuts.

"Sisters!" Sister Angela shouted, startling us.

"Sister Karol," she said, giving me The Eye. "What year were you born?"

"Nineteen forty-six," I said, as if proving my point. "December 10."

Mugs laughed out loud, and then quickly apologized.

"Sister Karol, if you were born in 1946, you are twenty-two years old," Sister Angela said, exasperated. "You'll be twenty-three in December."

"Oh," I said, feeling exceedingly stupid, "Thank you, Sister." I could hardly explain that for some reason, I never know how old I am. I'm always off by a few years—and always older.

In a neon-lit closet with no windows, I sat on a folding chair eight hours a day, feeding thousands of medical records, page by page, into a fancy copy machine. Mugs supplied me with snacks and water on her rounds, while I entertained myself reading clinical details of medical procedures. I excelled at my job, doing ten times the work expected. Even so, I felt punished by the time there.

Not only was working in a closet with toxic fumes from copy toner a life-threatening nightmare but going home to the convent usually made every day worse. Mugs and I really felt like felons on a work release program, coming back to prison every night. While no one in the convent admitted it, we were actually grounded for the summer. Unlike the other sisters at Saint John's, we had no access to any of the three cars; nor did sisters invite us out with them, not even to the grocery store. Our unspoken rule of the summer was "Work, eat, then go to your room."

Some sisters never spoke to us, not even around the dinner table. In fairness to those who did, I admit that it wasn't just us who got the silent treatment. During our stay, several sisters weren't on speaking terms, and two nuns hadn't spoken to each other in over a year. Imagine living that way. And for all the talking that did occur at the dinner table, there was no real communication. No one asked "How was your day?" and nothing of interest or consequence was ever discussed. Typical dinner table conversation went something like this:

"Well, that was some storm we had last night," Sister Benedicta said. She talked only about weather. "Knocked my violets to the floor . . ."

"And someone left a car window open," Sister Joan Ann added. "The seat was soaked when I got in this morning."

"Did you fill the tank?" Sister Casmira asked, clearly with an agenda.

"Yes, I filled the tank!" Joan Ann shot back, with an agenda of her own.

"Well, I was just asking," Casmira answered, ticked. "Because last Wednesday I got in the car and the tank was empty."

With hate in her heart, Joan Ann looked ready to stab Casmira with the steak knife.

"Did you see the price of gas?" Sister Amata announces, always desperate to derail conflict. "I think we should try to cut back."

"I can't cut back," Sister Dolores, who rarely spoke out, responded, "I need a car for home visits."

"What about carpools?" Sister Amata continued. "I hear they really work."

"Well, they wouldn't work for me," Dolores declared once and for all.

"The violets can't be saved . . ." Sister Benedicta mumbled, picking up where she left off at the start. Shaking her head, she kept mumbling, "Can't be saved . . ."

On and on and on, day after day, streams of unconsciousness crossed at the dinner table like ships in the night. Sometimes no one talked at all, indicating they were all mad about something. Mugs and I sat at the end of the table, our designated space, whispering to each other. It's not that we didn't want to share; I just didn't want to engage. I always feel it's best to avoid personal contact with some kinds of craziness, and that convent was loaded with it.

"Maybe we should try to make the conversation more interesting," Mugs suggested, feeling somewhat responsible.

"I'm not going there, Mugs," I said, when we considered talking about world events. "I think it's better not to say anything. Don't speak unless spoken to. Let 'em go. We're just visiting."

After dinner the remarkable insanity continued. Everyone headed for one of a dozen reserved La-Z-Boy chairs parked in a semicircle before a big-screen color TV. For me and Mugs, it was standing room only unless we brought in a dining room chair, which we didn't. With talking and laughing outlawed in the TV room, the sisters watched game shows and sitcom reruns in silence. That ruled us out, but we didn't want to be there anyway. What good is a recreation room if you can't recreate? Mugs and I couldn't even pretend to live that way.

To entertain ourselves after dinner, we frequently went to the physical therapy lab in the hospital. The staff befriended Mugs and me and looked forward to our therapy sessions. We blew off steam on the treadmill, pretending to run as fast as we could out of Anderson. On our list of "what we hate in Anderson," Saturday evenings ranked as most dreadful. Not only were we confined to the house, but everyone was required to watch *The Lawrence Welk Show* because one of the sisters knew his family. That did it for me. I'd rather go to sleep before sunset. Every Saturday night after dinner I'd ask Sister Angela for permission to go to bed early, feigning weariness after a stressful work week.

"You may go," she'd say, as if exceedingly pleased over the success of her "beholder" duties in having us asleep by 9:00 P.M.

In the entire eight-week internment, we left the convent twice. Because we weren't allowed out on our own, Sister Dorothy Marie volunteered to chaperone. Once we drove to the Dairy Queen for banana splits, and once to the grocery store for snacks—the holy grail of St. John's Convent.

"What's the big deal about snacks?" I asked Dorothy on our first of two field trips.

She explained that the convent kitchen was off-limits between meals. Sister Felicia, the house cook, kept a meticulous inventory with no pity for the fool who snuck food without permission. Snacks were available in a dining room cupboard, some labeled with sisters' names so no one else would take it. It looked as if everybody had her own food. I'd never seen anything like it. Even Mugs, who grew up in a family of twelve, found it unusual.

"There goes another one," we'd say with every bit of nun nuttiness we witnessed, "right over the cuckoo's nest."

In helping prepare a summer survival kit, Dorothy took us to the supermarket to stock up on snacks. She stretched the trip to include a city tour. At that point, even Anderson felt like New York City. She felt as sorry for us as we did, agreeing that we were unjustifiably incarcerated, and she offered to do what she could to help. From day one, Dorothy appeared to be someone we could talk to honestly.

"How can you live like this?" I asked her the minute we got in the car and cleared the convent grounds. "No one speaks. They don't like each other. . . ."

"I can see why," Mugs added. "You're the only likable one. The others are so miserable."

"Welcome to community living," Dorothy said. "It's not like Saint Mary's, is it?"

"Is it like this everywhere?" Mugs asked. "Are people that unhappy?"

"Some are," Dorothy said, adding, "and nearly every convent has them."

Mugs sank in the backseat, moaning, "Oh my God . . ."

"What do you do for fun and friends?" I asked, feeling sorrier for her than us. "How do you survive?"

"I have very good friends at the hospital," Dorothy explained. "They're my real community."

"Any of the nuns?" Mugs asked.

"Oh my, yes," Dorothy responded. "Only a few are mean and incorrigible. Some of us have lived together for ten years; we've grown on one another. Listen, if you want community, you can find it anywhere."

"But how can you live in that convent?" I asked again. "How can you come home to that insanity every night?"

"Get used to it, honey," Dorothy said. "Those are your sisters. That's community life."

After a summer's hell on earth in Anderson, Mugs and I returned to Saint Mary's. The night before we left, there was no going-away party like the one we had in D.C. with Maurice, Mel, and Ann. Mugs and I left St. John's Convent the same way we arrived: without notice. We returned to Saint Mary's with horror stories of community life in miserable convents, terrified over what likely awaited us in the year ahead—an abysmal experience the likes of which we had just got a glimpse.

In retrospect, I can see that we were put in the worst convents that summer for a reason; it was an internship in the harsh reality of community life. For five years we lived happily ever after in a community of peers, but now we faced convents where we'd be a minority of one; our friends would not be with us. We each stood alone before the abyss we faced in the year to come. In the summer of 1969 we returned to Saint Mary's from our prison work camps as college graduates with most Solemn Souls, fully ripened and ready to go.

Our year ended just as it began, with Gertrude and Vincent Clare meeting each of us with a welcome-home group hug, then announcing immediate departure to Lakeside. Unlike the previous year, we returned with good reports from the designated summer "Eyes." We must have been good because the Beholder didn't demand to see any of us. Even so, Gertrude knew how difficult the summer had been (I was still angry over not being at Woodstock), and she wanted us to spend our last days together at Lakeside. Before parting ways, Gertrude and Vincent wanted us to return to the beginning, to reflect on the best and worst parts of year, and prepare for the new life ahead.

After five years of seeing one another day and night, we were together at Lakeside like war buddies about to be split up. We didn't need to plan our days because by then we knew the group's flow of when to move, what to do, and where to go. What I'll never forget are the nights around the fire—on the beach or in the cabin during a thunderstorm. We sipped beer and wine, talking dreamily and sharing the best and worst parts of the year. We knew one another so well by then that we told the same story, adding something only we remembered.

In response to Gertrude's asking me the best part of my year, everyone yelled and cheered when I said *Mission: Impossible*.

Watching television began as a big bone of contention between us and Gertrude from day one. We wanted the freedom to watch anything at any time, and Gertrude vetoed the idea.

"You need to be studying or relaxing with one another," she said, "not watching TV."

"But some shows are very good," I countered, pushing for any TV time more than the nightly news, which we already watched. "How about if we watch one or two shows together? You know, like a community TV night?"

"What if someone doesn't want to watch your show?" Gertrude asked.

"They don't have to," I said, "but that's not even a problem because we already have consensus on one show."

"Which is?" Gertrude asked, looking trapped.

"Mission: Impossible!" we yelled, startling Gertrude and Vincent, who both burst out laughing.

"Just give it a chance," I begged. "Watch it once and see for yourself. You'll love it."

We had a lot riding on the season premiere of *Mission: Impossible*. Fifteen minutes before showtime, the crowd gathered and rearranged the furniture around the TV. Crackers and cheese, along with chips, dips, and pretzels, topped TV tables scattered between the chairs. Two reserved rocking chairs sat front row center, giving Gertrude and Vincent Clare unobstructed viewing pleasure. They promised to arrive with a surprise, heightening the suspense.

Seated and ready, we yelled down the hallway for all stragglers because the opening minutes of *Mission: Impossible* are essential. In the first sixty seconds, an agent finds the cassette tape describing the impossible mission (should they decide to accept it); then the tape suddenly disintegrates. We wanted Gertrude and Vincent fully focused.

"Here we come!" they said.

In they walked with a cooler of ice cold beer and big bowls of fresh popcorn. What could our Jesus do more?

"We brought the party!" Vincent said, grinning and holding up a beer to an outburst of cheers.

"No mission is impossible for us!" Gertrude added, laughing out loud when she saw the rocking chairs. "Look at the chairs set up for the old ladies," Gertrude said, pointing to the rockers.

"Come on, sisters, get in," I said, taking each by the elbow, ushering them to their seats. "I'll even give you a little push to get you started."

That night was one of the best of my life, not only because of what happened at that moment but because of what that night turned into. *Mission: Impossible* became the highlight of our week. Every episode, regardless of how incredible, showed how to overcome insurmountable obstacles and be fully ready in seven days for something more difficult. Working as a team, the M.I. agents modeled community survival skills under extreme circumstances. Becoming the theme of our year, *Mission: Impossible* symbolized everything we hoped for and feared about life after college.

Within weeks, our favorite TV show turned into a community holy hour otherwise known as Beer Night. Gertrude and Vincent surprised us weekly with beer or wine and snacks. While attendance was never mandatory, no one missed a night; some even cut class-required lectures for an evening of *Mission: Impossible*. What began as a favorite TV show turned into an enchanted evening. We made a flexible rule of no talking during the show, but during commercials we'd discuss the status of the mission as though the outcome depended on our input. We laughed so much on those nights, falling asleep with some moral to the story given to us by Gertrude and Vincent. Every night after the show they left us with pithy little sayings, "weekly words to live by," such as "Nothing is impossible for those who believe," "When the going gets tough, call your sisters," and "When life gives you lemons, make vodka lemonade."

Throughout the year, such small events stood for such big feelings. Like the night—after constant begging by Sisters Gretchen and Suzanne—Gertrude let us watch the Academy Awards. It was the year Barbra Streisand tied for the Oscar for best actress in *Funny Girl*. She wore a black dress that turned transparent from the stage lights. Live on national television, Barbra Streisand appeared nearly nude, and we saw it happen.

While I learned several big life lessons that year in the juniorate, it was the everyday blessings that ripened me most. A sweet richness grew among us, week after week around the TV, into what felt like the true sacrament of sisterhood. On those nights, without a doubt, God was with us in the pleasure of our company, the show, the running viewer commentary, the endless laughter, and the "weekly words to live by." Those are the magic ingredients that nourish souls on levels deeper than anyone on the outside can possibly know or imagine.

On our last day together at Lakeside, we planned a vow-renewal ritual on the beach at sunset. We built a fire, surrounding it with nineteen stones facedown—one for each of us—and each one painted with a gift or a fruit of the Holy Spirit.* We also made little tinfoil boats big enough to hold a votive candle and wrote our wish for the new year on a small piece of paper.

Nancy strummed "The Water Is Wide" on her guitar, while we put heartfelt wishes in our tin boats, lit the candles, walked out into the water, and set the boats on a receding wave. They looked like a fleet of souls sent off to the unknown land of the year ahead. Then we renewed vows for three years. As in the peace pipe ceremony at a powwow, we each picked a stone from around the fire. (I got Long Suffering and wanted to trade it for another but couldn't.) Then each of us recited the following formula, handwritten and signed on white lined paper, while the others softly hummed the melody of "Ave Maris Stella":

In the name of the Father and of the Son and of the Holy Spirit. In the name of our Lord Jesus Christ and under the protection of Mary, His Immaculate Mother, ever Virgin, Mother of Sorrows, I, Sister Karol Ann Jackowski, make for three years the simple vows of poverty, celibacy, and obedience, in the Congregation of the Sisters of the Holy Cross, promising to persevere in it for three years, in the exercise of the

---

*According to Catholic teaching, the seven gifts of the Holy Spirit are Wisdom, Understanding, Counsel, Fortitude, Knowledge, Piety, and Fear of the Lord. The twelve fruits of the Holy Spirit are Charity, Joy, Peace, Patience, Benignity, Goodness, Long Suffering, Mildness, Faith, Modesty, Continence, and Chastity.

employments which, according to the Constitutions, my superiors may
assign me. Such are the obligations which I take before God and in the
presence of Sister Gertrude who accepts them in the name of God and
of the Congregation of the Sisters of the Holy Cross. Amen.

Then into God's hands we commended our spirit, and called it a night.

A strange, sacred sadness swallowed us on our return to Saint Mary's, a culmination of denied separation anxiety that had been building all summer. The time we dreaded for so long had come. The following day we began parting ways. Because I wasn't going anywhere that warranted bus, train, or air travel, I endured every tearful good-bye at the South Bend airport with Gertrude and Vincent at my side. I was the last to leave.

Two days later, after taking me out to lunch as though it was our last supper, Gertrude and Vincent dropped me off at the Saint Joe High School Convent parking lot, nearest to the convent entrance.

"I'm scared," I said, sniffling and whining, wanting them to save me from I-don't-know-what.

"Oh, go on," Gertrude said, "you'll be fine! They'll love you."

"And we'll see you next week at the picnic," Vincent added, referring to the annual welcome picnic for new postulants. "We're just up the street, you know."

The divine comedy of that particular moment made me laugh.

"Don't remind me—it's too depressing," I said, bemoaning the closeness of Saint Mary's. "In five years, I've gone nowhere."

"Now, that's not true," Gertrude said, trying to make me feel stronger than I did.

"You know that's not true," Vincent added, cheering me on.

"You're right," I admitted, lifting my suitcase, "that's not true."

With greater clarity, I added, "In five years, I've gone to the corner."

chapter seven

approaching forever

Get a hold of yourself! It is I. Don't be afraid.

—JESUS, MATTHEW 14:27

I t's a good thing I couldn't see my future in 1969. If I knew then, at the age of twenty-four, that I wouldn't get past the corner until 1991, I would have pulled an immediate Ellen Gibson, changed clothes, waved good-bye, and ended the story there.

I arrived at Saint Joe's High School Convent two weeks before school started, wanting enough time to get settled personally and prepared professionally. I felt like a freshman with first-year jitters, needing to "get a hold of myself," pull myself together before the school year began. My whole life was packed into one suitcase, several boxes, and a trunk—all of which appeared neatly stacked in the corner of my new room, which I called Cinder Block #203. Built in 1953—the bomb shelter era—of yellow brick and gray cinder block, the two-story, flat-roofed concrete convent stood like a walled-in fortress plopped down on the northwest corner of U.S. 31 and Angela Boulevard, one of the busiest intersections in South Bend. I lived there for two strange years.

A ten-foot-high yellow brick wall surrounded the convent. I suppose the intent of the brick was to block out noise (which sort of worked), as well as to provide privacy for cookouts and sister sunbathers (which rarely worked). The wall was most effective in daring students to jump up for a peek at nuns in shorts and bathing suits. And every time that happened, Sister Edna, the freshman English teacher, yelled, "I'm calling the police!" That, of course, only served to escalate the student challenge, making matters far worse. The "nun-wall jump" became a varsity sport with points awarded for whom you saw: the older the nun, the more points awarded. For example, I'd probably be a 1, whereas Edna would be a definite 10, or more. She may even have been an instant win.

Since I was living on the second floor, my room faced U.S. 31, the Notre Dame golf course, and round-the-clock traffic, including a caravan of semis headed south. After a week of restless nights, I realized the youngest sisters in the house got the noisiest rooms. That didn't bother me, but sleeplessness did. I need sleep. I love sleep. Now I even work in bed. It took months before I slept through the night; and even then, if there was an accident (and there were many), nights were endless. After five years of being able to hear pins drop at night, I suddenly felt as if I slept in a turning lane. I began the school year very tired and really didn't get much rest until the end of Notre Dame football season.

At the crack of dawn on home football weekends, horn-honking traffic backed up outside my bedroom window for miles in every direction. Rabid Notre Dame fans could easily sit in cars for hours with nothing to do but stare at our convent and honk the horn in order to whip up Fighting Irish frenzy; some horns honked the school song. That was my alarm clock. On those loud weekends, everyone became a Notre Dame fan, whether you wanted to or not.

As a reminder to drivers that someone lived within earshot of their honking, I often thought of doing little shows or posting inspirational messages in my bedroom window, but I never dared. We lived too close to The Eye. Still haunted by the Augusta Hall curtain incident, I had learned the lesson, but the temptation lingered.

Similar in design to a cellblock, the convent's bedroom floor was a rectangle of twelve bedrooms lining the perimeter of the second floor. Instead of a guard station in the center, there were two sets of shared bathrooms, each accommodating six sisters. Nine of us lived up there in 1969. Spare rooms were used by sister visitors but never friends or relatives. It would be another ten years before that changed, and in some convents bedroom floors remain cloistered. No outsiders allowed.

Our concrete rooms measured approximately eight by ten feet; they were equipped with bed, dresser, closet, sink, desk, bookcase, and chair. Each room's walls were painted in strange colors. My room was such a sad shade of blue that when I walked in for the first time and sat on the bed, I started to cry. I walked the edge of tears all day, but that weeping blue room pushed me over the edge. The next day I repainted the sad blue cinder blocks white. It took four coats to cover up all that sadness. All went well with white until I woke up the next morning, stood at the sink, looked in the mirror, and got the queasy feeling of gas station bathrooms. On the third day I mixed white paint with a little too-bright yellow, making a mellow yellow I called Sunshine; and that's the color it stayed.

All interior walls were constructed with cinder block, each painted with some pastel mystery shade of pale green, sad blue, too-bright yellow, blah beige, or Pepto-Bismol pink. Going from room to room on the guided house tour made me feel dizzy and slightly nauseated, especially when we began with the pink guest parlor on the ground floor, a strange little square airless room with plastic plants, a tabletop statue of Mary, cobalt-blue Naugahyde lounge chairs, and a wall-hung shiny gold crucifix. If I'd been a guest, I wouldn't have wanted to stay long.

Also on the first floor were the superior's office, a huge stainless-steel kitchen, and a bright dining room with one long table seating twelve. The south wall of the dining room and community room (one opened into the other) was floor-to-ceiling glass, letting in precious sunlight and a well-manicured lawn with gardens of flowers and plants. Either at the dining room table or in one of many La-Z-Boy recliners in the community room, you could look out on the walled-in backyard at a rose garden and tomato plants. It was a little patch of paradise. When the automatic sprinklers turned on and wouldn't turn off, we called the yard Walled-in Pond.

Two bedrooms were located on the first floor, near the chapel; one was for the superior and one for Sister Bernadetta (Bernie), the school librarian, who suffered terribly with emphysema and couldn't climb stairs. Sister Angela, assistant principal at the school, lived in the superior's room to help take care of Bernie. When Ange was away, we all kept a constant eye on her. Everyone loved Bernie and Bernie genuinely loved everyone.

My favorite room in the house (besides my room) was the little stone chapel tucked in on the southeast corner of the building. I loved that we entered God's house through our house, the community room. The proximity of the chapel to where we ate, relaxed, and lived the rest of our life gave the first floor a strange hushed atmosphere. Sisters spoke in low tones, even whispered, creating an unwritten rule of silence, as though we might disturb God. I'm sure we already did, but not by talking and laughing.

I always felt the chapel was the still, silent heartbeat of the convent. While the youngest traditionally sat in the first pew, the superior always sat in the last, regardless of age, as if tending the flock. Being the youngest, I shared a slippery pew up front with Sister Mary Ann O'Neil, ten years my senior. Whoever waxed the oak pews for the Feast of the

Assumption overdid it: I nearly slipped to the floor, and had to put my feet on the kneeler to brace myself, a survival skill learned as a postulant in the Church of Loretto. In 1964, Mary Sue and I overwaxed the pews for Christmas and several old sisters slid down and couldn't get up. Solution to the slippery pew slide: feet-on-kneeler brace.

The simple oak altar looked like an old dining room table with a long plain white tablecloth. Two small side altars enshrined wooden carved statues of Mary and Joseph, illuminated by the warm glow of votive candlelight. Thanks to the sacristan, Sister Edna, there were always live plants or bundles of fresh flowers at their feet (donated by local funeral homes). At least God's house was filled with more wood, flowers, and candlelight than concrete, making divine warmth palpable. In addition to the room of my own, that was the only other room in the house about which I could say there was a *there* there.

The sisters I lived with that year were a motley mix, some clinically dysfunctional. In those days, dysfunction was more the norm in community life than the exception. After decades of living secluded lives in silence, antisocial behavior was all some nuns knew. They didn't know how to carry on an interesting conversation, speak to laypersons without condescension, or disagree respectfully. Disagreement of any kind was phase one to full-blown conflict, which must be suppressed, no matter what. God forbid that there ever be differences among us. What would people think? After centuries of living together, we were incapable of building community and unable to accept diversity and love one another as sisters. A banner I made hung on the wall at the foot of my bed: GOD BLESS OUR UNHAPPY HOME.

Complicating any real chance of community life is the fact that sisters were assigned to convents because of their jobs at schools or hospitals, not because of personal compatibility or liability. For example, when I received the job at Saint Joe High School, it was a foregone conclusion that I'd live in the school's convent. We went where the job was and lived with whoever else ended up in the same place. Sometimes you hit the jackpot and got a great group of women, as we did at Saint Peter's; other times you end up in convents like the one in Anderson. Saint Joe's was not unlike Anderson in that both were the painful living consequence of random selection.

Sister Johanna, I learned on my first day at Saint Joe's, was "superior in absentia"—meaning she didn't live with us. Even though our community lives had normalized considerably by 1969, it was unheard of that anyone would live somewhere else, much less the superior. But Jo did. She worked at the high school as dean of girls, ate lunch and dinner with us, and then went to Saint Mary's, where she stayed with a friend who taught at the college, Sister Lucille.

I found this out on the first day after my welcome barbeque dinner and party in the backyard, behind the wall. Like a good young sister, I was helping with clean-up when Jo called me to her office and closed the door. The cinder-block office, painted beige, didn't look lived in at all: no papers or mail on the desk, no notepads or pens, no coffee cup, no plants, and, most telling of all, no telephone. This was the office of no one at all.

Jo was in her forties and looked blank and a little wild-eyed, as if she couldn't get out of there fast enough—the picture of someone who'd be writing postcards from the edge.

"How are you doing, hon?" she asked, grabbing her purse from behind the desk. "Is everything okay? Need anything? Do you have enough money?" she asked in rapid succession.

"I'm mostly tired," I said, wanting to let her (and me) go. "It's all pretty overwhelming."

"Once you get unpacked and settled, you'll feel much better," she said, clearly distracted while digging in her purse for car keys.

"I'm sure I will," I responded, not wanting to keep her. "Thank you for asking."

"Listen, hon," she said, handing me a white card with a handwritten phone number on it. "If you need me, here's the number. But I'll see you in school on Monday."

Not knowing what to say because I didn't understand what she was telling me, I stared at the number and mumbled, "That's fine."

"I'll explain it all to you someday," she said, almost teary-eyed. Noting my confusion yet anxious to leave, she added, "I don't live here. I can't. I stay at Saint Mary's."

I was stunned. All I could say was, "Oh."

What I wanted to do was yell, "You can't live here? What do you mean? You're the superior!" At that point, I only wanted her to leave. She looked as if she was beginning to fall apart, and I didn't want that to happen in front of me.

"Take this," Jo said, slipping twenty bucks into my jacket pocket. "I'll see you Monday."

It was 8:00 P.M. when Sister Johanna walked out the door, into her car, and drove off to Saint Mary's. (How she owned her own car, I didn't know, but she did, and no one seemed to object.) On the first night of real convent life, my new superior told me living conditions in the house were so unbearable that she couldn't stay there. It felt as though she said, "Welcome to Saint Joe's. I'm having a nervous breakdown. Here's twenty dollars. Take care."

Sisters Rosella and Mary Ann waited for me in the community room with three glasses, a bowl of pretzels, and what was left of a big jug of wine. Rose was a sixtysomething bundle of joy with a keen sense of humor and a heartwarming laugh that I found to be infectious. She taught remedial English at the high school, and the students adored her. Mary Ann was taller than I, and Sister Bernadetta called both of us a "tall drink of water." She taught Spanish, was blessed with an operatic singing voice, and was closest to me in age. Both would become lifesaving friends.

"She doesn't live here," I said, chuckling in disbelief. "What's up with that?"

"What did she tell you?" Rose asked, pouring me a glass of wine while Mary Ann pulled up a La-Z-Boy chair, breaking the perfectly formed semicircle of recliners around the TV. Everyone else went to chapel or to bed.

"She wanted to know if I needed anything," I told them. "Then she gave me a phone number where I could reach her, and slipped twenty bucks into my pocket."

After taking a big gulp of wine while easing into a recliner, I added, "She said she can't live here . . ."

Rose and Mary Ann looked at each other, turned to me, and spent the next three hours sipping wine and helping me feel welcome.

"How can they appoint someone in Jo's condition to be superior?" I asked. "She clearly can't do it."

"That's another story for another night," Rose said.

"But not tonight," Mary Ann said, "I'm beat."

"Well, this place seems like a real nuthouse," I said. "How do you survive?"

"Like this!" Mary Ann said, "We get together like this and laugh."

"Well then, I'm in," I concluded. "This I can definitely do."

That was my true welcome to Saint Joe High School Convent. And in a pure act of divine intervention, Sister Rosella lived on one side of me in Cinder Block #202 and Mary Ann on the other side in Cinder Block #204. They felt like guardian angel bookends. Knowing that they were there, I wasn't as scared as I was when the day began. I saw the mess I moved into clearly, but I didn't feel alone.

Eleven and a half of us lived in Saint Joe High School Convent in 1969; the half being our superior in absentia. Adding significantly to the strangeness of the situation was the fact that I lived with two of my high school teachers: Sister Mariella (originator of the Rat Test) and Sister Marita (biology), neither of whom I had gotten along with very well.

"It's not fair!" I told Gertrude after she informed me in June whom I'd be living with. "No one should have to live with former high school teachers. That's cruel and unusual punishment. It's not right."

"But they're not your teachers anymore," Gertrude said, "they're your sisters."

"They're both!" I shot back, clarifying my point. "That's too weird to live with."

"Well, start getting used to it, Kare," she said. "Someday you may have to live with a former Superior General."

That silenced me. I nearly fainted at the thought.

I remembered that conversation when I arrived, but it made no difference. They were still my teachers, especially since they'd be voting on me for final profession. For me, the whole year was one long daily exam. Before final profession, every professed sister you lived with was sent a form by the Superior General to vote on whether or not they'd want to live with you forever and ever, amen. (But we didn't get to vote on them.) One dissenting vote could kick you out. Once again, my high school teachers would be grading me. Sister Mariella continued to treat me like a fifteen-year-old with ratted hair, and Marita rarely spoke to anyone at all, including me. All year part of me felt as if I was still in high school.

Leveling off the strangeness in our convent were Sisters Bernadetta, Clare, and Marie Bernard—the silent saints among us—all in their sixties. Bernie worked part-time in the high school library, Clare taught remedial math and English, and Marie Bernard was our housekeeper. While we worked outside the convent, Marie worked inside, keeping things spotless. If I came home during the schoolday for a moment of peace and quiet, Marie joined me with coffee and cookies. Since Marie was home alone all day, I imagined she talked to angels. She always looked as if she did, since she had pure white curly hair, an everlasting smile, and a face that radiated kindness.

Clare lived around the corner from me in Cinder Block #201. Her room was full of flowering plants that she sang and talked to long before the rest of the world discovered the benefits of doing this. Every evening Clare stopped by my room to ask how I was, stayed for exactly fifteen minutes, and parted with the mutual promise that we'd pray for each other. After Clare left, my day felt blessed.

Bernie was the angel living beneath me. I could hear her at night gasping for air, and Angela rising to help her. I'm sure the whole house woke with Bernie, praying that the agony would end. Every breath Bernie took was a struggle to bring in air and let it out, yet she never complained or whined. Bernie showed how to grow old with dignity, which I hoped to do someday.

Marie, Clare, and Bernie showed me nothing but extraordinary kindness and heartfelt concern, possibly overcompensating for how mistreated and abused I was by Sister Edna's daily reprimands. She was what I called the convent queen of mean, and she appointed herself my personal Eye of the Beholder. She drove me nuts. At least once a day Edna pulled me aside to correct something. My skirt was too short, my veil too sheer and revealing, and my classes too loud and rowdy.

"It sounds like a party in there," she said one day, pulling me out of a particularly enjoyable religion class. Edna stood there shaking her head in disapproval while waiting for an explanation, as though she was my boss.

"You call that religion?" she asked with biting sarcasm.

I actually did call that religion, but I never said what I wanted to say to her face. She didn't scare me, but she did have a vote on my future and I didn't want to give evidence of insubordination.

"Thank you for telling me, sister," I'd say, calling all angels to hold my tongue.

Sister Angela and others often intervened in my defense when Edna picked on me in public. Even Sister Ann Francis, who bore her own brand of passive-aggressive unkindness, stood up for me on occasion (like when she needed a ride to the mall).

When I'd complain about Ann, Bernie defended her, saying, "Oh, but she does so many acts of kindness."

What I wanted to say was, "Those aren't acts of kindness, they're 'acts of Ann Francis,' " but I didn't. I was not about to cast that stone.

Any personal endorsement of me by other sisters infuriated Edna. She'd stomp up to her room and slam the door. Sister Angela was my constant defender. I hugged Ange in gratitude every time for saying what I wanted to say to Edna but couldn't. Being assistant principal of the school, Ange became the virtual superior in the convent, and she smiled like an angel at everything I did and said. That kind of sisterly love continued throughout my life until the day Ange died.

Looking back, I thank God for putting so many angels into the divinely mad mix of nuns at Saint Joe's. Without angels at my side that year, I surely would have bolted, either begging for a room at Saint Mary's or calling a taxi to the South Shore train station and going home. Those angels saved my soul.

Our school days began with morning prayer and mass in the chapel at 6:30, followed by breakfast. Sister Mariella cooked a hot breakfast daily and generally took charge of the kitchen—the importance of which she exaggerated greatly and took much too seriously. For example, if you were in the kitchen between meals, Mariella demanded to know why. She could be sound asleep and still hear the fridge door open or the pantry door close, causing her to jump up and nab the culprit. No one was allowed in the kitchen when Mariella cooked, until she called for the servers; even then, we could enter only one by one. A crowded kitchen was the setting for disaster, the likes of which I witnessed several times.

Anything relative to food or the kitchen needed Mariella's approval. I knew that better than most because I was assigned the dreadful task of taking her grocery shopping—always a "young sister" job. If I slipped something into the cart, like Popsicles, she'd make me take it back, then reprimand me like a five-year-old about staying close to her and the cart and not getting anything not on her list.

"We can't afford it," she'd tell me.

I never said anything at the time, but we were talking about ninety-nine cents. I could have afforded that. When we got home and I carried in the groceries, she'd stand there as I unpacked bag after bag, showing me where to put everything, as though I couldn't figure it out on my own. Every kitchen cupboard was labeled with its contents. Mariella went crazy with the labeler, sticking black plastic strips on every cupboard: CUPS, DISHES, GLASSES, CANNED GOODS, PAPER PRODUCTS, JUICE, etc. She'd call for a house meeting if, God forbid, a can of peas appeared in the JUICE cupboard.

The biggest problem with Mariella and the other convent bullies was that no one challenged them. Mariella became a kitchen bully because the community let her. I was in no position to be the first to take her on, at least not until I was finally professed. She too had a vote that I needed.

Depending on class schedules, some ate breakfast quickly in order to be in school by 8:00 A.M., whereas others sat around leisurely, reading the morning paper or chatting with the chaplain, who usually stayed for a good Mariella breakfast. To her credit, she was a very good cook, making divine buttermilk biscuits, even though she obsessed over things like butter.

I was in a hurry one morning, sitting down at the end of the table, wanting to just grab toast and coffee. I took a piece of toast, buttered it, spread jam on it with somebody's homemade raspberry preserves, and savored the first bite as Mariella screamed.

"*Crumbs in the butter?*" she shrieked. "*Crumbs in the butter?*"

I choked on my toast, as if I was maybe swallowing material evidence. Everyone at the table froze, then turned and looked at me.

"What'd I do?" I asked, sipping water to stop choking.

"*Crumbs in the butter!*" Mariella repeated, walking over to me with evidence in hand. All eyes followed her.

"Did you do this?" she asked, in a full-blown reprimand. I had seen that angry face many times in high school. Suddenly I felt like fifteen.

"Do what?" I asked, looking at a stick of butter on a plate.

What I did was leave toast crumbs behind while buttering my bread: a class A felony in Mariella's kitchen. Of course, I should have cut square patties and put them on my plate before buttering the bread, thereby avoiding the contamination of communal butter with my crumbs.

Bless me, Father, for I have sinned.

Not only did I leave crumbs in the butter but, in her eyes, I also mutilated it. Because the butter was hard rather than cut into thick unspreadable little squares, I skimmed thin slices off the top, making a little dip in the butter's surface, giving it the wide U-slope of a skateboard ramp.

"And that!" she said, pointing at the dip in horror. "That is NOT what convent butter looks like."

I almost laughed in her face at this, but I was now savvy enough to know not to. At that moment Mariella represented nothing other than one vote I really needed.

Just get up and go, I thought, as though prompted by angels.

"I'm sorry," I said, standing up to leave, trying desperately not to laugh, "I have to go. It won't happen again. Have a good day, everybody."

With the exception of Sister Edna, everyone at the table that morning rolled their eyes and felt bad, telling me so throughout the day. It was not unusual for something disruptive to happen at the table, and I wasn't the only one who took refuge from convent insanity at school. We all had our turn leaving the table for one reason or another, and tended to bury misery with work. That's what happened in dysfunctional convents all over the country. If the living situation was unbearable, sisters spent as much time as they could at work, sometimes going back to school after dinner and not returning until late, when everyone would be asleep. O unhappy day.

A few sisters taught part-time, but those who worked full-time were usually gone from 8:00 A.M. to 5:00 P.M. We gathered for vespers—evening prayer—at 5:30 in the chapel, followed by dinner. Our evening meal, always a feast, was cooked by Lottie, the part-time chef, who also worked weekend nights as a lounge singer in Mishawaka. I adored Lottie and tried to get home from school early just to chat. We hit it off so well. Lottie, a single parent, raised a little girl with her mother's help. She placed her daughter's picture on the counter facing her as she cooked. Every day Lottie sang the blues while making dinner, my favorite song being her version of Nina Simone's "I Want a Little Sugar in My Bowl." But best and most memorable of all, Lottie had a gold front tooth with a cutout star.

"Wow! What is that?" I asked the moment we met.

"When I sing, the lights hit the gold and it sparkles," she said, smiling. I wanted one.

Lottie came to us with a wealth of southern cooking experience, making the most miraculous meat loaf and mashed potatoes, macaroni and cheese, pot roast, chicken-fried steak, corn chowder, ambrosia salad, banana cream pie, pineapple upside-down cake, and fudge-nut brownies. Most of us treated Lottie like a queen to make up for the abuse she suffered under the micro-supervision of Mariella and the condescending racist criticism of Ann Francis, both of whom treated her like an underprivileged teenage trainee.

Even our superior in absentia made it a point to give Lottie huge financial bonuses every now and then. She did that with me too, though I'm not sure why. For reasons I never questioned, Johanna kept giving me money—twenty dollars, fifty dollars, and if I went away for a weekend, two hundred dollars. I suppose, like a bad parent, she did so to soothe her guilt over her total absence in my young impressionable religious life, as though money would somehow cover it. I never cared about the money one way or another; it just felt strange. But Lottie really appreciated Johanna's generosity and, by her example, showed me how to do the same. Lottie was the superior I wished we had.

After dinner most of the sisters turned on the TV, sat back in their designated La-Z-Boy rockers, and then watched the news and game shows. Inevitably an argument erupted over someone's giving the answers too soon, as if to show how smart she was. Within the hour most stomped off to bed angry, leaving two or three behind, usually Mariella, Ann Francis, and Edna. They deserved one another, like just desserts.

After dinner and on weekends, I often went back to school for club meetings, athletic events, or to my office to prepare lesson plans. I taught junior girl's religion, and senior boy's (the football team) sociology. I hated lesson plans, but I never dared walk into a classroom without one. Every night I dreaded having to plan what I'd teach the next day. Something in me resisted the thought of planning today what I'd say tomorrow. I taught very well anyhow because I loved the kids and what we learned, but not even excellent student evaluations changed my mind about what I wanted to do next. Because so much of my own high school education happened outside the classroom, that's where I wanted to spend my time. That's the kind of teaching I did, counseling students the rest of the day. That's the kind of teaching I love.

Even in class we ended up discussing what happened the night before, an impromptu lesson plan I called "most current events." For example, junior girls lacked interest in learning about the "holy trinity," but they couldn't stop talking about the only thing that mattered day and night: parents, boys, and sex. And the football team couldn't care less about sociology, but they wanted to stay after class to continue discussing their big concerns: parents, girls, and sex. That was the trinity that junior girls and senior boys wanted to talk about endlessly. So we did.

I buried myself in after-school work mostly to avoid spending time at the convent—as did every sister in the house who had the energy. Going home at the end of the day felt like going to another job. Living in that house was hard work and a constant drain of energy. The job of trying to build community is a thankless, exhausting task when not everyone wants to. Some sisters felt too old and too tired, wanting only to be fed, taken care of, and left alone. The rest of us pulled together as best we could. We built community with one another, including a few Holy Cross Brothers who lived on the other side of the high school, as well as lay faculty who befriended us. For many sisters across the country, "inclusiveness" became the survival skill of the 1970s. That was the year my understanding of community grew to include not just nuns but everyone.

It wasn't utter chaos in our convent without a superior, but at times we came close to bedlam, especially on weekends and holidays. Friday night became departure night. Half the house bolted on weekends, with no one seeming to care whether you hung around or not, so why stay? Many didn't, but I did. I had to. Being temporarily professed, we didn't have the liberty (or the money) to come and go as we pleased. Several sisters left each weekend to visit nun pals in happier convents, and every now and then, one or two snuck out at night going who knows where. Being a late-night person who couldn't go anywhere, I saw and heard it all.

Holidays became another occasion for mass exodus. For example, I assumed we'd spend Christmas in the convent, but I ended up (happily) going home to my family in East Chicago. In a house meeting to discuss the holidays, it became clear that no one wanted to spend Christmas together. Sisters decided instead to be with family, friends, or other sisters in other convents. No one wanted to stay at our convent for the holidays. We planned to celebrate with one another when everyone returned in the New Year.

While we did not live according to the Constitutions, "in a spirit of union and community," we did struggle to live with one another anyhow, day by day. In that kind of madness, I sorely missed my friends. As letters and phone calls revealed, all of us were living in nuthouses, trying to survive. Sharing our misery offered divine comfort. But in another way it showed the sorry state of convent living in 1969, which was sobering and depressing. My friends and I asked ourselves the same question that year: Is this how we want to live our lives?

In an effort to pull us together and cheer us up, Johanna announced at a house meeting that we'd be having weekly happy hours on Fridays, with cocktails, cheese, and crackers, followed by dinner.

"The liquor cabinet in my office will no longer be locked," Johanna told us, in the event that we wanted happy hours when she was gone. "We're all adults. We can enjoy a drink every now and then without a problem."

We must have looked like bug-eyed kids given a key to the candy store, because she added quickly, "Just keep in mind that this is for communal use, not personal use."

That was wishful thinking.

At the first happy hour, beer, wine, scotch, gin, vodka, Southern Comfort, and mixers like club soda and tonic water were lined up on a table in the community room. Plastic trays with Ritz crackers topped in multiflavored processed cheese squiggles sat nearby with a Mariella special, "Ants on a Log"—celery sticks filled with cream cheese and topped with three black raisins.

I offered to fix drinks, but the sisters preferred to make their own, and within minutes I knew why. One sister put a few ice cubes in a tall glass, filled the rest with vodka, tossed in a few olives, looked at me with a big grin, and announced as though she made magic, "A martini!"

My stomach turned at the sight. "Many martinis!" I said.

"How about some crackers with that?" I suggested, wanting to get food in her before the martini hit.

"No, thank you," she responded, still smiling. "I have snacks in my room."

She didn't stay for dinner, taking the giant martini up to her room, humming all the way. We didn't see her again that night.

Within a week, the liquor cabinet was empty. While designated for communal use, some sisters hit the sauce personally with happy hours every night. A couple did so secretly, late at night, but one sister quite openly made a big scotch and soda after dinner and took it up to her room.

"Good night, ladies," she'd say, raising her glass, "sweet dreams."

You may find this hard to believe, but I was the one concerned over the kind of drinking going on. I mentioned it to a few others, who didn't see a problem. I even suggested to Johanna that we have a house meeting to talk about gallons of alcohol disappearing in a week. Gossip was spreading like wildfire about who took it, and I felt something needed to be done. I didn't want the alcohol locked up again, but I believed we had to talk about the problem.

"I think some of these women are alcoholics," I told Johanna. She looked at me as if I was young, inexperienced, and exaggerating—which I was, of course, except for exaggerating.

"I'm not imagining this, Jo," I said, explaining, "last night I heard a crash in Clare's room. So did Rose. We knocked, but she didn't answer. When we went in, she was on the floor, drunk. She got up to vomit and fell."

"Oh, she just had a little too much," Jo said, dismissing the seriousness of the problem. "I've known Clare for years."

"But she has a little too much every night," I said, pressing the issue. "I see her. I'm the one who cleaned her up and got her back into bed last night—and she's taking medication. She shouldn't be drinking at all. And she needs to hear this from you."

But she didn't hear it from Jo. God love her, our superior had her own edge to walk and couldn't go further. It would be years before Clare got the medical help she needed. Like many alcoholics, Clare found ways to live with the problem and hide the consequences, and most convents, like ours, provided the perfect setup. We were experts at leaving one another alone and avoiding conflict. That year three sisters suffered from alcoholism, and none of them received the assistance you would expect in the sisterhood—that is, not until years later when they had to be hospitalized.

I talked to Clare about her drinking the day after I picked her up off the floor and put her to bed, and every other time I had to intervene on her behalf. She always thanked me, promised not to drink as much, and assured me it wasn't a problem.

"When it comes to alcohol," I told her over and over, "believe me, Clare, I know. You have a problem."

Nothing alcohol-related was ever discussed at a house meeting that year, other than plans for parties and holidays. We were the house of chronic denial. I kept talking to Clare, as did Rose and Mary Ann, but nothing changed; and Johanna couldn't handle any of it. Day by day we saw less and less of our superior at the convent.

"I can't cope," she'd tell me at school every time I'd ask her to intervene. "I'm sorry, but I just can't."

I seemed to be the only one who wondered seriously why she was the superior. None of us could cope, but we were doing it anyhow. But Jo really couldn't—it simply wasn't in her. She couldn't manage anything other than making it through the day, so the rest of us did the best we could to hold the house together. Jo restocked the liquor cabinet as needed and happy hours continued. The same sisters poured tall glasses of vodka, gin, and scotch and then went to bed. The day the liquor cabinet was unlocked at Saint Joe High School Convent is the day all kinds of silenced demons were unleashed.

In 1970–1971 two acts of divine intervention saved our souls. The first, arriving in late spring of 1970, appeared to us in the form of a dog, a mutt from the farmers' market in Mishawaka we named Dulcinea, after the heroine in *Man of La Mancha*, Dulcie for short. The second appeared to us in a new, thirtysomething superior named Michelle Harmon, who joined us in the fall of 1970. With the arrival of Dulcie and Michelle, everything began to change for the better.

We talked for months about getting a dog. Mary Ann, Rose, and I started discussing it before Christmas. Having grown up with dogs (my first was a beagle named D.J., for "Dog Jackowski"), we felt it might lift our spirits in ways we couldn't. At first we ran the idea by sisters we knew loved dogs: Bernie, Clare, Marie Bernard, Marita, Angela, and Johanna. Strengthened by their approval, we brought the idea up at the dinner table. Edna and Mariella were definite nos, while Ann Francis lingered on the fence, tending toward no. Edna and Mariella said they'd pack up and leave if we got a dog. In my eyes, that sealed the decision. We had to get a dog.

We continued talking about a dog, with those in favor becoming more vocal in their support. Even Ann Francis came around, raising the level of yeses to nine and a half out of twelve, an overwhelming majority. We did not plan to get a dog the day Mary Ann and I went to the farmers' market. On the way into the market, we saw a box labeled FREE PUPPIES, surrounded by a group of children begging parents for the one puppy that wanted them. Inside the cardboard box a litter of mutts, looking like little black Labs, begged to be given a happy home.

"What do you think?" Mary Ann asked, as we looked at each other with the same thought in mind.

"I don't know," I said, envisioning the consequences. "Let's think about it. If there are any left when we leave, it'll be a sign."

Well, on the way out, there was one puppy left in the box—the runt.

"It's a sign!" we said, looking at the solitary orphaned puppy.

We took the runt home and named her Dulcinea, after Don Quixote's impossible dream.

Thank God it was a Saturday and most nuns were gone. Since she was small enough to fit in the pocket of my hooded sweatshirt, we snuck Dulcie in and out of the convent, keeping her a secret until Monday, when everyone would be home. We banked on the ooohs and aaaahs of supporters to drown out the dissent of Edna and Mariella. The chaplain, Jim Daley, a diocesan priest from Iowa studying theology at Notre Dame, was also in on the plan, vowing clerical support when the time came. We kept Dulcie in our rooms to stop her from crying and took her out behind the high school for housebreaking lessons, where no one would see. The following Monday morning, after mass at breakfast, Mary Ann made the announcement.

"We have a surprise for everyone this morning," she said, excited. "So stay where you are and we'll be right back."

While Mary Ann and I went for Dulcie, the nuns at the table were buzzing. Rose, Johanna, Bernie, and Ange knew what was happening, but the others didn't. Not a clue.

"Okay," I yelled in advance, "close your eyes and don't open until I tell you."

"Oh, goodie goodie goodie," Jim yelled back in advance support. "I love surprises."

We were counting on his priestly blessing to silence the anticipated anger of Edna and Mariella. Both acted like angels in front of "Father" and wouldn't dare misbehave.

Mary Ann and I walked in through the community room.

"You can open your eyes now," I announced, standing at Mary Ann's side.

"Meet Dulcinea!" Mary Ann said, holding the puppy up for them to see before letting her down on the floor.

Jim was the first to jump up from his chair, squealing with delight.

"Oh Dulcie!" he said, picking Dulcie up and letting her lick his face. "Welcome to Saint Joe's. Bless you."

Two things happened. First, the other sisters gathered around to ooh and aah over Dulcie, feeding her scrambled eggs and sausage, and second, Edna and Mariella stood up and left the table.

"Think they're going to pack up and leave now?" I asked Mary Ann as we both noticed their departure.

"We should be so lucky," she said.

Dulcie came to us in the spring, near Easter, and what she brought to our convent was something we were dying for: new life. Rules were set to keep Dulcie away from Edna and Mariella. By common agreement, she was not allowed in the dining room, kitchen, or chapel, although several times I found Dulcie in the chapel sitting at Bernie's feet as she prayed. Dulcie became Bernie's guardian angel, following her everywhere, hopping on her lap or jumping up at the foot of the bed when the emphysema acted up. Only Bernie dared to let Dulcie in the dining room and kitchen, sneaking her snacks from the fridge, like lunchmeat and hot dogs. Mariella wouldn't mess with Bernie.

In ways that only a dog can, Dulcie brought joy to our world. Sisters took turns walking her, playing with her, but Mary Ann and I cleaned up the yard. She slept in nearly all of our rooms, favoring Bernie's, and only once making the mistake of walking into Edna's room.

"Get that damn dog out of here!" Edna yelled, standing outside her room in the hallway.

"Oh, my God," I said to Rose, whom I was talking to at the time. "Edna said 'damn.' She's really mad."

"You stay here," Rose said, "I'll get Dulcie."

Edna was the only one who continued to hate Dulcie, even to the point of kicking her, which Bernie saw happen. I walked in on the two of them and never heard Bernie that angry.

"What are you doing?" Bernie yelled. "Don't you dare kick her!"

"Get that dog away from me!" Edna yelled back. "I told you I don't like dogs."

"You don't have to like her," Bernie said in a scolding tone of voice. "But you have no right to be cruel to her. How dare you kick one of God's creatures?"

Picking Dulcie up, Bernie was in tears. Edna turned around and walked away, saying nothing.

"I'm sorry you had to see that, Bernie," I said, walking over to console her, "but I'm glad you did. Who knows what she would have done to Dulcie if you hadn't stopped her?"

Even Mariella came around to loving Dulcie. It began with Dulcie sitting a few feet in front of Mariella, just staring at her.

"Don't even look at me," Mariella told Dulcie. "It's not going to work. Don't give me that look . . ."

"She's talking to her," I whispered to Bernie that night. "That's it. Dulcie won."

Dulcie lay down, put her head between her front paws, and fell asleep looking at Mariella. Day by day they grew closer and closer until one evening, while Mariella was watching the news, Dulcie hopped up in her lap. Expecting an outburst of anger, we froze.

"Well, well, well," Mariella said, not moving, "what have we here?"

"Looks like you have a new friend," I said. What it really looked like was a miracle.

"Well, she better just sit still," Mariella said, looking delighted and embarrassed at the same time because we had seen her change her mind.

Everyone but Edna found a friend in Dulcie, and everyone but Edna became kinder and gentler as a result. Whatever it is that dogs do to heal us, that's what Dulcie did for us in the spring of 1970. She brought new life to a group of women who badly needed it, lifting our spirits and delighting us in unexpected ways. By the fall of 1970 Dulcie was one of us, sort of. We still kept the dining room off-limits when we were at the table, and Mariella becoming the first to fill Dulcie's bowl with only the best table scraps. Dulcie did wander into the chapel with the rest of us for morning prayer, mass, and vespers, but sometimes she'd be in the chapel alone. Maybe that's where she too went for peace and quiet. I imagine even Dulcie needed to get away from us every now and then, especially Sister Edna.

Something must have happened between Edna and Dulcie that no one saw because when Edna entered the room, Dulcie growled and bared her teeth—something she did only to Edna. And Edna all of a sudden kept her distance. I think the older Dulcie got, the more Edna feared being attacked in her sleep. Whatever happened between them, both made it a point to keep their distance, in much the same way as I did with Edna.

In the fall of 1970, Sister Johanna requested and received a leave of absence from the Sisters of the Holy Cross (leaving the community shortly after), and Sister Michelle Harmon became our new superior. Having studied psychiatry at the Menninger Foundation, Michelle arrived far better equipped to deal with our house of chronic denial. She and Dulcie bonded instantly, which was a divine sign for everyone but Edna. Michelle and I bonded instantly too. Little did I know then that Michelle and I would become lifelong friends.

Not only did Michelle convene weekly house meetings, but she made us talk to one another about what we could do to improve the quality of our community life. We began slowly by changing the daily schedule to rise later, with morning prayer at 7:00 before breakfast, and mass at 5:15 P.M. before dinner. For those like me who love to sleep, an extra hour every morning makes all the difference in the world. I could wake up at 6:30 A.M. and be seated in the chapel for morning prayer with time to spare.

In an act of total bravery, Michelle also tackled the alcohol problem head-on, speaking with each of us individually about what we wanted to happen. As a result, Friday-night happy hours continued, though the days of unlimited alcohol ended, as did the habit of pouring liter-size cocktails and going to bed. When we drank, we drank together. Frequently we'd have pizza and beer or wine and cheese. On special occasions we'd whip up a batch of whiskey sours or manhattans, but never again did we see a table full of vodka, scotch, gin, Southern Comfort, and bourbon, accompanied by the free-for-all that followed. I'm sure the sisters who wanted to drink alone in their rooms found a way to do so, but at least we were no longer aiding and abetting the problem.

Whenever a conflict brewed, Michelle called us together to resolve the difficulty. Nothing ever reached the breaking point under her leadership. Gradually, day by day, nearly everyone became comfortable speaking her mind, learning to disagree without personal animosity. Even the silence of those who couldn't speak received respect. No one was forced to do anything.

Having lived a lifetime of silence, many sisters struggled to speak, especially if their opinion differed from the majority. And those of us who always spoke our minds learned to be patient and accepting of those who couldn't. When we began to talk to one another, to listen to one another, and to respect, even treasure, the differences between us, community was born. Blessed be.

In less than a year, our dead house came back to life, and our unhappy home turned into a hospitable convent. Previously known as departure night, Fridays became community nights with open happy hours that sometimes included faculty, friends, Holy Cross brothers, and sisters who for the first time came to our convent to spend the weekend. Rosella's best friend, Sister Ildephonse from Michigan City, was a frequent guest. Ildie was also a "tall drink of water" with a sense of humor that reminded me of an older and wiser Ellen Gibson. She never realized how funny she was, but no one made an ordinary story as funny as Ildie could, and no one made it funnier than her sidekick, Rose. When Ildie came for a weekend, no one left the house, and our happy hours lasted until well after midnight, with endless laughter we came to call "The Rose and Ildie Show." While a year before I could hardly bear to spend time in the convent, with the arrival of Michelle, the convent became home. That's the kind of difference one person can make in community life.

Even Mariella relaxed her grasp on the kitchen, allowing us to add what we wanted to the grocery list, snack when we wished without permission or explanation, and even invite outsiders to dinner. We began sharing responsibilities for grocery shopping, cooking breakfast, and preparing dinners on weekends. Now that sisters stayed home on weekends, we began planning meals together. Flexibility entered our lives with Michelle, and though it took a few sisters some getting used to, we wallowed in what it did to enrich community life.

Of all the joys Michelle brought to our life that year, a particularly fond one of mine was the car she bought for two hundred dollars—a big pea-green tank of a Ford that no one would drive except her and me. I loved that car. The turn signals were located on the hood above the headlights, flashing as though in a parade every time we made a turn. If you lifted the floormats from the front passenger side, you could see the ground through a rusted-out hole. If the nice convent car wasn't available, the other sisters would rather stay home than risk being seen in the green Ford but not Michelle or me. The Tank was our first choice. We used to joke that no one would even steal that car—until Christmas, when I found out that was no joke.

I drove the Tank home the day after Christmas. I parked the car on the streets of East Chicago beside our house on Northcote Avenue, woke up the next morning, and the car was gone. I ran outside to look around, thinking maybe I had parked out front, but the Tank had disappeared.

"It can't be stolen," I told my dad, "no one would want that car."

"Well, it's gone," he said. "We better call the police and file a report."

The police came to the house, took the information on the car as if it was no big deal, and started to leave.

"Wait!" I said, stopping them. "What about my car?"

"Your car is gone, Sister," one of them said.

"You mean I won't get it back?" I asked, heartbroken.

They laughed as though that was the funniest thing they had ever heard.

"Not in this city," they said. "If we find the car at all, it'll be stripped and on cinder blocks in some alley. Sorry, Sister."

I called the convent to tell Michelle our dear car was stolen. Because it was the Tank, no one else cared, but we did. All day I walked around lamenting the loss and finding it hard to believe that anyone would steal that car. Around 5:00 P.M. the same day the phone rang.

"It's the police," my mom said, smiling while handing me the phone. "They found the car."

"Found the car!" I screamed, grabbing the phone. "Did you really find my car?"

The East Chicago Police had indeed found the Tank.

About fifteen minutes later the police came to the house, picked me up, and drove me six blocks, where the car sat parked in an alley, untouched. Nothing was missing, damaged, or stripped off. Even the tires were intact. In East Chicago, that's a true Christmas miracle. Only the registration papers were removed from the glove compartment and left on the front seat.

"I've never seen anything like it," the cop said. "We rarely find stolen cars this soon, and never in this condition."

"What do you think happened?" I asked, elated to have the Tank back. "Do you think they saw what a piece of crap it was and just left it here?"

"Not at all, Sister," the cop said. "If the car works, they don't care what it looks like. They steal for parts."

"What happened, then?" I asked.

"I don't know," he said, shaking his head. "Maybe they looked at the registration, saw that the car belonged to nuns, got spooked and ran."

"Really?" I asked, not mentioning that my veil was also in the glove compartment. I kept it there for emergencies, like getting stopped for speeding.

"Really, Sister," he said, "I don't know how else to explain it. God was clearly on your side. Merry Christmas."

That became the big joke with the green Ford. No one would even steal it, and if they did, they'd give it right back. When I returned to Saint Joe's, the sisters planned a little welcome-home party for me and the prodigal car. We celebrated that the Tank, which had been lost, was found. None of that would have happened the year before—neither the car nor the party. I am not exaggerating when I say that Michelle Harmon made all the difference in our world.

THE DECEASED

As soon as a sister dies, the prayers for the dead will be recited. One or more sisters shall watch and pray beside the body until burial. . . . When the superior receives word of the death of a sister, the psalm, "Out of the depths I cry to You, O Lord," is recited at the first common exercise following notification. At the time of the funeral the body of the deceased is taken to the church, where a sung requiem Mass shall be offered. After Mass and the final absolution, the body is carried in procession to the cemetery.

—CONSTITUTION 45: 278–280

In the spring of that year, March 12, 1971, Sister Concilio died. When a sister dies, the entire community mourns and celebrates the loss. I had seen that happen my first week in the convent when two sisters passed away. Sister Anna Raphael died the day we entered, September 14, 1964, and Sister Fausta followed two days later. We spent half of our first week in the convent at funerals. At the time I didn't realize that, as was not the case in most families, death occurs frequently in the sisterhood, most often in January after the New Year. I suppose having survived another year, some couldn't face doing it all over again.

The ritual for burial of a sister was unlike anything I experienced before or since. It made no difference whether or not you knew the deceased personally: she was your sister, and everyone who could gathered for the burial. As a postulant, I didn't know what to expect at my first funeral other than communal sadness and sobbing, but what I witnessed instead was a ritual so beautiful that, without sounding morbid, I began to look forward to it over and over again.

Concil was the first of my friends to die. I was with her three days before she passed, saying good-bye and fetching the pink poodle, and I sat with her in the three days after. I loved that sisters sat with the deceased until their burial, keeping the spirit company as she crossed over, praying for a speedy entrance into everlasting life. At night we moved the body to the Adoration Chapel in the convent infirmary where sisters attended round the clock. As postulants and novices, we sat in the chapel with many dead sisters, most of whom I didn't know at all. Regardless of what they were like in life, they all looked kind and gentle in death.

At first, sitting in the dark with a dead body spooked me so much that I'd close the coffin lid during my time. I imagined I saw them move and feared their eyes would pop open and they'd sit up. We did our own embalming in those days, and I didn't trust it. The mortuary was in the basement of the convent infirmary across the hall from the furnace, where I took "bags" to burn. The mortuary door remained closed, but after a sister died, I knew she was in there being prepared for viewing. Eventually I found comfort in the presence of my dead sisters, sometimes talking to them, asking them to pray for my perseverance. I needed all the help I could get, and I saw the dead as a direct line to divine intervention.

Because Concil was so well known and loved, family and friends from all over the country arrived for her burial. The Church of Loretto was packed. I was one of six sister pallbearers to carry her body into the church. A solitary tower bell rang a single mournful tone as we entered, while the sisters chanted Psalm 130, "De Profundis"—"Out of the depths I cry to You, O Lord." Sister Marie Cecile played the organ and bells as though her soul created every sound. Only she could pull heavenly music out of sisters, like me, whom she said "sang all three parts at once."

With the music, the rising clouds of incense, and a church full of soulful voices, I sometimes wondered if I too hadn't died and gone to heaven. You couldn't be there and feel otherwise. It was hard to tell if tears were those of sorrow or joy because we felt both. We mourned the loss of Concil while rejoicing that one of our sisters went home to God. The final blessing of the body occurred as we sang "In Paradisum"— "May the angels conduct you into Paradise"—which was followed by a procession to Our Lady Queen of Peace Cemetery.

As the community left the church, sisters and friends lined the road to the cemetery—about three city blocks—chanting Sister Marie Cecile's "Ave Maris Stella," the hymn we sang at every major turning point in our lives as Sisters of the Holy Cross: reception, profession, jubilees, and burials. The hymn our sisters sang as we entered the community is the same hymn they chanted at our burial, the same hymn I first heard when Sister Madeleva's body was brought back to Saint Mary's on that hot summer day in July 1964.

While the tower bell continued its tolling, we carried Concil's body through a nun-lined path to the cemetery, with sisters and family following as we entered. In those days, we all gathered around the grave site for the final blessing, stood by as the body was lowered into the ground, all the while chanting, "Ave Maris Stella." Sisters, friends, and family sprinkled into the grave rose petals or handfuls of the earth that would cover her. I loved that we put our sisters into the ground surrounded by those who had gone before her, and covered her with roses and earth. Unbeknown to anyone but me, Concil was also buried with a mini-bottle of Canadian Club.

I began to experience death differently after entering the sisterhood. No longer was it a moment to be dreaded, feared, or mourned. I began to see death as a divine turning point in this life, to be celebrated, and I found in the days and years to come, all of the things death cannot take away. Not even death could remove my loving memories of Concil, the awareness of her presence, or the amazing coincidences and signs alerting me that she was near. The veil between Concil and me remains so thin that I feel her at my side even more so now than I ever did in this life. Blessed be.

With every funeral of sisters I didn't even know, I felt as though I was given another angel at my side. That's probably why I spent so much time in the cemetery and came to love and visit cemeteries wherever I go. Some sisters look for churches in cities they visit, I look for cemeteries. Whenever I walked through the arches of Our Lady Queen of Peace Cemetery, I felt welcomed home by the sisters resting there, even protected. I entered another world when I visited them and I too, was granted peace when I left. Though we buried our sisters' bodies, we set their spirits free. In the sisterhood, that is always reason to celebrate and rejoice.

The other loss suffered that year came with the mass exodus of friends from the sisterhood. Nearly all of my close friends left the Sisters of the Holy Cross between 1970 and 1972, and not just those in my class. Sisters Miriam Edward and Christopher Marie left, as did my favorite high school teachers, Sisters Michaela and Angeline. (Ange left to join the Sisters for Christian Community.) In my class, Mugs, Nancy, Judy, Sue, and Jane all left, as did several others from our group. Unlike the death of Concil, this was a loss I mourned with no reason to celebrate. With every one of my sisters who left, I felt more and more alone.

Across the country, these were the years when the "bleeding of the sisterhood" began, resulting in the loss of over two hundred thousand nuns. Many of our best, brightest, and most creative sisters, including most of the Saint Mary's College faculty, left at that time. The most significant loss occurred among women in their twenties, thirties, and forties, leaving behind a widening gap between young and old. In my thirty-three years as a Sister of the Holy Cross, I was usually the youngest in the convents where I lived, with decades between me and the next oldest. Most of the "middle-aged" left.

A majority of women I know left the sisterhood because they couldn't live any longer in dysfunctional local communities. While we all asked the question "Is this the way I want to live forever and ever, amen?" many arrived at the conclusion that it wasn't. It couldn't be. Living in convents filled with the kinds of problems I experienced at Saint Joe's, many sisters saw no hope for the kind of change that would make a significant difference. Some buried misery in work, as I did, finding comfort in the friendship and companionship of colleagues. Over time, many fell in love with coworkers, leaving to pursue relationships or marry, some with priests who eventually left the priesthood.

With the radical changes in religious life called for by Vatican II, thinking sisters began questioning the value system in religious life, and many found it wanting. Disagreements about where priorities were placed, where we experience true community, and how normative gospel values were, motivated many women to seek religious life elsewhere. Tensions escalated between sisters wanting to open convent facilities to local community needs and those insisting on maintaining exclusiveness for sisters only. No outsiders allowed. "Loving our neighbor" was fine and good as long as they didn't disrupt convent life. As my friend Judy Baldwin explained:

> The last straw for me was a big community meeting where the keynote guest speaker ripped the young nuns for wanting to change things. A bunch of old timers (many of whom I lived with at the time) jumped on the bandwagon. I maintained sanity by spending most of my time with the kids or people like (Holy Cross sisters who also left) Mardi Hack, Eleanor Van Deelen, and Vicky (can't remember the last name). By the time the end of the year came, I was ready to go and lots of the sisters wanted me to go. So I left a note saying good-bye and Godspeed. On the front of the note was, "Damn everything but the circus." That was 1970.

Of all the changes young sisters advocated, opening convent doors in a gesture of hospitality terrified the older sisters. Adult relationships with clergy and laity was an entirely new experience for most—exciting for some, frightening for others. We hardly knew how to relate well to one another, much less to outsiders. At Saint Joe's arguments erupted every time someone suggested inviting friends or family to dinner, happy hours, even to spend the weekend. I welcomed outsiders into our lives because even the meanest of nuns tended to behave better in their presence. I began to see then, as I firmly believe now, that whenever we get together with our own kind to the exclusion of everyone else, it brings out our worst features. That's why diversity is such a divine blessing. It helps all of us behave.

Constant battles over maintaining the status quo and opening our lives to others wore many women down to the point that the only option that made sense was to leave the sisterhood in order to live the religious life they envisioned. The women I know who left moved not only out of the convent but also away from an exclusively Catholic world, opting to follow the gospel call to welcome and serve everyone in need. The wake-up call to justice and equality heard in this country during the 1960s and 1970s resounded loud and clear in the sisterhood, with those involved in social justice issues facing additional tensions in traditional convents. Conscientiously objecting to the resistance of communities that refused to step forward and speak out against war and injustice, many sisters saw no other Christian choice but to leave.

Any major shift in consciousness enables us to create a new relationship to the life spirit within, as those engaged in protest marches, antiwar demonstrations, and calls for nonviolence knew all too well. Inner-city nuns, like the missionaries in Third World countries, possessed a highly developed social conscience dedicated to the multidimensional cause of social justice. This irritated the lives of sisters who objected to public displays of dissent and protest. In most convents, socially active sisters were a minority, eventually forced to leave by the majority of socially unconscious sisters who made their daily life miserable.

It wasn't long before sisters involved in the peace and justice movement realized their own freedom of conscience was at stake. Some superiors banned sisters from signing petitions and participating in demonstrations, while others felt, as I did, that sisters must take their place in the front lines of any movement that works toward justice, equality, and nonviolence. Sisters who disobeyed superiors paid a dear price, often receiving the silent treatment, a particularly insidious manner of convent shunning. When it was clear that never the twain shall meet, socially conscious sisters prayed for grace, shook the dust from their feet, packed their bags, and left.

In the 1970s deep-seated attitudes of racism, sexism, and self-righteous Catholicism appeared in many convents, forcing thousands of sisters to leave the sisterhood in search of truly Christian communities. Ironic as that may sound, many sisters found leaving to be God's truth and theirs. One way or another, the women I know left convents in order to pursue the religious life to which they had felt called in the beginning.

Moved by the Holy Spirit within, some left because the life didn't change quickly enough, whereas others left because they could not live with the changes called for by Vatican II. Those who stayed clung to the belief that religious life would or wouldn't change. Tensions between the two would last for decades, leading to a historic decline in membership from which nearly all religious communities never recovered. Once external differences are stripped away, most sisters questioned the life to which they felt called. These were days of corporate soul-searching in the sisterhood. When the manner of our lives became more ordinary, sisters began asking, "What's the difference between us and every other single Christian woman?" Thousands of nuns found no difference at all and left.

As we began to witness the "bleeding of the sisterhood" in the early 1970s, I nearly bled to death over the loss of my dearest sisters and closest friends. I felt as if part of me left with every one of them, pushing me into a soul search of my own. As one by one, they left, the stunning news of their departure struck a soulful blow, moving me to the brink of seeking the answer to the ultimate solitary question: Why stay?

In the year before my final profession, 1971–1972, three choices helped answer that question. First, in the summer of 1971, I began my master's degree in theology at Notre Dame, studying mysticism. Second, in the fall of 1971, I was sent to East Chicago to be dean of girls at my alma mater, Bishop Noll High School. And third, in the summer of my final profession, I spent six weeks with the IHMs (Immaculate Heart of Mary Sisters) in Monroe, Michigan, at their newly established House of Prayer.

Rather than bolt with my friends in a movement of solidarity—a daily temptation—I followed my soul's call to travel within and listen more carefully to where I was being led. Filled with anger over the loss of so many friends, I found it difficult to see clearly. I despised the nuns who made life so miserable for my friends that they felt forced to leave, as well as the sisters who stood by silently and let that happen. I looked at those sisters and saw nothing other than a clear-cut indictment of our proudly proclaimed commitment to live "in the spirit of union and community."

In 1972, the summer of our final profession, seven were left out of the fifty who had entered the Sisters of the Holy Cross with me in 1964. That I would be one of them was a divine mystery I didn't understand. Given every reason over the years to be sent home, I hadn't been. And given every reason to leave, I didn't. The biggest mystery in my life that year was my still being a nun. Before I stood at the altar of God and promised to live as a sister forever, I needed to know why I wanted to stay. With nearly every external reason stripped from my life, I needed to look deep within to see what was left. Studying mysticism appeared as one way to begin the journey within.

I needed the approval of Mother Octavia to begin graduate studies at Notre Dame. At first I thought, "Fat chance." No way would The Eye grant me that permission, especially since only finally professed sisters received the benefit of graduate school. I suppose the community didn't want to risk investing financially in sisters who might eventually leave, and I surely must have been high on that list. But having studied mysticism on my own at Saint Mary's, I felt called to pursue the inner life in that way more deeply. Convincing Mother Octavia of that felt like a foolish dream.

Though I don't recall the exact conversation, other than expecting a big superior "No," I somehow received the blessing of the Beholder and began my master's degree in theology during the summer of 1971. I can attribute the surprising support only to the intercession of Michelle Harmon, chosen by Mother Octavia as one of six sisters trained in corporate renewal, a program to travel the country helping dysfunctional local communities adjust to the changes.

Having studied the works of John of the Cross and Teresa of Ávila, I chose to study the fourteenth-century mystics, in particular Julian of Norwich from England and Marguerite Porete from Belgium—two women mystics I had never heard of. Mystics are simply those believers who descend into the depths of the soul through solitude and prayer and experience the kind of freedom of spirit one finds in union with God. Some, like Teresa of Ávila, lived in monasteries with other sisters; others, like Julian of Norwich, lived alone in hermitages. Both lifestyles appealed to me, and for years I felt torn between a communal life of prayer and service, and a contemplative life lived in solitude. I even considered joining a contemplative community of sisters in Connecticut, attracted to one of their publicized works: tending sheep. In living alone now, I still struggle to maintain balance between the call to solitude and the call to community. With one foot in each world, I relish the best of both.

The strong call to solitude I felt in 1971 had everything to do with how much I missed time alone in my two years at Saint Joe's. Consumed by work at school and stress in the convent, I was starving for solitude. That's what attracted me to the mystics. They too followed the soul's call, being led into solitude in order to hear the voice of God more clearly. What also attracted me to the mystics was their fierce independence from corrupt church authority, which is probably why we were never encouraged to read their writings. The truths mystics reveal tend to dismiss church rules as unnecessary, sometimes even contrary to the voice of God. Needless to say, most Catholics grow up never even knowing they exist.

Julian of Norwich, for example, in her one and only book, *Revelations of Divine Love*,* speaks of God as Mother, writing over and over that "love is all that matters;" even concluding "sin is no blame but worship." Anyone who experiences sin (when it leads to insight) as worship is guaranteed to be ignored, if not condemned by the Church in every age. Even seven hundred years later, referring to God as Mother remains a big papal no-no. While "change" is revealed every season as a sacrament of nature, it remains sinful in the eyes of most organized religions.

The Belgian mystic Marguerite Porete ended up condemned for heresy and was burned at the stake for hearing voices she claimed to be divine, especially her revelations about the "free spirit" letting all souls enter in union with God. In *A Mirror for Simple Souls*,† she writes:

The soul at the highest state of perfection and nearest the dark night is beyond noticing the rules of the Church. Commanded by pure love, the Church cannot control her.

In the end, that's why Church authorities killed her. Their God forbids such freedom.

After his "dark night of the soul," John of the Cross also concluded that love is the one and only answer to everything: loving God, loving neighbor, loving life, and loving self. The divine light he saw in the darkness was this: "Love and do what you will." He, however, was canonized a saint, not burned at the stake; nor was Teresa of Ávila. Both were in charge of Carmelite monasteries and abbeys and were well regarded by the Catholic Church.

In stripping away everything that doesn't matter, mystics found the

**Julian of Norwich: Showings*, trans. Edmund College and James Walsh (New York: Paulist Press, 1978).
†Marguerite Porete, *A Mirror for Simple Souls*, trans. Charles Crawford (New York: Crossroad, 1990).

one and only truth that does matter. I needed to do that too. I needed to find within me the only truth that mattered. I needed to discover all over again the religious life to which I felt called in the beginning. Because I needed to find out if "the call" was still there, I turned to the mystics to help me see more clearly, love more dearly, and follow more nearly.

Oddly enough, I returned to the beginning in more ways than one. In the fall of 1971, I packed my bags, left Saint Joe's, and moved back to East Chicago as dean of girls at Bishop Noll High School. I didn't live at the high school convent, full of older sisters, but moved into Saint Patrick's Convent; located in an inner-city part of town called Indiana Harbor, or simply The Harbor. Originally an Irish parish, Saint Pat's grew into a mixed community of native Italians and Hispanics. I liked being connected to an inner-city parish as much as I liked the sisters who were sent there with me.

Six of us lived at Saint Patrick's convent, only one of whom I knew before moving in, my pal Sister Suzanne Brennan, who was one year behind me at Saint Mary's. The others were Sisters Joan Mader, Geraldine Bloom, Mary Ann Lamping, and Carmencita. Joan, Geraldine, Suzanne, and I worked at the high school, and Mary Ann and Carm worked in the parish. In spirit we were all the same age, or close—something I hadn't experienced in two years. I found myself at home with them, no longer needing to escape convent misery with work. Mercy.

Saint Pat's convent was a big old two-story brick house that at times felt haunted. Whoever lived there before left traces of energy behind, and all of it felt good. We lived surrounded by kind spirits, even though the physical closeness of neighbors kept the house naturally dark and hidden from natural sunlight. The guest parlor, chapel, community room, dining room, and kitchen were located on the first floor, with all bedrooms on the second floor. I lived across the hall from Suzanne, with Geraldine and Carm as neighbors. We shared one bathroom, which I don't recall being a problem. I don't recall anything that year being a problem, which itself was sanctifying grace.

While I think our superior was Joan Mader, it seemed as if no one was—in my life, that's the highest "superior" compliment. With the six of us pretty much of the same mind, we decided everything together and rarely experienced the kind of conflict that might warrant "superior" intervention. An added bonus for me came with my job as dean of girls. I had no teaching responsibilities, so my dread of lesson plans disappeared, as did the anxiety of coming home to a conflict-ridden community.

Being the dean of girls for one year made it clear that I was not called to the work of disciplining high school students. The proverbial "sins of my past" were heaped upon me that year. Not only did my high school reputation as a hell-raiser precede me, but it shot any chance of my credibility as disciplinarian. For example, part of my job was to stand in the hallway to check the length of uniform skirts, which, when the girls were kneeling, should touch the floor. My brothers, David the freshman and Hank the senior, would sneak up from behind, swat me on the fanny, and yell, "Hi, sis!" Any attempt at seriousness on my part was also met with playful ridicule by brothers and sisters of my high school pals, who'd say, "Oh, come on, we know what you did in high school."

With no credibility as a disciplinarian, I struggled daily to do my job well, chalking up several major successes—one a major drug bust and the other a dress code victory.

The drug bust, I must admit, was purely accidental. Cruising the hallway one day outside the cafeteria, I spotted a few girls huddled together suspiciously, but when I got closer it looked as though they were sharing Hershey's Kisses. It wasn't until I asked for one that the look on their faces alerted me that something big was amiss. They looked as if they saw a ghost. What I thought were Hershey's Kisses turned out to be "uppers" wrapped in tinfoil. Among the students, my credibility as dean soared, but only I knew the truth: I was lucky.

The dress code victory occurred in the spring, the day after the Academy Awards when a braless Jane Fonda received the Oscar for best actress in *Klute*, dressed in a black silk blouse unbuttoned to the waist. About a dozen girls appeared in school the next day braless with uniform blouses unbuttoned to the waist. Before the homeroom bell rang, all were marched down to my office by shocked and horrified old nuns who expected me to expel every one immediately. When the girls walked in, I knew they were pulling a Jane Fonda.

"What's going on?" I asked the group as they stood giggling before me, only slightly embarrassed.

Denise Patterson, a wildly funny girl, spoke for the group. "The dress code doesn't say anything about wearing a bra or buttoning our blouses," she said, correctly. "So we're not breaking any rules, Sister."

"You've got to be kidding," I said.

They weren't.

"Button up and come with me," I said, grabbing car keys out of my purse.

"Where are we going?" Denise asked, slightly nervous.

"I'm taking you home to get dressed," I said, calling their bluff. "I find it hard to believe your parents saw you leave the house that way this morning."

Of course I was right. The bras were in their lockers.

"Go get them," I said, sounding stern. "Put them on, button up, and come back here."

"Yes, Sister," they said, looking more embarrassed.

"Do this again and I will call your parents," I told them. "Understood?"

"Yes, Sister," they repeated.

"And Denise, since you're the spokesperson for the group, I'm making you responsible to see that this never happens again."

All she could say, all any of them said, was "Yes, Sister."

That was the day I came home and announced to my sisters at the dinner table, "I think we should abolish high school and put teenagers and their runaway hormones on an island for four years. Bring them back when they're eighteen and ready to study."

Every day we told stories like that around the dinner table, sometimes sitting for hours over the day's silliness. The most hilarious stories always came from Geraldine, without a doubt the funniest sister I've ever known. She joked about teaching remedial English for three minutes and entertaining her students for the remainder of the period just to keep them from bolting.

"They have the attention span of a gnat," she'd say. "After three minutes they line up at the door waiting to leave."

One afternoon Geraldine called me to intervene when two girls in her last-period remedial English class, Denise Patterson and Mishka Borum, accused a shy, lonely classmate of sexual harassment. Because Denise and Mishka were frequent visitors to my office, we knew one another well.

"Tell me what happened," I said to the girls out in the hallway. "What have you done now?"

"John Silas had his hands all over us, Sister," they claimed, trying not to smile.

"Oh, for God's sake," Geraldine said, "John Silas doesn't even know he has hands. Stop torturing that poor boy."

That was the end of that. They intended simply to get out of class.

Ger also struggled her entire life with her weight, which she turned into comedy for those she lived with. She enrolled dutifully in Weight

Watchers that year. Suzanne and I were determined to help her, even to the point of not having sweets in the house—for me, the ultimate sacrifice. One night Suzanne came to my room: she spotted Geraldine tiptoeing downstairs in the dark with a flashlight. We followed her minutes later, finding her sitting in the dark community room eating M&M's with peanuts, which she had hid under the sofa cushions.

"Geraldine!" Suzanne said, startling Ger. "What are you doing?"

"Don't you dare take them away from me," she said, grabbing the M&M's, jumping up, and running into the kitchen.

We chased her around the dining room table, waking Joan, who came down to see what was going on.

"She's got M&M's!" I said, running after Ger. "Get her!"

Joan rolled her eyes, shook her head, and went back to bed.

Another night Suzanne and I found Ger in a dark kitchen heating up a can of El Paso taco filler.

"Stay away from me," Ger said, threatening to burn us with the hot pot.

"We're doing this for your own good," Suzanne told her. We won that battle, allowing Ger three heaping spoonfuls before turning over the rest to us.

I think of that whole year as one big laugh and a big breath of fresh soulful air. In returning to my beginning, I saw family and friends whenever I wanted, and discovered once again the joys of community life. My family loved having me near, and I loved being able to join them for holidays and birthdays. Most important of all, even in my hometown of East Chicago, I found myself at home with my sisters. That divine truth was still there. I still found myself called to life in community with the Sisters of the Holy Cross. It felt as though the God who called me to sisterhood in 1964 returned me to the beginning so that I could hear more clearly the sound of "forever and ever, amen."

PERPETUAL PROFESSION

*About three months and a half before the expiration of temporary vows,
the sisters may make a petition in writing to the superior general for admission to perpetual profession. The superior general, after considering
the recommendations of the provincial superior, and the formal reports
from the superiors of the houses from which the sisters lived, may, with
the advice of her council, admit temporarily professed sisters to perpetual profession.*

—CONSTITUTION 11: PROFESSION OF VOWS

My year as dean of girls at Bishop Noll ended a three-year tenure in
high school work. In my letter to Mother Octavia requesting to be admitted for final profession, I also asked to spend the summer in retreat
at the IHM's House of Prayer in Monroe, Michigan, and to study full-
time the following year, completing my graduate degree in theology. My
friends thought I was crazy, but what did I have to lose? If I wasn't accepted for profession, it wouldn't matter, and if I was, why not? Besides,
it's not as if I was asking to go to Disneyland.

After receiving my letter, Mother Octavia responded with a brief
one-liner that in essence said, "Please see me." My heart sank. One-liners
that say "Please see me" never sound good, and those who saw the letter concurred. This could be it. All who petitioned for final profession
needed to meet with Mother Octavia eventually, but only I received an
immediate "Please see me" response. I began thinking she might say,
"Since you're already in East Chicago, why don't you just go home."

"Don't you have a photo album you can bring along?" Paj asked in
jest, trying to humor me.

"Very funny," I said. "But I'll never make that mistake again. All I'm bringing with me this time is me. This is showdown at the OK Corral."

I wasn't anxious about my meeting with Mother Octavia. That was a first. Clearly, something in me had shifted. I felt as though I had nothing and everything to lose. Having done my best to be a good sister, I cast my fate to the wind, commended my spirit into the hands of God, and sat myself down, eye to eye with the Beholder. Sitting before Mother Octavia on the desk was my bigger and fatter file. It had grown significantly since the last time we met.

First we dealt with the contents of the file. One by one, Mother Octavia flipped through the evaluations of all the sisters with whom I had lived during the past three years. Much to her scowling dismay, all reports were glowing except one, which she pulled from the pack to read more carefully. Knowing that one negative vote could send me home, I braced myself for the worst, thinking, "It must be Edna."

It was.

"Sister Karol," she said, holding the dissenting vote. "Sister Edna doesn't think you are fit to be a Sister of the Holy Cross."

I wanted to say, "The feeling is mutual," but didn't.

"That doesn't surprise me, Mother," I responded calmly. "Sister Edna and I didn't get along very well. Does she give a reason?"

Handing me the form so that I could see for myself, I burst out laughing. In big, bold, underscored words, Edna wrote: "THE DOG IS HER GOD!"

"Excuse me for laughing, Mother," I said, because she hadn't even cracked a smile. "But do you really believe this? Do you think I want to be a nun because I love dogs?"

What I wanted to add but didn't was the fact that if all the sisters at Saint Joe's voted on Edna, she would have been sent home. Feeling brave and dying to hear her say something positive, I asked, "What do the other sisters have to say?"

She really didn't have to tell me, because I already knew. Most of the sisters who evaluated me showed me their comments before mailing them, even my old high school teacher, Sister Mariella. Over time we became friends.

"The other sisters strongly support your admission to final profession," she said with downcast eyes. "And in consulting with the council, we concur."

I could hardly believe it. My soul soared so high I nearly floated off the chair and flew out the window.

"Thank you, Mother," I said, beaming.

"Now, Sister Karol," she said, changing the subject as though she couldn't let my happiness linger too long, "let's talk about your summer plan to join the IHMs at their House of Prayer. What's wrong with Mary's Solitude?"

Mary's Solitude is the retreat house the community built above the convent garage. We called it Our Lady of the Garage. The two sisters in charge of the retreat house at the time were caretakers more than anything else, neither of whom I'd look to for a retreat. But I decided not to bring that up.

"There's nothing wrong with Mary's Solitude, Mother," I said. "It's just that I'd like to go somewhere different, and I've heard such good things about the IHMs new House of Prayer."

"Well, Sister," she said, looking miffed, "maybe you'd like to join the IHMs if you think so highly of them."

That was a cheap shot, but I didn't say so.

"If I wanted to join the IHMs, Mother," I said, "I wouldn't be here now. Besides, aren't we all sisters?"

She stared at me with The Eye in such a way that I feared she was changing her mind about my acceptance.

"Very well," she said, without a smile, looking unnerved by my response. "You may go."

She also said, "You may go," when I pressed my luck and asked about studying full-time in the fall. Only finally professed sisters were allowed to go to graduate school.

"Thank you very much, Mother," I said sincerely. I was truly grateful because she single-handedly could have thrown me out.

"You're very welcome, Sister Karol," she said, breaking into a slight smile.

And for the first time ever, in the Eye of the Beholder I did feel very welcome.

The six weeks I spent with the IHMs at their House of Prayer became my way of preparing for final profession. It was like a forty-day deep breath of fresh air, enveloped by the kind of silence and solitude that granted me a peace that not only surpassed my understanding but felt everlasting. What I remember most is arriving in Monroe, Michigan, at the IHM Motherhouse, not knowing anyone—an experience I grew to love—and leaving with the heartwarming feeling of belonging to another community. My circle of sisters grew to include all those I met that summer, especially Sister Martha Rabaut, one of the spiritual directors with whom I lived. When I think of the angels who crossed my path, entered my life, and made a difference in my world, Martha was the angel in the summer of 1972.

While I arrived at the House of Prayer tired and scattered at the end of the school year, and a little nervous over final profession, I returned to Saint Mary's feeling grounded and indestructible. I welcomed six weeks of silence, solitude, and prayer like an old friend I hadn't seen in years. Four of us lived in a brick duplex not far from the Motherhouse, where the House of Prayer was located. We lived in natural silence, not the novitiate kind with a mandatory no-talking rule. Our silence came from within and served as the open door to solitude and prayer. We prayed together every morning and night, taking turns preparing the prayer service, and joined the others at the House of Prayer daily for Eucharist. We also took turns cooking, which I loved, and had the kind of fun that I came to recognize as the presence of God. Fun became a true sacrament that summer.

Located near Detroit, the House of Prayer is a stunningly beautiful renovated red barn located in a solitary spot at the Motherhouse, surrounded by hermitages. I still have dreams about sitting on the carpeted floor around an altar made with an old wagon wheel left in the barn before its renovation. I understood for the first time the feeling of sanctuary, of being embraced by a sacred presence made up of the God within and the holy spirits surrounding me. In my dreams I live there. The barn enchanted me in ways many churches don't. I walked into the barn every day and felt welcomed by God and God's sisters. It's no exaggeration to say I found heaven on earth that summer.

I don't recall how I knew about the IHM's House of Prayer, but I do remember the feeling of having to go there as though something waited to be found. Led by what I now see as holy spirits, I did find with the IHMs what I needed to return to Saint Mary's and join my six sisters in making final profession. I left the House of Prayer feeling ready to take the final step. Everything in me felt more permanent and unshakable when I left, as though I had entered rooms in my soul so deep and indestructible that no one or nothing could disturb me. And it's a good thing I did, because when we returned to Saint Mary's to prepare for final profession, it felt as though we had stepped back five years into the novitiate.

I was the last of the final profession candidates to arrive at Saint Mary's, several days after the others. Given that only a handful of us were left, I was sorely missed, especially by Paj. Ten of us professed final vows on

August 15, 1972, the Feast of the Assumption of Mary—seven in our class and three from previous classes consisting of sisters who needed more time to decide and were granted two-year extensions.

From our class, Sisters Michele Idiart, Ellen Bush, Francis Virginia, Linda Sartori, Beth Mulvaney, Paj, and I returned, with Michael Ann, Diana Cundiff, and Ros Smith joining us. Our superiors for the summer were Sisters Francis Helene and Vincent Clare, our old pal from the juniorate; both of them accepted very well the fact that we acted as though we didn't need them for anything other than helping us have a good time.

We lived in single rooms above the old convent laundry. Newly renovated and called Basil Hall after the community's founder, Father Basil Anthony Mary Moreau, the building was located next door to Our Lady of the Garage. Sister Mary Jo Delaney, a missionary on leave from Brazil, also lived with us. Because we looked at the month before profession as a time of reunion and vacation, it was hard to rally the dead seriousness expected of us by Mother Octavia and imposed on us by Sister Francis Helene.

Vincent Clare knew us well enough to not push the seriousness, and Francis Helene caught on quickly. After seven years of dead seriousness, how much more serious could we be? What could possibly happen in one month that would make our souls more fit for final profession? We felt our presence was proof enough of the seriousness needed to say "Forever and ever, amen." Vincent Clare knew exactly what we needed from our days in the juniorate: sky, sun, water, and sand, far from the Eye of the Beholder. She and Francis Helene packed us up and took us to Lakeside.

With no agenda other than being together, we took long walks on the beach and spent late nights sitting around a fire talking about how we decided to stay after all our friends had left. Beneath all the suffering and sadness, I like what happened to me in the convent. The person I turned into was a pleasant surprise. In seven years I had become far more tolerant, socially conscious, understanding, braver, less self-centered and judgmental, more creative, even funnier. I didn't lose my fun self in the convent, as I feared might happen, but I found ways in which fun can become a sacrament. In 1964 I had begun with a blank soul and ended up seven years later with a spiritual life that transformed me into a far better person than I imagined I ever could be.

Having fooled around in life before entering the convent, I also found myself much more serious about higher education, discovering in my years at Saint Mary's that I had a fine mind eager to learn. I became surprisingly disciplined about work that I loved, turning into a highly skilled administrator, counselor, and organizer. Had someone told me in high school that I'd be studying mysticism and wanting to live in a hermitage, I would have laughed at them; yet that's exactly what happened to me. I took to the contemplative life eagerly and felt myself at home in religious life in ways I never knew before. Much to my surprise, and that of everyone who knew me, my searching soul found what it longed for in the sisterhood. When such profound changes take place, there's a great sense of freedom and release as life loses many of its complications. In our Lakeside days I discovered an Emily Dickinson poem (#410)* that said it all:

> The first Day's Night had come—
> And grateful that a thing
> So terrible—had been endured—
> I told my Soul to sing—
>
> She said her Strings were snapt—
> Her bow—to Atoms blown—
> And so to mend her—gave me work
> Until another Morn—

*The Complete Poems of Emily Dickinson, ed. Thomas H. Johnson (Boston: Little, Brown, 1960), p. 195.

And then—a Day as huge
As Yesterdays in pairs,
Unrolled its horror in my face—
Until it blocked my eyes

My Brain—begun to laugh—
I mumbled—like a fool—
And tho' 'tis Years ago—that Day—
My Brain keeps giggling—still.

And Something's odd—within—
That person that I was—
And this One—do not feel the same—
Could it be Madness—this?

When we returned to Saint Mary's from Lakeside, calm and re-freshed, the work of preparing for final profession began. We decided to make our own invitations and commemorative cards and write our own vows—all of which needed Mother Octavia's approval. We groaned collectively on hearing that news. Invitations previously used by the community looked like obituary cards, and the vow formula used for a hundred years meant little to us. I was picked to design the invitations, while we decided together on the vows, spending way too much time arguing over every single word. I recall a few sisters storming out of the room because their suggestions were vetoed, infuriated further by the laughter of the rest of us.

"Oh, come on," I said repeatedly. "Lighten up. We're talking about sixty seconds of our life."

Well, some sisters couldn't lighten up, taking the whole moment far more seriously than the rest of us. (They also left a few years later.) The fact that I could not become serious was a particular worry for Francis Helene, who insisted on repeated rehearsals in the Church of Loretto during the eight-day retreat preceding final profession. We practiced marching into the church, filing into our pews, and one by one going to the altar, kneeling down before an imaginary bishop, and reciting our vows. I was the worst. Everything proceeded as planned until I got to the altar, knelt down, and began to recite my vows. With dead seriousness I enunciated every word clearly and soulfully until I got to the heart of the matter.

"I, Sister Karol Ann Jackowski, of my full and deliberate will, vow celibacy, poverty, and obedience . . . *forever?* Who put that in there?"

Everyone laughed, my laughter magnified by the microphone, but Francis Helene looked worried.

"You've got to do it right once," she told me. "Come on, get serious."

So I went back up to the altar, knelt down before the imaginary bishop, and spoke softly and seriously into the microphone.

"I, Sister Karol Ann Jackowski, of my full and deliberate will, vow celibacy, poverty and obedience *f-f-f-f-f-f-f-f-f-f-f-f* . . ."

Once again we started to laugh. I truly couldn't say "forever," not even in rehearsal. By that time we were out of control, and my perfect rehearsal wasn't going to happen.

"I'll be fine, Francis," I told her. "Don't worry. I won't blow it."

Every time she looked at me, I saw worry.

"I'll be fine," I kept telling her. "Trust me. I'm not going to laugh."

I spent most of my eight-day retreat walking the nature trail or sunbathing in the cemetery. I visited Concil there every day, asking her help in getting me through the vows. Lake Joy was off-limits, except for one day when we were allowed to swim in silence. I didn't even bother. Eight days of silence before final profession was a bad idea. Forcing us to wallow in the gravity of what we were about to do only increased our already high level of anxiety. Nearly every day I found Paj out in the sun, hitting tennis balls against the brick wall of the steam plant.

"Are you okay?" I asked. "You look crazy."

"I'm bored with God," she said. "I just want to get this over with."

Getting it over with is what we all wanted, but final profession is a high holy moment in the sisterhood, not to be gotten over with that simply. We were the stars of the show that day, with sisters, friends, and families from all over the country coming to honor and celebrate with us. That's the part of final profession I looked forward to.

For the Sisters of the Holy Cross, the Feast of the Assumption of Mary is one of the holiest days of the year. Traditionally it's the day novices profess temporary vows, we profess final vows, and professed sisters celebrate jubilees of ten, twenty-five, fifty, sixty, even seventy years. The whole day becomes one magnificent celebration of sisterhood. Just as they did the day we received the habit, sisters, family, and friends lined the path as we and the jubilarians walked in procession to the Church of Loretto.

I remember sunshine that day, and thanks to Joe Bonadies, the college gardener, we were surrounded by a campus full of trees and flowers exploding with the fullness of summer, as though heaven and earth couldn't wait to celebrate with us. Church bells rang the happy sounds all morning as the community buzzed with excitement. All stops are pulled out on that day. Even infirm sisters get dressed and come to the church, and those who can't, get dressed just to listen to the ceremony in bed. August 15 was the Feast of Forever and Ever, Amen.

When we stepped out the door of Basil Hall, the chanting of "Ave Maris Stella" had already begun. Something in me still melts when I hear that hymn, but when it's sung in harmony by hundreds of sisters I literally felt lifted up. I counted on that feeling to get me through the ceremony without breaking up when I came to the moment of "forever." As we entered the church, I spotted my family and friends, all of whom stood, waved, blew kisses, and took pictures. I smiled, waved, and took a deep breath. This was no rehearsal. This was it.

"Get a hold of yourself! It is I. Don't be afraid."

Leading the procession, we filed into the front pews. I was seated next to Paj, the only one of our friends left. Sister Marie Cecile pulled the most divine music out of the organ while choirs of sisters sang, with some ringing handbells. That's what choirs of angels must sound like; I couldn't imagine a more heavenly sound. Gold vases of white lilies surrounded the altar, with clouds of frankincense rising and filling the church. The bishop, dressed in his festive best, stood before the altar smiling. In a matter of minutes we would be kneeling before him. Out of body is how I felt once we took our seats, taking deep breaths and focusing only on getting through the moment of "forever." With Paj at my side, I felt confident that all would go well. It had to.

The profession of vows took place after the reading of Scripture and the homily, neither of which I recall. The one clear memory that never fades is the moment we walked to the altar, one by one, and professed our vows. I was nearly last and the wait was torturous. I knew everyone in our group, especially Francis Helene and Vincent Clare, braced themselves for my profession, praying with me that I'd make it through without laughter or fainting. At that point, both felt possible.

When my time came, I heard whispers of "Good luck," "We're behind you," "You can do it," and "Go, Kare." I started to smile and stopped myself. I couldn't go where a smile might lead. This was not rehearsal and we were not alone. The entire congregation, especially my family and friends, were hanging on every word I said.

"Get a hold of yourself! It is I. Don't be afraid."

With vow paper in hand, I walked up the altar steps and knelt before the bishop. You could hear a pin drop. I focused on keeping still so my shaking hands wouldn't skew my vision. After taking the deepest breath of my life, I said: "In the name of the Father and of the Son and of the Holy Spirit, I respond to the call to live a vowed life in community, and wish to consecrate myself to the service of the Church, under the special protection of Mary, our Compassionate Mother. With my sisters as witness, I, Sister Karol Ann Jackowski, of my full and deliberate will, vow chastity, poverty, and obedience . . . At that moment I paused, took a deep breath, and whispered in a barely audible voice, *"Forever . . ."*

I heard sighs of relief from my sisters. Seeing the end in sight, I continued, picking up the tempo: ". . . according to the Constitutions of the Sisters of the Holy Cross. Trusting in the strength of the Holy Spirit, I will be faithful in these vows until death. I ask Mother Octavia to accept my commitment in the name of the Church and the Congregation. Amen."

I don't recall what the bishop said in response, but I do remember rising, turning to face the congregation, and smiling as though I had won the biggest contest of my life. I'd done it. Francis Helene and Vincent Clare looked equally happy and relieved, as did my sisters who went before me. When I returned to my pew, I felt their silent applause, but when the last sister, Beth Mulvaney, professed her vows, the entire congregation erupted in applause after every Sister of the Holy Cross stood up and professed: "We wish to live and die with you."

My brother David mistakenly stood up and made that profession with them. A moment I still treasure. Once the applause died down, the bishop spoke to us, quoting Scripture:

"There will be gifts for you," he said, "gifts that no one can take away."

Paj and I jokingly started looking under the pew for the gifts, but there weren't any.

"No one will take our gifts away," I whispered, "because no one else wants them."

Everyone within earshot of my whisper started giggling, mostly with relief that the worst was over and the celebration could now begin.

The rest of that day is one big blessed blur of flowers, cards, real gifts, a banquet, family, high school friends, and all the sisters from the past seven years embracing me with their blessing, especially Francis Helene and Vincent Clare, and even my nemeses Sister Edna and the Beholders, and Mother Octavia and her council. Mercy.

The whole day felt like a divine embrace that never ended, and the day after, I went home for a two-week vacation with my family. I do believe we were given a sanctifying grace at the moment of final profession, which I count on daily to lift me up and carry me through the years to come. In making a promise forever, I felt I received a divine promise of eternal life in return. How do I know that everlasting grace is real and not a figment of my fertile imagination? I'm still here forever and ever, amen.

afterword

How this book got written is a story in itself. Truth be told, I never thought I'd be able to write a book now about what happened over forty years ago. Pulling memories from such thin air felt impossible. I'm sixty now and my memory of life as an eighteen-to-twenty-five-year-old isn't what it used to be. I feared not having anything to say. With every book I write, I call on holy spirits to guide me; but with this book, and the spiritual direction of psychic Kathy Cazana, I called on many more holy spirits for help. At the risk of sounding ridiculous, I listened to dead people in writing this book.

Part of the spiritual exercise I do before beginning to write involves altering my consciousness and dipping into its stream. In meditation on this book, I called to mind every person I wrote about, living and dead, praying that they help refresh the memory, no matter how awful or painful. Regardless of what you believe about an afterlife or communicating with the dead, I must tell you that the deceased sisters I call by name in this book came to mind immediately, each one ready to help me envision the story I wanted to tell.

Because I use imagination to put me in touch with old memories, I relied on the Ignatian method of meditation called composition of place, or application of the senses.* It's similar to what we know today as visualization or what Carl Jung refers to as active imagination. While Ignatius used this method of meditation to get in touch with divine truths in gospel stories, I used the seven steps to get in touch with the divine truth of buried memories. This is how it works:

1. Recall a memory or story.
2. Put yourself there.
3. Pray for the grace to see clearly.
4. See yourself in the story. Who else is there? What do you see?
5. Listen to what the people are saying. What do you hear?
6. Look at what the people are doing. What do you feel?
7. In response, what do you say and what do you do?

Ignatius believed that the use of imagination would put us in touch with the divine mystery of what happened at that time. With imagination being "the Divine Body in everyone" according to William Blake, it's no wonder the method is a timeless treasure. Some memories became so clear that I recalled exactly what we said, enabling me to create dialogue and describe experiences reflecting what happened and how we felt. So when I began to put words in someone's mouth, what I heard as a memory became clear.

Even memories of the novitiate, of which I felt I had no recollection whatsoever, appeared in broad daylight like a lost treasure I never ex-

---

*Developed by Saint Ignatius Loyola, founder of the Jesuits, a Roman Catholic order of priests.

pected to find. Incidents came to mind that I hadn't thought of in decades, some more clearly than others but all from the same pool of hidden memories. Frequently, one recovered memory opened a door to a litany of stories and released a flood of precious memories. That's how well the seven steps worked.

Out of respect for living and dead sisters and the hidden life they chose in the sisterhood, I changed some names, while others remain as they are. In the event that I didn't see and hear my deceased sisters correctly, or portray them kindly enough, I ended every workday (and this book) infinitely grateful to all mentioned for helping me write this book of precious memories, praying to be excused for all storytelling inaccuracies in my sixty-year-old mind. I pray the same of you.

a litany of thanks

First and foremost, I thank my family and friends, who changed my life and became part of my story. All those I call by name in this book carry with them the precious memories that grant my life its mystery. I thank them for the memory, as well as the help in remembering, praying that you, the reader, come to know and love them as I do. That's this book's greatest blessing; at least it is for me.

Blessed be.

First and foremost, I thank Laurie Liss, my agent, and Jake Morrissey, my editor; both holy spirits in my current life story. This book was their idea. Laurie sealed the deal on December 24, 2005, and Jake blessed it with the perfect title. Thanks to Laurie and Jake, I got what I wanted for Christmas that year. This is it.

Blessed be.

First and foremost, I thank these sisters for refreshing my memory: my best friend, Vern Hargrove, who saved everything I sent since 1964, and Sisters Mary Ann Pajakowski, Judy Gallavan, Margaret "Mugs"

Gallagher-Smythe, Nancy Ottoboni, Jane Huynh, Suzanne Brennan, and Michelle Harmon, whose conversations and e-mails resurrected forgotten memories, filled in the blanks, and verified stories I couldn't believe were true. They are the unseen authors of this book.

Blessed be.

First and foremost, I thank these earthbound angels for the kind of support every writer needs to thrive: Sally Davies, Adri Trigiani and Tim Stephenson, Michael Patrick King, Mary Feeley, Corrine McGuigan, Virginia Bell, Christene Barberich, Joanna Brett, Darren Walsh, Kathy Cazana, and my Sistern for Christian Comments in Sophia's Circle. I'll be thanking you for the rest of my life.

Blessed be.

And finally, first and foremost, I bow in thanks to the deceased loved ones who guided the writing of this book, especially the most delightfully vocal: Molly Sullivan and Sisters Joseph Marie, Concilio, Mercita, Rosella, and Gertrude. I called their name and they were there. Forever and ever, amen, I thank them all for saving my fun-loving soul and blowing such divinely inspired winds beneath the flapping wings of this book.

Amen.